Michael Gray's pioneering critical study of Bob Dylan's work, *Song & Dance Man*, was published in 1972. A revised and updated edition, *The Art of Bob Dylan*, appeared in 1981.

He has been the manager of singer-songwriter Gerry Rafferty and post-punk band Flag of Convenience, and in 1985 published a critical biography of Frank Zappa, *Mother! The Story of Frank Zappa*. He is currently working on an African travelogue and a comic novel.

John Bauldie was born in 1949 and lives in Essex. A former lecturer in English literature, he is currently working as a freelance writer. He likes Phil Ochs, David Blue and Bolton Wanderers.

All Across the Telegraph

A BOB DYLAN HANDBOOK

Edited by

MICHAEL GRAY and JOHN BAULDIE

Introduction by

BOB WILLIS

Futura

Contents

Thanks and Acknowledgements

For help with the establishment and maintenance of *The Telegraph* magazine I should like to thank Graham Brandwood, Bob Carroll, Dave Dingle, Clinton Heylin, John and Celia Lindley, Ian Woodward, and all contributors and subscribers for loyal enthusiasm. For long-time friendship thanks always to Bill Allison and Michael Krogsgaard. (*JB*)

For help with putting this book and/or me together I thank John Bauldie and all the writers whose work is included, plus Sarah Beattie, Andy Benson, Dave and Jackie Giff, Peter Harrison, Dave Laing, Sharon Linney, Ron Lowe, Angela MacRobbie, Peter Narváez, Cle and Debbie Newhook, Robin Piper, my sister Valerie, David Willis and Bob and Juliet Willis. (*MG*)

Acknowledgements are also gratefully given to the following: the exceptionally generous-minded Allen Ginsberg, plus Full Court Press, NY NY 10013, and Some/Release Press, 309 West 104th Street, (apt 9D) NY NY 10025, USA; Ilene Cherna; Clinton Heylin; Dave Dingle; Garner Simmons for the extracts from his book *Peckinpah – A Portrait in Montage*; W.W. Hutchinson (for comments on Pat Garrett etc.); John Way (for the basis of Note 23); Robyn Flans and Ronald Spagnardi for Levon Helm's interview, used by permission of Modern Drummer Magazine, 870 Pompton Ave., Cedar Grove, NJ 07009, USA; Tony Jowett, for his 'Note on Bob Dylan and Bob Marley'; the authors and publishers of all source-works quoted, as detailed and credited in the Notes (page 273); Susan Hill, Rowena Webb and Jane MacAndrew at Sidgwick & Jackson; Private Eye for permission to reproduce Ken Pyne's cartoon; for the material in *1960s: . . . And Who Was Mr Jones* by Jeffrey Jones, from *Rolling Stone*: Straight Arrow Publishers Inc., © 1975; the copyright holders of extracts reproduced from David Bowie's 'Suffragette City' (© 1971/2, Titanic Music Ltd/Chrysalis Ltd), 'Record-Company Sales Force Instructions' (© Columbia Records/CBS Inc); Liam Clancy, by Bob Dylan' (© Landseer Films Ltd., 1984); and David Blue's 'Cupid's Arrow' (© 1976, WB Music/Good Friends Music). Photography credits are listed with The Contributors (page 283).

The editors and publishers also wish to express their thanks to the undermentioned copyright owners for the use of material written and composed by Bob Dylan. Quotations are taken from Bob Dylan recordings and may in some cases differ from the printed sheet-music versions.

Introduction

Bob Willis

I am frequently asked what has been the most thrilling experience of my life so far. Most people expect me to reply that it was taking 8 for 43 at Headingley to help England defeat Australia in 1981, or becoming a father for the first time, or meeting the Queen to receive my MBE. All tremendous thrills, of course – but the most honest answer would probably be having a seat right on the stage at St James' Park, Newcastle, on 5 July 1984 when Bob Dylan played to a huge and ecstatic audience during his European tour of that year.

It was an indescribable thrill to be there, and a couple of times my good friend Ian Botham had to restrain me from rushing forward and seizing the microphone to announce the next number.

My unwavering enthusiasm for Dylan and his music began way back in 1963 when, as a 14-year-old schoolboy, I first borrowed and then bought my first album: *The Times They Are A-Changin'*.

In the years since first hearing those nervous, riveting early songs, I have bought all the albums and attended many Dylan concerts in England, Australia and New Zealand. Like so many fans I have followed the twists and turns of his remarkable career with a devoted fascination and in awe of his mystery and magic. I have played his music – some would say relentlessly – on cricket tours around the world and in many quiet, private moments.

There was a period when I didn't take any other music with me when I was touring. I played my Dylan tapes on England's tour of India in 1976–7, and then in Pakistan and New Zealand in 1977–8. They also made three trips to Australia with me, in 1978–9, 1979–80, and 1982–83. I'm a notoriously early riser, and I used to psych myself up for the day's test match cricket with an hour or two from Bob Dylan. People would always know which room was mine just by walking on past the music along the corridor. I still play it frequently today and find my passion undiminished, my pleasure entirely fresh and exuberant.

In 1965, when most of England's top cricketers seemed to have at least three initials, I added 'Dylan' to my own name by deed poll, and I have always been pleased to see R.G.D. on the scoresheet or in the newspaper.

The first time I saw Dylan live was at the Royal Albert Hall in 1965, and I'm glad to be able to report that I also saw the controversial concert he gave there a year later with The Band.

In 1969 I risked being sacked by Surrey County Cricket Club when I went to attend a Dylan concert on the Isle of Wight and almost failed to get off the island in time to resume the match.

I never had much success with converting cricket people until Ian Botham came on the scene. I met Ian for the first time out in Australia. We played a Centenary Test in Melbourne in 1977, and then that winter when we went to New Zealand I dragged him along to Dylan's Western Springs concert. We didn't have good seats, because we had to wait until after the cricket match before we could sort anything out. Some of the local press were trying to engineer Bob Willis Meets Bob Dylan but, if anything, I was even less keen on this than he was, in the circumstances. I couldn't imagine anything worse than meeting Dylan in the company of the Auckland sports media. I wasn't going to get involved with that. So we had no contacts for tickets and just went along and bought what we could get at the last minute, and we were miles away. But Ian really enjoyed it. I went on to Australia and saw Dylan again in Melbourne. Tony Greig got me a ticket about four rows from the front, which was terrific. Until St James' Park six years later, that concert in Melbourne in March 1978 was the closest view I'd ever had.

I was very fortunate that when we came back that summer, although cricketing commitments made me miss Dylan at Blackbushe, I managed to get to his Earls Court shows on four consecutive June evenings during a test match against New Zealand. Dylan's inspired performances appeared to help me bowl faster than normal.

Throughout Bob Dylan's 25-year recording career there have been books attempting to analyze the man and his work, and of course he is a frequent subject for newspaper and magazine articles. But while journalistic writing about Dylan usually misunderstands him entirely, I'm afraid I also find that reading through heavy tomes about him gives me little pleasure. I always prefer just playing the music.

But pleasure is just what repeated browsing through *All Across The Telegraph* has been giving me – and I think this is because as well as being an excellent anthology of writing about the man's music and life, this book tackles Dylan in the right spirit, with the eccentric mix of emotions you actually get from listening to his records. It catches something of the fun, and the exuberant extremism, as well as the sense of awe and the intensity, which all comes into the real experience of being a Bob Dylan enthusiast.

There has certainly never been any book quite like it. If it affords you anything like the pleasure it has given me, you will be well rewarded and well equipped to sustain either a growing or a fully-fledged preoccupation with the most unusually talented voice of our time.

Bob Willis, MBE
Birmingham, England,
November 1986

Preface

This book is a best-of selection, taken from the first twenty-five issues of a unique magazine – a critical quarterly devoted solely to the life and work of Bob Dylan.

It is testimony to the special nature and scope of Dylan's vast talents that such a magazine should not only survive but flourish; so is the fact that this journal, *The Telegraph*, is but one venture in a burgeoning literature about this major twentieth-century figure.

In launching such a magazine in the first place, and in running it for the last five years, *The Telegraph*'s editor, John Bauldie, has needed many special skills (and not always easily compatible ones) which must come into play when a critic takes on a living artist in such a sustained way.

To succeed in this exacting critical task you must be good at hustling as well as making critical judgements. You have to deal with determined distrust from the artist himself while maintaining some sort of working contact, however mutually wary, with that artist's retinue of lawyers and copyright-protectors. You have to pull together all sorts of documentation and arrive at much assessment despite the unavoidable way that so much misinformation emerges through the distortions of press hype, record-company ignorance and train-spotter obsession.

To have managed all this and run a magazine at the same time, with the resourcefulness to make it reliably illuminating and with a sense of humour which has kept the whole enterprise sharp and sane – sane in spite of the necessary fanaticism – is an impressive achievement.

Those who, like me, worked alone on Dylan projects in the past have had extra reason to be glad of *The Telegraph*: it has replaced a sense of isolation with the welcome communality of a regular forum.

But critical quarterly or no criticial quarterly, there is an overriding compensation for the difficulties and dodginess of dealing with a great living artist, and that is (to state something so obvious it often goes unnoticed) the artist's aliveness. In the case of Bob Dylan, who is so mercurial and so *prolific*, it feels very exciting and, as Christopher Ricks remarks somewhere, a privilege, to be alive at the same time as him.

Of course you can feel that way without being any sort of critic, and this book is intended for anyone who has ever, even briefly, felt that way about Dylan and his music. Certainly you don't need to care about the ups and downs of the critical life, nor do you need to know anything whatever about *The Telegraph* magazine, to enjoy this book.

I should make clear that the selection of the material here, and in most applicable cases its revision, is mine – that while John Bauldie has been a tireless and invaluable consultant on it, in addition to having always been responsible for the magazine, this book is, in the end, my own responsibility.

Hence there need be no apology for the inclusion of several pieces of work by John Bauldie himself. They are there at my behest, not his, and – as will readily become apparent to the reader – on merit. Indeed my pleasures in editing this book have included knowing that it will bring Bauldie's own work as a writer to a wider public, and having been able to combine contributions by new names with those by some well-known and distinguished ones.

The book is sub-titled *A Bob Dylan Handbook* because what it offers isn't just critical assessment, nor just biography, but an assemblage of all sorts.

Some of it is solid information on key areas and crucial periods in Dylan's life and career. Some of it is exclusive interviews with people who have worked with Dylan, and/or been around him, at significant times in his creative development. Some of it is critical essays. Some of it is fragments, snippets, clippings and other oddments. And of course, there are the obligatory rare photographs.

The result should be a book you can dip into, flip through and get surprise and pleasure from; it also aims to be an authoritative reference work: at the time of writing, *the* most accurate and reliable scrutiny yet of its charismatic subject and his extraordinary first twenty-five years' worth of creative work.

Michael Gray
Merseyside, England
December 1986

An Enlightening Thing?

I don't think you can end with hero-worship, or any kind of worship; but . . . I used to worship Woody Guthrie, Robert Johnson. I know what hero-worship is. I also know that it's an enlightening thing . . . It's nothing that holds you back.

Bob Dylan, 1978

Spotlight on Bob Dylan: A Comic Strip Serial

Just a wandering guy with a guitar—but he became a rock'n'roll super star!

From *The Hornet*, 1974

Bob signed Al Grossman as his personal manager and, before long Dylan the changed his name to that because of his love for Welsh poet, Dylan Thomas) was a household name. Grossman also acted for Peter, Paul and Mary and they gave Dylan free publicity at all their gigs.

WE'D NOW LIKE TO SING "BLOWIN' IN THE WIND," A SONG WRITTEN BY THE MOST IMPORTANT FOLK ARTISTE IN AMERICA TODAY—BOB DYLAN!

HOW MANY ROADS MUST A MAN WALK DOWN BEFORE THEY CALL HIM A MAN? HOW MANY SEAS...

The crowning moment of Bob's early career came at the 1963 Newport Folk Festival. When he began to sing "Blowin' In The Wind," everyone joined in!

The release of Dylan's second album, in 1963, turned him into a cult hero. The L.P. was snapped up and protest songs like "Masters of War," "Blowin' In The Wind" and "A Hard Rain's A-Gonna Fall" soon became standards. But Bob was getting into rock. His first rock album "Bringing It All Back Home," was also his first million seller!

Bob made another piece of music history in 1966 when he released "Blonde On Blonde" —it was one of the industry's first double albums! It was a rock album of the highest calibre and included great songs like "I Want You", "Rainy Day Women Nos. 12 and 35", "Leopard Skin Pill-Box Hat" and many more. But, not long after the album's release, came tragedy. Bob was involved in a motor-bike accident and broke his neck!

I'M GOING TO CRASH!

In August, 1969, Bob appeared at the Isle of Wight Festival. He is reputed to have earned £35,000 for his sixty-five minute performance!

I WON'T BE ABLE TO PERFORM FOR A LONG TIME BUT AT LEAST I'LL HAVE PEACE AND QUIET TO WRITE!

Apart from a couple of singles, "Watching The River Flow" and "George Jackson" in 1971, no new material had been issued for some time. Then in 1973 came the soundtrack album "Pat Garrett And Billy The Kid." Dylan not only wrote the music for that film but also appeared in it as Billy's friend, Alias.

WHOA BOY!

In January of this year Dylan fans' dreams came true. He released a new album, "Planet Waves" on new label, Asylum, and an instant No. 1) and embarked on a mammoth U.S. tour with The Band. For the twenty-one city tour with 658,000 seats available, over SIX MILLION people are reported to have applied for tickets!

DYLAN ROADSHOW

THIS GUY DYLAN'S A REAL NUISANCE! I'VE NEVER SEEN SO MANY TICKET APPLICATIONS!

Look out for another super "Spotlight" feature soon, lads!

1950s: Did Bob Dylan Really Play Piano for Bobby Vee?

Yes. Journalist-biographer Anthony Scaduto quoted a 'Dinky-town friend' as saying:

> He had this whole mythology about being Bobby Vee, the rock singer. He used to go to parties and introduce himself as Bobby Vee or have friends point him out to strangers as Bobby Vee . . . one of the Bobby Vee stories was that Dylan used to play with him – sometimes went on for Vee when he was sick. And we would believe them. At least in the beginning.

and Izzy Young noted Dylan as saying: 'I played the piano with Bobby Vee. Would have been a millionaire if I'd stayed with him.'

Not unnaturally these stories are taken to be threads in the myth that Dylan wove around himself. But when they get tested out, many of them turn out to be true. Dylan really did bum around a lot, really did meet a lot of old blues singers – and he really did play piano for Bobby Vee.

Here (from a combination of two interviews) is Bobby Vee himself:

> After we cut 'Suzie Baby', which was about five months after Holly's death, we started working in the [North Dakota] area and the record looked like it was doing well, and we had a vision of success in the group. And we worked June, July, August, somewhere around there and we thought to ourselves that maybe we should add a piano, y'know, to the band. It was just a rhythm section at that time, and in doing that we would probably have the ultimate rock 'n' roll band.
>
> So we sort of asked around the Fargo area and a friend of ours suggested a guy . . . that had been staying at his house, and was working at a café as a busboy – the Red Apple Café in Fargo – and so my brother met with him and they went over to the radio station to use the piano and they sort of plunked around a bit and played 'Whole Lotta Shakin' ' in the key of C, and he said, he told my brother that he had played with Conway Twitty, which was a lie

18

[but] . . . for openers he thought 'phew!' He didn't even want to audition the guy – he got the job.

. . . And so we went out and bought him a shirt: it was a small investment to make him a member of the band.

So he was identical to us – looked like he'd always been there – and went out and played a couple of small jobs in North Dakota, just tiny places. . . .One was in a church basement, the other in a little pavilion.

He was kind of a scruffy little guy, but he was really into it. Loved to rock 'n' roll. He was pretty limited by what he could play. He was pretty hot – in the key of C. He liked to do handclaps, like Gene Vincent and the Bluecaps, who had two guys who were hand-clappers. He would come up [to my microphone] and do that every now and then, and then scurry back to the piano.

He was Bob Zimmerman at the time – that was his name. He wanted us to use the stage name of Elston Gunn for him.

. . .[We] realised that . . . he didn't have a piano and we weren't in a position where we wanted to buy one; lug a piano around with us . . . that was really too much of a hassle.

So we decided to work as a four-piece band and we told him that, er, y'know, we decided not to use the piano. And he was a bit disappointed at the time, and eventually left Fargo. . . We paid him $15 a night, so we paid him $30 and he was on his way.

. . .He left Fargo and went down to Minneapolis and went to school . . . and then . . . about a year later we were out in Long Island or Staten Island, playing. And one of the guys in the band saw him in the audience – this was before he was popular – and he said, 'I saw Bob Zimmerman, in about the second row.' And we all said, 'No kidding? I wonder how he got so far east?' 'Cos he was just a spacey little guy, y'know, just sort of worming his way around. And then about a year after that I was in Greenwich Village and I saw an album – his first album cover. And I realized that was him.

Liam Clancy, by Bob Dylan

Recorded by David Hammond and Derek Bailey, Slane, Ireland, 1984

The times I remember the Clancy Brothers most was not mostly in the clubs where we played but in those bars: there was a bar called the White Horse Bar and . . . you could always go there, any time, and they'd be singing, you know, Irish – the Irish folk songs. Actually I learnt quite a few there myself.

. . .I never heard a singer as good as Liam ever. He was just the best ballad singer I'd ever heard in my life – still is, probably. . .

Liam always sang those ballads which always would get to me . . . I'd never heard those kind of songs before . . . close up, you know. I'd heard them on record but I hadn't heard them close up.

All the legendary people they used to sing about – Brennan on the Moor, or Roddy McCorley . . . I wasn't aware of them, when they existed – but it was as if they'd just existed yesterday . . . I would think of Brennan on the Moor the same way I would think of Jesse James or something, you know. They just became very real to me.

. . .I ran into Liam in an airport somewhere last year; I can't remember where. . .

Bob Dylan, by Liam Clancy

Recorded by Patrick Humphries, London, October 1984

. . .I was coming through La Guardia Airport about six months ago, and I had the bodhran on my back, and the guitars, and the next thing I felt this body behind me, and I got this great hairy kiss on the cheek. Now when that happens in New York you're going to turn round and belt whoever it is. So I turn around and it's Bob Dylan.

We stood talking for a little while and suddenly the whole thing flooded back to me – what it was all like at that time. He says: 'I love you guys. And I love [Robert] Shelton for bringing me to your first concert in [New York] Town Hall. You know what I remember about that concert, Liam? You sang a commercial about Donnelly's sausages!'

For a lot of people, certainly English onlookers, that whole period in Greenwich Village in the late fifties and early sixties was a golden period...

It was. It was a certain sort of spontaneous combustion. It's a thing that happens around the world at different times. It happened in Paris in the twenties when Hemingway was writing: a mini-renaissance. It moves from place to place, and there are people who try to find out where it's going to happen next, to follow it. But you can't control it, you can't predict it. What was happening in the Village at that time – it was a surprise to find yourselves in the middle of it...

Do you know what Dylan was when he came to the Village? He was a teenager, and the only thing I can compare him with was blotting-paper. He soaked everything up. He had this immense curiosity. He was totally blank and was ready to suck up everything that came within his range.

What did you feel about Dylan's electric set at Newport in 1965? That seemed to be the divisive event in the folk music fraternity...

I was actually filming at the Newport Festival that year. I was up a 12-foot platform filming with a telephoto lens, so I could zoom in close. And Dylan came out, and it was obvious that he was stoned, bobbing around the stage. Very Chaplinesque, actually.

He broke into that 'Tambourine Man' and I found myself standing there with tears streaming down my face, because – I saw the butterfly emerging from the caterpillar. I also saw, for the first time, the immense value of what the man was about. When he sang 'my ancient empty street's too dead for dream-

21

ing', I *knew* it was Sullivan Street on a Sunday. So it was not only a street, it was our street. I suddenly realised that this kid, who had bugged us so often, had emerged into a very major artist.

Clichés That Come To Pass

Christopher Ricks

The distinctive poignancy of American English within American writing has much to do with its making its own transience an acknowledgement and not just an admission. The sense that some of the most vivid words in today's American language are – to take up the terms in which T.S. Eliot disparaged American slang – 'inherently transitory', 'certain to be superseded', 'certain to pass away' and 'cannot endure': this sense can then itself constitute some of the great effects of distinctively American writing, so that the deterioration of the language becomes, though always a loss, the source of new gains.

Every user of language, whatever his or her politics, is engaged not only in conversation but in conservation. In any language, 'the conservative interest' predominates.

The terms are those of Henry James: 'The conservative interest is really as indispensable for the institution of speech as for the institution of matrimony.' But the *extent* to which the conservative interest within language predominates varies greatly from one society to another. It predominates more in Britain and in British English than in America and American English.

The American poet Ed Dorn has said:

Our articulation is quite different from other people's; we arrive at understanding and meaning through massive assaults on the language, so no particular word is apt to be final. It's rapidly rerun all the time. And I think that can be healthy usage. On the other

22

hand, there's so much of it that it gets the reputation for being loose. A lot of it in fact is.

Put like that it might sound blithe, but the best American poets convey the poignancy of there being nothing final. Dylan, for instance. 'It's rapidly rerun all the time'. With personal experience and with American technology in his mind's eye, Dylan sings, in 'If You See Her, Say Hello':

> Sundown, yellow moon
> I replay the past
> I know ev'ry scene by heart
> They all went by so fast.

There is no such thing as a video of the heart; replaying the past really does depend on knowing every scene by heart; but what makes this heartfelt is the unspoken 'And yet' between the lines

> I know ev'ry scene by heart
> They all went by so fast.

'*And yet* they all went by so fast'; not 'because they all went by so fast'. You'd have been right to expect that it would have been by their having gone by so slowly that they were known by heart. It isn't that by some audacity 'fast' means 'slow' (black English sometimes likes 'bad' to mean 'good' – 'Lenny Bruce was bad'); simply that you have to be quick on the uptake as Dylan kisses the joy as it flies, in both senses of *it flies*.

Again, in 'Is Your Love in Vain?' he sings: 'Are you so fast that you cannot see that I must have solitude?' – where fast means slow on the emotional uptake because of being so determinedly ahead of the game. To say of someone, especially of a woman, that she was 'fast' was itself once a fast (indecorous and suggestive) thing to say; but this sense faded. The language, sensitive to these glowings and fadings, is in sympathy with the love-experience which likewise has its glowing and fading.

'No Time To Think'. That is the title, and the refrain, of a Dylan song. But in terms of the transitory language, it is not that there is no time to think but rather that one of the things that must be promptly thought about is that there's no time. The

refrain in this song is always 'And there's no time to think' –
until the last verse. Then the refrain-line both expands and
contracts: it expands, in that it takes over the whole of the last
verse; it contracts, in that in the final end when it is time for the
last refrain, time so presses ('no time to lose') that instead of
'And there's no time to think' the refrain is curtailed to 'And no
time to think'.

> No time to choose when the truth must die
> No time to lose or say goodbye
> No time to prepare for the victim that's there
> No time to suffer or blink
> And no time to think.

The point is not that British English is insensitive to time (no
language ever can be); rather that, because it gives a less
important role than does American English to the passing or
transitory or obsolescent, there are certain effects cut off from it
– effects which cannot as clearly be seen and shown from the
vantage point of this one form of English as from the other.
Effects, for example, of rueful admission: of American English
itself conceding that much of it not only is not built to last, but is
built not to last.

Some love affairs are like that, and a poet or singer is likely to
create something worth his and our while when his love affair
with his medium, language, is intimate with this sense of what
a *while* is (in language and in life) that something should be
worth it. Dylan sings, as no English singer quite could:

> You will search, babe,
> At any cost.
> But how long, babe,
> Can you search for what is not lost?
> Ev'rybody will help you,
> Some people are very kind.
> But if I can save you any time,
> Come on, give it to me,
> I'll keep it with mine.
>
> ['I'll Keep it With Mine']

An English counterpart could have effected the ghostly musical

24

presence there of 'keep. . .time'; but could not have trusted British English so perfectly to combine, as American English here does, the smallest social offer and the largest offer of salvation:

> But if I can save you any time. . .
> But if I can save you   anytime. . .

It is not only the compacting of the two senses within the one line which shows the sheer egalitarian width of American English, but the compacting within the second sense – 'But if I can save you anytime' – of the most serious magnanimity with the casual largesse of conversation – 'any time' in that sense is pure American in the way in which, socially at ease, it fosters such ease. It can even be printed as one word in American English; when *sung* by Dylan it is not unmistakeably two words as it is when he prints his words. Within art (and the daily language too can be used with art), 'any time' gets some of its force, breezily fresh, from the sense that it is not itself a phrase which could have figured in American society and American English '*any* time'.

'No particular word is apt to be final,' said Ed Dorn. But *finally* to be apt, that is a different matter; and the word 'final' or 'finally' stands differently to experience in American English for this very reason: that a consciousness of how little is final in words or out of them pervades the saying. (And of course nothing is 'final' in a performing art.)

Dylan's song 'Rambling Gambling Willie' has the line: 'When the game finally ended up, the whole damn boat was his'. The game didn't just end, it ended up; and it didn't just end up, it finally ended up. ('No particular word is apt to be final.') There is a mild surprise at it being possible to say 'finally ended up' without blankly repeating yourself; and yet it makes perfect sense, since a gambling game is always beginning and ending again, until the last hand, when it finally ends up. In this, the gambling game is like the song itself, which is always coming to an end with each verse (ending with the refrain 'Wherever you are a-gamblin' now, nobody really knows'), but does finally end up.

Or again, Dylan sings to Ramona: 'You've been fooled into

25

thinking/That the finishing end is at hand'. Not one of those temporary or tentative ends, but the finishing end. In 'All I Really Want To Do', Dylan sings:

> I aint lookin' to block you up,
> Shock or knock or lock you up,
> Analyze you, categorize you,
> Finalize you or advertise you.
> All I really want to do
> Is, baby, be friends with you.

– where 'finalize' gets its pouncing power not just from being a word that was American before English (though Australian before American), but also – given the American sense of how even finality fleets away, like an advertisement ('Finalize you or advertise you') – from being such a shrug of a word. And one might (in passing . . .) notice Dylan's dexterity with the phrase 'knock you up' – which is apocryphally taken as getting the Englishman into trouble – when he offers an early call in the morning:

> I aint lookin' to block you up,
> Shock or knock or lock you up.

The sly propriety tactfully, pregnantly, separates 'knock' from 'you up' for a couple of words; after all, the preceding 'shock' would more suggest 'shock you' than 'shock you *up*' (though one of the things that Dylan is doing is giving a shake to the phrase 'shake you up'). Nobody need feel embarrassed; it all goes by so fast.

You can hear the acknowledgement of the transient, the obsolescent, in the imaginative use in American English of such a sturdily old-time phrase as 'come to pass'. In British English, this could be well-used with simple archaic dignity, with the sense of something more grave than any simple happening: under 'come to pass', in Collins' *Dictionary* (1979), the phrase is flatly reduced to '*Archaic*. To happen'. But the creative use of the phrase within American English is likely to pick up the poignancy of 'come *to pass*', a poignancy which the English poet may believe has to be spelt out rather than intimated; spelt out, for

26

instance, as Christina Rossetti does when she makes her two-stanza poem 'May' turn upon a change of these words:

> I cannot tell you how it was;
> But this I know: it came to pass –
> Upon a bright and breezy day
> When May was young, ah pleasant May!
> As yet the poppies were not born
> Between the blades of tender corn;
> The last eggs had not hatched as yet,
> Nor any bird foregone its mate.
>
> I cannot tell you what it was;
> But this I know: it did but pass.
> It passed away with sunny May,
> With all sweet things it passed away,
> And left me old, and cold, and grey.

This is altogether more explicit, more explicated even, than the American way with the phrase. There is a poem by John Crowe Ransom, 'Spectral Lovers', which has the stanza

> And gesturing largely to the moon of Easter,
> Mincing his steps and swishing the jubilant grass,
> Beheading some field-flowers that had come to pass,
> He had reduced his tributaries faster
> Had not considerations pinched his heart
> Unfitly for his art.

'Jubilant' swings on into 'Beheading some field-flowers', but does sadden at 'that had come to pass'. Ransom uses the phrase with an Anglophile elegance that is yet tinged with what is now an unEnglish shivering of the phrase.

Dylan, in 'I Pity The Poor Immigrant', ends his vision of this suffering with this turn of phrase:

> I pity the poor immigrant . . .
> Whose visions in the final end
> Must shatter like the glass.
> I pity the poor immigrant
> When his gladness comes to pass.

'In the final end' finds some resilience in the fact that this is itself nearing the *last* ending of a verse; furthermore, its doubling ('final end') is effectively American. Moreover, those last lines of the song, 'I pity the poor immigrant/When his gladness comes to pass', sharply challenge the British English sense of the phrase. You can of course imagine kinds of gladness for the happening – the arrival – of which somebody is to be pitied (sadistic kinds, for instance); but the pressure of the phrase is essentially to make you acknowledge that gladness comes *to pass*. 'We Poets in our youth begin in gladness;/But thereof come in the end despondency and madness'.

'The conservative interest' is present in the old-world phrase 'come to pass', but in the Dylan song it does not predominate. Something has happened since the old days of the phrase: has come to pass.

Sometimes, though, Dylan does need to help the conservative interest predominate. Then he will move from a quintessentially American phrase like 'big dreams' to a British English way of speaking:

God don't make promises that he don't keep.
You got some big dreams, baby, but in order to dream you gotta
  still be asleep.
When you gonna wake up, when you gonna wake up,
When you gonna wake up
Strengthen the things that remain.

                              ['When You Gonna Wake Up']

There the language to which he means to awaken his audience is not American English, with its 'big dreams', but the conservative interest and conserving force of the *Revelation* of the King James Bible: 'Be watchful, and strengthen the things which remain, that are ready to die.' The biblical line is itself one of the things which remain; and it impinges newly within a sense of the language itself as elsewhere so 'ready to die'.

For American English is especially alive with words and phrases that are ready to die, that are busy being born and busy dying. This can be a great resource, provided that the words and phrases admit it – not so much admit that they *have* seen better days as admit that before very long they will have seen better days.

28

In every language there are clichés (phrases which have seen better days), and slang. Clichés and slang can be very different, but they are both likely to have a short life-expectancy, if life is vividness and vitality. Then they can become zombies and ghosts: dead but they won't lie down, like that phrase itself. In every language an artist, or an imaginative conversationalist, can unexpectedly show that they are not really dead but sleeping; or not quite dead, and so can be given the kiss of life; or quite dead, but can be resurrected. Yet it is in American English, with its constitutional need to be novel – since how else could it free itself from British English? – that there can most often be created this particular poignancy, of a language acknowledging that much of it is not long for this world, and building an art which lasts out of a medium which admits that many of its characteristic components will not last. 'The order is/Rapidly fadin' ', sings Dylan, with some unexpected play of *rapidly* against what is usually that slow process, *fading*. Or, in one of the loveliest lines on *Infidels*:

> Only a matter of time till night comes steppin' in.

1960s: William Zantzinger Did Kill Poor Hattie Carroll

William Devereux Zantzinger killed poor Hattie Carroll at 1.40 a.m. on 8 February 1963, at the Spinsters' Ball – an annual charity event sponsored by post-débutantes – at the Emerson Hotel in Baltimore. That year's event was to benefit the Baltimore League for Crippled Children and Adults.

Zantzinger attended the function with his 24-year-old wife, the former Jane Elson Duvall. The couple had met at school – Friends School, Washington DC – and William Zantzinger had gone on to the University of Maryland. His father, Richard C.

Zantzinger, was a Maryland socialite and a former member of the State Planning Commission.

The Spinsters' Ball had begun at about 10 o'clock on the Friday night and was due to run until about 2 a.m. on the Saturday. Two hundred people had invitations to attend.

The Zantzingers drove there from the 600-acre family farm at Mount Victoria: a farm which produced tobacco, corn and grain.

At about 1.30 a.m. a 30-year-old black waitress, Mrs Ethel Hill of Belkthune Avenue, Baltimore, was clearing a table near the Zantzingers when she was approached by Zantzinger himself. He asked her something about a firemen's fund. Then, as the police reported it later, she was struck across the buttocks 'with a cane of the carnival-prize kind'. She tried to move away but Zantzinger followed her, striking her several times across the arm, thighs and buttocks.

Mrs Hill wasn't seriously hurt, but her arm was injured. As Zantzinger was taken back to his table by his wife, he struck *her* over the head with a shoe.

Ten minutes later Zantzinger went up to the bar and ordered a bourbon and ginger ale. The barmaid was Hattie Carroll, a 51-year-old black woman who had worked at the Emerson Hotel for six years as an extra employee for special functions and 'ballroom events'. She was a member of the Gillis Memorial Church and was active both with the Church and in local social work. The mother of eleven children, Hattie Carroll lived with two of her daughters (a 14-year-old and an 18-year-old), her other nine children all being older and married. She suffered from an enlarged heart and had a history of hypertension.

When William Zantzinger ordered his bourbon and ginger ale, Carroll was slow to respond and fumbled with the glass. 'Just a minute, sir,' she said. Zantzinger shouted back: 'When I order a drink, I want it now, you black bitch!'

Carroll said she was hurrying as best she could. Zantzinger struck her across the neck and shoulders with his cane. She shouted for help and then collapsed into the arms of a fellow-worker. A hotel official called for an ambulance and for the police. When the police later found the wooden cane, it was broken in three places.

The ambulance took the unconscious Hattie Carroll to the Baltimore Mercy Hospital. The police arrested Zantzinger and charged him with assault. As they escorted him out through the hotel lobby, the policemen were attacked by Zantzinger and by his wife. Patrolman Warren Todd received multiple bruises on his legs; Zantzinger received a black eye.

Zantzinger and his wife were taken to the Pine Street police station where Jane Elson Duvall Zantzinger was charged with disorderly conduct and her husband with the same offence plus two charges of assault 'by striking with a wooden cane' Ethel Hill and Hattie Carroll. Mrs Zantzinger was released on providing a $28 collateral.

William Zantzinger was held overnight in police custody. He appeared in the Central Municipal Court the following morning – still wearing tails and a carnation, though without his white bow tie. He pleaded not guilty to the charges and was released on $600 bail.

At 9.15 that same morning, Hattie Carroll died in the Mercy Hospital, never having regained consciousness. Suspected cause of death was a brain haemorrhage caused by a blow to the head.

Zantzinger had already been released from custody by the time the police were told of Hattie Carroll's death. A warrant for his re-arrest was issued, this time on charges of homicide. When the police from Charles County went to the Mount Victoria Farm, some seventy miles south of Baltimore, neither of the Zantzingers was at home. The police therefore put out an APB.

Judge Albert H Blum, who had presided at Zantzinger's court hearing that morning, said later that he had left instructions that he was to be notified if Hattie Carroll's condition worsened, so that he could if necessary increase the amount of bail required. Hattie Carroll actually died while this hearing was in progress, but the news of her death didn't reach the court.

Zantzinger was to be charged with first- and second-degree homicide. It was the first time in the history of the State of Maryland that a white man had been accused of murdering a black woman.

The trial took place in June 1963. A three-judge panel found Zantzinger guilty only of manslaughter. The homicide charges were dismissed and sentence deferred until August, when Zantzinger was sent to prison with a six-month sentence.

With time off for good behaviour, he was home in time for Christmas.

William Zantzinger has continued to prosper. Aside from his farm and inherited wealth, he also owns W & Z Realty in White Plains, Maryland. In 1984 he was elected Chairman of the Board of Trustees of the Realtors' Political Action Committee of Maryland.

Bob Dylan's Neglected Newport Year: 1964

Bill Allison

Although we have some knowledge of Dylan's appearance and the songs he sang at the 1964 Newport Folk Festival, certain aspects of his performance and its aftermath pose questions. What was Dylan doing at the time? What was the contemporary reaction? How have those performances been chronicled since? And why have they been so often overlooked?

1964 was a crucial year for Dylan. The 24-year-old was learning to cope with all the pressures of being Bob Dylan – public, private, past and present. But more than this, Dylan was also searching for a road into his own future. He was entering a period of transition that would take him from being a 'folk-singer' writing 'protest songs' in touch with the demands of his audience – writing the 'topical' songs they wanted – to being a creative artist and poet, attempting to tune in to the demands of the universe: not only the vast outer universe of history and space, but also the complex inner universe of self.

The times they *were* a-changin' and we were seeing another side of Bob Dylan. His performances at the 1964 Newport Folk Festival were an integral part of this transition period.

The Newport '64 programme tells us that Dylan was scheduled to make two appearances. The first of these was on Friday 24 July at 1.30 p.m. in the grounds of St Michael's school, Rhode Island Avenue, Newport. This was a 'workshop' featuring 'broadsides' and topical ballads. It was hosted by Pete Seeger. Fourteen artists were billed to appear: Johnny Cash, Len Chandler, Jimmie Driftwood, Bob Dylan, Seamus Ennis, Sara Gunning, Phil Ochs, The Chad Mitchell Trio, Tom Paxton, Frank Profitt, Malvina Reynolds, The Rodriguez Brothers, Bill Thatcher and Hedy West. Given equal billing, this would mean that each artist could perform only two or three songs.

A newspaper clipping from the *Providence Journal* tells us that Dylan was:

> One of the highlights of the afternoon ... beginning with a new song, 'Hey Mr Tambarine Man' [sic] and following it up with a comical protest to capital punishment, 'The Iron Lady', referring to the electric chair. He had the crowd on their feet for the first time during the performance...

When I first read the cutting, I was excited – not only the first recorded performance of 'Mr Tambourine Man' but also the discovery of a previously unknown Dylan song. However, much more prosaically, the reporter simply got it wrong. It was Phil Ochs who both sang and wrote 'The Iron Lady'. Whether the audience stood for him rather than for Bob Dylan is, therefore, unclear.

Dylan did, in fact, sing two songs at this workshop – 'It Ain't Me Babe' and 'Mr Tambourine Man'. He was using Newport 1964 to sing major new songs in public for the first time.[1]

Dylan was also scheduled to appear on 26 July at 8 p.m. on the main stage in Freebody Park. This was the main festival performance area. On the soundtrack of the film *Festival*, a documentary chronicling the Newport events, we hear Ronnie Gilbert introducing Dylan, who begins to play 'All I Really Want To Do'. Reviewing this, the *Providence Journal* says:

> [Dylan] started off with 'All I Really Want To Do Is Baby Be Friends With You' [sic] and then sang a song 'To Ramona', which drew the blonde Mary Travers of Peter, Paul and Mary out to the area of the recording vans where she draped herself over a stepladder, utterly absorbed in Dylan's performance. After singing 'Hey Mr Tambourine Man' and 'Signs of Freedom Flashing' [sic], he left the stage, but the fans would not be quieted, so he came back on with

Joan Baez who joined him in 'With God On Our Side'. Before the fans were subdued he had to come on briefly again to thank them and tell them he loved them.

Although this takes care of the two scheduled appearances, the newspaper report carries a passing reference to a *third*, unscheduled appearance – on the evening of the workshop session, Friday 24. The report says:

Dylan, appearing better dressed than he did last year or at his brief appearance on Friday night, obviously is the voice of the youth of America. . .

This 'brief appearance' was at the end of Joan Baez's set in the main park. They sang 'It Ain't Me Babe' together, Baez having invited Dylan on to the stage.

It has taken over twenty years for this information to be drawn together, and for a sizeable amount of misinformation about what Dylan sang in which set to be put aside. Why have Dylan's 1964 Newport appearances been so overlooked, by chroniclers and commentors alike, when they come from such a crucial time in Dylan's development?

First, consider the contemporary reaction to Dylan's performances. Although the *Providence Journal* stated that the crowd cried out for more, we read little to suggest this elsewhere.

Critical writing about 'the folk scene' in the United States in the sixties appeared in three widely-read journals: *Sing Out!*, *The Little Sandy Review* and *Broadside*. The reaction in all three publications was quite hostile.

The 'folk' and 'protest' movements of the period saw themselves as part of a mission – a mission they felt could change society for the better. (It is difficult now to conceive of, or exaggerate, the level of optimism of these times. Sic transit.) The 'folk' fraternity saw Dylan and his topical work as being major forces in this movement. Imagine, then, the bitterness when Dylan seemed to be abandoning and rejecting them, as he did at Newport '64, by singing his new, introspective, non-political songs – even at the workshop for 'broadsides'.

This feeling of abandonment and betrayal was reaffirmed and, indeed, intensified with the release of *Another Side of Bob*

Dylan in August 1964, and it erupted in the pages of the main 'folk' journals. Spectacularly, there was an article in the November 1964 edition of *Sing Out!* which took the form of an open letter to Bob Dylan written by the editor, Irwin Silber. This dealt with what Silber thought was the general drift of Dylan's work. Of Newport 1964 he wrote:

> I saw at Newport how you had somehow lost contact with people. It seemed to me that some of the paraphernalia of fame were getting in the way.

(Compare this with the newspaper report of the crowd demanding more from their 'spokesman' and of Dylan telling them he loved them.)

Silber suggested that Dylan had blown it and that the system had chewed him up. If 'the paraphernalia of fame' alluded to Dylan's shift towards modish clothes, and to his having, by the time of Newport '64, an entourage (mostly Bobby Neuwirth), then Silber's further charge – 'You're a different Bob Dylan from the one we knew. The old one never wasted our precious time' – was plainly an attack on the new material. Silber felt that inward-looking, own-experience songs were valueless, and seems to have been suggesting that Dylan had somehow cheated the audience by gathering them together to expect one thing and then giving them something else.

Here, in fact, was the first example of the mismatch between what people wanted from Dylan and what he wanted to give – the great mismatch that would so often recur throughout Dylan's career.[2]

Many of the themes that appear in Silber's *Sing Out!* article reappear in *Broadside* issue 53, 20 December 1964. A piece by Paul Wolfe on the 'new' Bob Dylan attempts to analyze Newport 1964:

> . . .the festival's most significant achievement was specific and twofold; it marked the emergence of Phil Ochs as the most important voice in the movement simultaneously with the renunciation of topical music by its major prophet, Bob Dylan. It was the latter event that proved most surprising.

Wolfe continues (compounding bad grammar with self-contradiction): 'Dylan's defection into higher forms of Art was predicted,' but adds:

> His new songs, as performed at Newport, surprised everyone, leaving the majority of the audience annoyed – some even disgusted, and in general scratching its collective head in disbelief. The Art that had, in the past, produced towering works of power and importance had, seemingly, degenerated into confusion and innocuousness.

Not only had Dylan abandoned 'protest', but the new songs – 'defections into higher forms of Art' – were poor songs. Wolfe compares them with the songs Phil Ochs sang. In this heavyweight protest championship of the world, Ochs wins on every count.

Ochs himself was unwilling to be a stick with which to beat Bob Dylan. Wolfe, saying he hopes Ochs won't follow in Dylan's footsteps, quotes Ochs' comments on Dylan in the Newport 1964 programme:

> I think he's slowly drifting away from songwriting because he feels limited by the form. More and more of his work will probably come out in poetry and free verse, and I would not be surprised if he stopped singing altogether, considering the over-adulation of his fans, and the lack of understanding of the audiences that identify with him.

(It's interesting that Ochs, here, ends by suggesting that what Silber called 'the paraphernalia of fame' was getting in the way from *Dylan's* point of view.)

Ochs also went into print in *Broadside* issue 54 (20 January 1965), with a rejoinder to the attacks by Silber and Wolfe – in the form of an open letter to them. Ochs said he thought they were like biology students trying to dissect Dylan: 'a rare prize frog'. They were annoyed because the frog kept hopping about in different directions while they were trying to dissect it. Ochs goes on, tongue-in-cheek, to reprimand Dylan for ignoring the reality of 'bombs and elections, folk-music critics and unemployed folk-singers' and then allies himself with Dylan's stance:

To cater to an audience's taste is not to respect them, and if the audience doesn't understand that, they don't deserve respect. As for Bob's writing, I believe it as brilliant as ever, and it is clearly improving all the time . . . How can anyone be so pretentious as to set guidelines for an artist to follow?

My major concern is how honest and well written I can make a song, not how well it can be used by the movement or how well it fits into the accepted pattern.

In another reply to Wolfe's article, one of the New World Singers, Bob Cohen, begins by saying that it is a mistake to see Dylan only as a writer and singer of protest songs:

For while he was writing and singing 'Blowin' In The Wind' and 'With God On Our Side', he was also singing and writing 'If I Could Do It All Over Again, I'd Do It All Over You' and 'Bob Dylan's Dream'.

Cohen says Wolfe's article is not criticism but 'fan magazine dribble made noble by his concerned progressive outlook'. Cohen argues for a broader perspective. It is dangerous, he suggests, to define and restrict. He implies that he'd thought the folk movement had grown out of that idea.

Wolfe replied to Cohen's article. He rejected Cohen's claim that Dylan wrote all kinds of songs. *The Times They Are A-Changin'*, he said, included only one non-topical song, 'Boots Of Spanish Leather'. If he had listened to it properly, wouldn't he also have listed 'One Too Many Mornings' and 'Restless Farewell' – the latter, of course a statement of Dylan's intention to move on?

The same edition of *Broadside* also contained 'a closed letter to myself' by Eric Andersen – which seems, on the whole, supportive of Dylan's position and new material as well as mocking of the entire debate. It ran:

the morning star is flickering over a bunch of lunch pails on their way to work. bob dylan is tucked away warm and sleeping. but the world is still staggering about its way. i look out my window and see all this. i can see clear down to the coast. i can see wide across the plain, over the hills, and deep in the wood berman gibson is still hollerin', dodging bullets, trying to tell the miners that jobs'll come

37

if they keep binding together and keep plugging away. i can still see sheriff rainey running around loose while a crowd of white mississippians are taking it all in like it was the ed sullivan hour. crosses are still finding wood, but no woody's. i'm still looking. down in the street there's a cop taking his ice from the number's runner. and in the ocean facing denver, the sea is filled with confused looks, disillusioned glances, messed up kids, hung-up adults, struggling farmers, workers, poets, painters, people, parents, writers, sinners, lovers, haters, saints, patriarchs and heroes alike. i look over the river. a couple of buildings are on fire; must be the sun coming up. dylan just got up to go to the bathroom. he stops first and looks in the mirror. 'i'm an artist,' he says. it's true. bob dylan is an artist and there's still problems. sincerely mine. eric andersen.

Further support came from Johnny Cash in the pages of *Broadside* – 'shut up and let him sing' – while in a later profile of Cash in *Rolling Stone* (January 1968), Jann Wenner tells us that: 'At the end of the Newport Folk Festival of 1964, Cash, who had just finished a compelling set of story-telling songs, gave his guitar to Bob Dylan, the traditional country singer's tribute to a fellow musician.'

Cash went on, after that Newport, to record 'It Ain't Me, Babe' and to release it as a single. It was a hit for him in the USA in November 1964, and remains interesting as a record that gave a 'rock' treatment to a Dylan song some six months before 'Mr Tambourine Man' was a hit for the Byrds. Was it the first folk-rock single?

It is clear that the only real support for Dylan, and the understanding of what he was attempting to do with his music at Newport, came from other singers and songwriters.

Yet this debate soon got swept aside. So soon after all this reaction to Newport '64 died down, greater battles began. Little wonder that the apparent black and white simplicity of *Another Side of Bob Dylan* has been comparatively neglected and the acoustic performances of Newport that year forgotten.[3] In a matter of months, electricity was to howl in the bones of everyone's face with Newport '65 providing a far more dramatic Dylan controversy.

The Mailbox Unlocked, Part 1

Dear *Telegraph*

I may be one of the few subscribers who has met and chatted with Dylan. I also appear in the film *Don't Look Back* – though if you blinked you'd miss me.

The meeting with Dylan took place at Heathrow Airport, London, as he was flying out at the end of the 1965 UK tour. I knew which flight he was leaving on because I checked the VIP flight lists. Amazingly, I found Dylan alone at the airline check-in desk. Albert Grossman, Bob Neuwirth and other members of the entourage were in another part of the building. I remember Dylan looking very dapper in dark glasses, leather jacket, blue drainpipe jeans and black winkle-picker shoes. I just went up to him and said hello. I asked him to sign his autograph on three album sleeves I'd brought with me, and he obliged. I found him very personable and polite.

My appearance in *Don't Look Back* came about at the very beginning of the tour, again at Heathrow Airport. A friend of mine, who was a reporter at the time, gave me a pass to go airside to meet Dylan's flight from New York. As a result we were probably the first people to see him on British soil that time. The film, quite near the start, has Dylan and Neuwirth walking up a ramp from the apron into the terminal building, singing 'London Bridge is Falling Down'. As the camera pans across, it shows us standing halfway up the ramp.

In the Ballantine Books' transcript of the film, the 'Young Man At Gate' pictured on page 18, facing Dylan, and quoted on page 19, is my reporter-friend. His name is Roy Shipston.

> Geoff Ward
> Ventnor
> Isle of Wight

1960s: Who and Where was Positively 4th Street?

4th Street is right at the heart of Greenwich Village. Dylan lived with 'Avril the dancer' on East 4th Street, had his photo taken for his union card in a booth on West 4th Street, and rented the apartment in which he first lived with Suze Rotolo on West 4th Street.

In 1965 when Dylan began to renounce the folk scene, or rather, leave it behind, there was a lot of predictable griping from some of the folkies. For the purposes of Dylan's response, '4th Street' is a kind of abstraction for that whole holier-than-thou, purist, he-was-an-*arriviste*-anyway scene, inside which many people had resented both Dylan's folk success *and* his apparent abdication from it.

The song was released in September 1965, and Scaduto writes:

> [It] moved a lot of temperatures up the scale. Dylan was either slicing up one specific individual on the Village scene or all of them, all of his friends and former friends. . . Everyone in the Village wondered who the song was about, and many took it personally and were hurt by it. Terri Van Ronk: 'Everybody was especially upset by the song because they felt *they* were the people he was talking about. We didn't think the nastiness was called for, or the putting down.' And Israel Young: 'At least five hundred people came into my place [the Folklore Center]. . .and asked if it was about me. I don't know if it was, but it was unfair. I'm in the Village twenty-five years now. I was one of the representatives of the Village, there is such a thing as the Village. Dave Van Ronk was still in the Village. Dylan comes in and takes from us, uses my resources, then he leaves and *he* gets bitter. *He* writes a bitter song. He was the one who left.'

But was Dylan's target a general one, or a specific one? The vindictiveness, the accusatory 'you' seems precise, doesn't it? Yet that is exactly what makes it so effective a curse upon the whole lot of them. It seems designed to provoke feelings of *individual* unease on a quite widespread scale: a lesson in the if-the-cap-fits process – the process Carly Simon invoked with playful knowingness in her later chorus of 'You're so vain, you probably think this song is about you'. Dylan knew 'Positively 4th Street' would set lots of people in the Village gnashing their teeth. No doubt he enjoyed contemplating the prospect of Izzy in a tizzy, and so on. But Bob Dylan has always chosen his targets with a kind of clear-sighted moral rigour. (Look, for instance, in *Don't Look Back*, which catches Dylan at exactly this period, at how his mercilessness with the phoney and para-sitical is balanced by immediate kindness whenever he encoun-ters warmth or open frailty in people.) In the case of the Village in 'Positively 4th Street', no doubt he felt adamantly that only the pious and teasable would feel savaged – and that they had it coming.

And after all, it might be mere insular egotism that 'the Village' assumed itself the target of the song at all. When, in Thompson's *Positively Main Street*, our hero Toby gets shown around Dinkytown – the bohemian section of Minneapolis where Dylan, as it were, dress-rehearsed, around the end of 1959, his prospective Greenwich Village début – the author is guided past the university by Ellen Baker:

'This,' Ellen exclaimed, 'is 4th Street.' She pulled to the kerb for a moment and put the car in neutral.

'You mean . . .?'

'Whether this 4th Street is "positively" the one, who can say but Bob? Everyone here in Dinkytown always thought their main drag was the one Bob sings about, though. It makes sense. Dinkytown is the student neighborhood where not just Bob lived, but everyone he hung around with. The Scholar and The Bastille coffee-houses were in Dinkytown. As you can see, now that we're on it, 4th Street would represent all that to Bob: the social scene, the university crud . . . the old folk people.'

Record-company Sales-force Instructions, 1965

This document was issued by Columbia Records (part of CBS Inc., the conglomerate that also owns CBS-TV in the United States) in 1965:

We have all tried 'different' avenues of exposure in promoting our artists and artist product. You have probably done some of these 'different' types of promotion on Bob Dylan, but have you tried . . .

Getting your accounts to position Bob Dylan product in other areas of their stores beside the folk music section, such as with The Byrds, Sonny & Cher etc. This will afford the customer a better chance to do some impulse buying.

Contacting musical instrument outlets and persuading them to use Bob Dylan display pieces in conjunction with their guitar, harmonica and sheet music displays.

Contacting radio personalities in your area that have 'Americana' type shows and pointing out to them the merits of featuring Bob Dylan in an American heritage theme.

Getting in touch with the casual wear buyers in department stores and convincing them to use Bob Dylan display pieces in their clothing displays. His dress may be considered 'kooky' by conventional standards, but kooky or not he is a motivating force on the youth of today, and they like to emulate their leaders.

Contacting the little theater groups in your area to convince them that readings of the lyrics of Bob Dylan songs would be presenting modern poetry in its finest form.

Getting in touch with the local newspaper culture editors and showing them the merits of doing a piece built around Bob Dylan, using a changing times theme.

Putting your ads in your local newspapers on Bob Dylan in unusual areas of the paper, such as on the sports page, the women's section or even the financial section . . . after all, he does mean money – for us at least.

Putting Bob Dylan displays with displays of men's boots (he wears them all the time), shades (he wears them all the time), or ANYWHERE that will attract attention.

1960s: . . . And Who Was Mr Jones?

There are several candidates for the status of Mr Jones in 'Ballad Of A Thin Man'. The first is the very famous dead man who may also have been the 'dancing child with his Chinese suit' in 'I Want You' – Brian Jones, the late Rolling Stone.

Jones' flatmate Dave told some stories about Dylan and Brian's close encounters a few years back in *New Musical Express*. Dylan apparently took an immediate liking to Brian Jones (and possibly admired the kind of clothes he was wearing at the time). Dylan and Robbie Robertson turned up at a New York hotel one day and got Jones to jam with them. The jam was so intense that Jones reportedly played his harp till his lips bled.

Dylan was a factor in Jones' paranoia. His flatmate recalls:

> Brian received a phonecall from Dylan asking him to join his back-up band. Brian was frightened of Dylan, though . . . Brian firmly believed that 'Ballad Of A Thin Man' was written as a put-down of himself. The line 'Something is going on here' [sic] 'but you don't know what it is, do you, Mr Jones?' used to pinprick his insecurity.
>
> Dylan, however, was still mooted to be best man at a wedding for Brian . . . [but] . . . no wedding took place.

So there's the first possibility.

Then there's Dylanologist A.J. Weberman's view, that there's a good case to be made for its being Max Jones, veteran jazz columnist of *Melody Maker* – a journalist with a pencil in his hand. But Dylan has made it obvious on visits to London that he was fond of Max Jones. (One example: he said hello to him from the stage of Earls Court, 26 June 1981.) So unless this affection was born of admiration for how Jones handled being attacked in the first place, he isn't the right man for the lob.

Let's turn to Dylan's own explanations.

In *Don't Look Back*, Dylan gives his picture of an ordinary man in the street (presumably an unhip person who in 1965 didn't perhaps know what was 'happening') as 'Mr C.W. Jones, you know, on the subway going to work . . .', so it could be that sort of general usage.

43

But Dylan has been asked directly who Mr Jones was at least twice. At Forest Hills, in August 1965:

> Q: Who is Mr Jones in 'Ballad Of A Thin Man'?
> A: He's a real person. You know him, but not by that name.

And at the San Francisco press conference of December 1965:

> Q: Who is Mr Jones?
> A: Mr Jones? I'm not going to tell you his first name, I'd get sued.
> Q: What does he do for a living?
> A: He's a pinboy. He also wears odd socks.

Then again, on the 1978 tour, Dylan introduced the song at the Nassau County Coliseum gig in Uniondale, New York (27 September) by volunteering this:

> I wrote this for a reporter who was working for *Village Voice* in 1963. He's still working for them. . .

So, as usual, not much help from the man himself, except that in this case, he does suggest that Mr Jones was indeed a journalist – leaving us to infer that 'with a pencil in your hand' was a specific reference in that direction. Add to that the implication given at the press conference that the surname really *was* Jones (and after all, it is just as possible that Dylan was playfully giving a straight answer here – a sort of double-bluff, as it were – as that he was playfully lying) and you're entitled to feel that Dylan's evidence supports, if anything, the candidacy of a claimant not yet mentioned: one *Jeffrey* Jones.

If you accept at all that Dylan was referring to a specific individual (albeit to designate a type and describe a syndrome) then Jeffrey Jones is the strongest possible candidate.

He stated the case for himself, ten years after the event, in *Rolling Stone* magazine, 18 December 1975. Here it is, only slightly abridged:

> It happened in the summer of 1965 at the Newport Folk Festival . . . Even now it is like owning up to a war crime to suggest that – I am Mr Jones.

44

I can't prove it, but I am convinced that Dylan used me as the unwitting model for his Mr Jones.

As a college student in the New York bureau of *Time* magazine, I concocted a story idea on the rebirth of harmonica in popular music. The article was to be built around a then obscure harp player from Chicago named Paul Butterfield who, I had heard, was going to make a big splash at the upcoming folk festival in Newport.

I sent the suggestion to *Time* . . . and to my surprise back came a memo advising me to go ahead. Attached to the memo was a yellow sheet of paper called a 'query', listing the questions that my reporting should answer and directing me to 'get quotes' from celebrities to support the story.

A week later I pirouetted slowly in the dust of a Newport, Rhode Island field, dazzled by the high sun of a July morning. In my pocket was the yellow query sheet. I'd interviewed Butterfield and things were going fine.

Suddenly I saw Joan Baez . . . She glided like a prophet, with a clutch of young girls as her train. They reached out but did not quite touch her, and cried ecstatically, 'Oh, Joan!' I saw then that my job was impossible. How was I, an awed college kid, to write anything authoritative:

'Hey, Mr Tambourine Man, play a song for me . . .' Bob Dylan's flat tenor voice rose above the throng seated at the perimeter of the storm-fenced festival arena. I walked towards the crowd, noting on my program that he was part of an informal 'workshop' session.

Near the workshop stage, next to a van filled with sound equipment, I met a high-cheeked woman with silver-blonde hair. It was Mary Travers, then of Peter, Paul & Mary I asked her questions prepared by *Time*. She asked if I would like to talk with Dylan. I nodded stiffly.

'Wait here,' she said.

Dylan had finished his set and was surrounded by chattering fans. Mary Travers grabbed his hand and led him to me.

We were engulfed by a swelling group of mostly teenage girls. Dylan pointed to the open side of the van. We climbed in and took seats amid hot amplifiers. Dylan's fans surrounded the vehicle, squealing his name, pounding the sides of the truck. The van began to rock.

'Yeah?' said Dylan.

As I opened my mouth to speak, he waved out of a window, then blocked the glass with a curtain and assumed a bored slouch.

'I'm doing this story for *Time* on the harmonica,' I said, 'and it seems to be, like, very important in folk music. I mean, after the guitar, probably the second-most-played instrument. They wanted me to find out what you think.'

'Yeah, man,' he said half-laughing, 'the harmonica is really big.'

The van rocked again.

'Well,' I asked, nearly choking on the crashing banality of every word, 'is it because of your influence?'

'No, man, the harmonica is just a good instrument, and it's been around a long while, you know what I mean?'

Dylan was polite, but impatient. I plunged on.

'*Time* has this way of doing stories where they use what they call a "peg", which is some person they build a story around. Paul Butterfield is the peg in this story, because they say he's going to be big. What do you think?'

Pause.

'Butterfield is great, man, great.' There was exasperation in his voice. 'Look,' he said, 'for me right now there are three groups: Butterfield, The Byrds and the Sir Douglas Quintet.' I couldn't tell if he was putting me on.

Dylan shot me a glance and I was rocked by a strange beauty in his ferret face, and by his eyes, which were alive and as maddeningly impenetrable as a cat's.

Dylan seized the silence.

'Is that all, man?' he said.

'Yeah, thanks a lot for your time.' I smiled wanly and extended a shaking hand. He took it limply. Then he climbed out the van door amid the fans, who swallowed him as he walked to a waiting car.

That evening, in the hotel dining-room . . . I heard laughing and a raucous shuffling of chairs behind me. Dylan – with an entourage that included Donovan, Bob Neuwirth and several slinky women – was being seated at the next table. I raised my hand in a tentative salute. Dylan hailed me with hollow delight.

'Mr Jones,' Dylan shouted from the chair he'd taken. 'Gettin' it all down, Mr Jones?'

There was laughter at his table.

'*Time* magazine,' he called with mock enthusiasm, 'You going to write a story for *Time* magazine, Mr Jones?

More laughter and jibes. I smiled and nodded, feeling like the village idiot, flattered by attention and defensively dumbstruck.

Later, in the lobby, I spied the elfin figure of Donovan. My multi-purpose query had instructed me also to keep an eye on Donovan. I approached him without hesitation. Already humiliated, I now felt recklessly brash. I followed at Donovan's side as he moved out the front door of the hotel and across an asphalt parking-lot towards a motel-like annexe.

'OK if I walk with you?' I asked cheerily.

'Well there's this party, you see . . .'

I stuck by him anyway, until we arrived at a room on the second floor of the annexe. Music and loud voices came through the door.

'Well, see ya now,' Donovan said as he knocked. The door opened and, as Donovan slipped in, I saw Dylan sitting on the edge of a couch, a girl by his side. The door closed quickly.

I waited five seconds, then knocked.

Five more seconds passed.

The door flew open. Bob Neuwirth came crashing out and fell flat on his back at my feet, staring at the ceiling. Dylan bounced up and down on the edge of the couch, laughing. Neuwirth suddenly scrambled to his feet, gave me a frantic look, then sprang back through the open door and slammed it, as though he were locking out a demon. I walked away.

The next day Butterfield's scheduled big splash was postponed by rain. Later, part of the Butterfield backed Dylan during his famous electric-axe inaugural . . .

It was a stormy coming-out party for what *Time* later called 'folk-rock' and I had missed the point totally.

Highway 61 Revisited appeared . . . [that] autumn. When I heard 'Ballad Of A Thin Man' I knew right then who Mr Jones was. I was thrilled – in the tainted way I suppose a felon is thrilled to see his name in the newspaper. I was awed too that Dylan had so accurately read my mind. I resented the caricature but had to admit that there was something happening there at Newport in the summer of 1965, and I didn't know what it was.

In retrospect, it has occurred to me that Dylan might not have known either.

Reels of Rhyme: Mr Tambourine Man

Aidan Day

'I don't know, different things inspired me . . .' said Dylan of the composition of 'Mr Tambourine Man' (written 1964, re-corded for *Bringing It All Back Home*, January 1965).[4]

Different things perhaps, and in another sense nothing external to inspiration itself. When the speaker of 'Mr Tambourine Man' invites the Tambourine Man to 'play a song for me', he is inviting himself to a mystery. 'Take me,' the speaker says, 'on a trip upon your magic swirlin' ship.' To hear the song would be to embark upon an interior voyage. What the speaker desires is the chance 'to fade/into my own parade': 'take me disappearin' through the smoke rings of my mind'. Within the fiction of the lyric the address to the Tambourine Man is an address made by the self to the self.

Specifically, Tambourine Man is called upon as a figure of the imaginative self or of the creative soul of the poet-speaker. The energy with which he is associated is the inspirational energy of artistic creation. In the third verse the achievement of poetic form is envisaged as resting upon the measure of the Tambourine Man's music: 'skippin' reels of rhyme/to your tambourine in time'. 'Mr Tambourine Man', as one commentator has aptly summarized, is a poet's 'invocation to his muse'.[5]

Muses, however, are not made to order. The point is highlighted in 'Mr Tambourine Man' by the way in which the governing verb of the refrain, '*play* a song for me', repeated ten times in the course of the lyric, becomes as much a plea as an injunction. The effect is reinforced by the repetition of the demand to be taken – 'Take me on a trip'; 'take me disappearin' ' – where the command is a request to be taken command of. In the last line of the last verse the imperative is a demand to be allowed. 'Let me forget . . .' Inspiration, it is implied, is something to be managed and simultaneously submitted to; something that can be directed but which must be cajoled into ravishing.

At one level, 'Mr Tambourine Man' is an account of what it is to be inspired from the immediate vantage point of not being so. Such distance is appropriate to a power that is figured throughout the lyric as preternatural in character. The images of the final verse especially convey a sense of something that moves and has its being deeper than the everyday world and self, and which escapes strictly logical formulation. To be drawn by the tambourine music is to draw deeply on the energies of the unconscious, where edges cannot be fixed. It is to negotiate the limits of finite structures, to the point where these begin to break down (the 'ruins of time') and where objects of common experience are, as it were, terrorized by a more-than-natural energy ('frozen leaves,/. . .haunted, frightened trees'). To be

48

taken up into the force of the creative moment would be to suspend ordinary suffering:

> Then take me disappearin' through the smoke-rings of my mind,
> Down the foggy ruins of time, far past the frozen leaves,
> The haunted, frightened trees, out to the windy beach,
> Far from the twisted reach of crazy sorrow.

The apotheosis envisaged in the remaining lines of this stanza has several defining features. There is the 'diamond sky': the crystalline perfection of an aestheticized nature. Like the 'Marbles of the dancing floor' in the City of Yeats' 'Byzantium', Dylan's 'diamond sky' is intimidating in its cold, unyielding brilliance. But its worth lies precisely in its transmutation of natural laws. The dance that takes place beneath the sky is an ecstatic one, the possessed dance of the creative moment itself, something larger than self-consciousness and reason. Imagination at this point overrides 'memory and fate', affirms a scope beyond the time-bound determinism of the natural self.

And as so often in Dylan, an image of circus, an image of carnival, finds its place in a picture of the subversion of the established and the known:

Yes, to dance beneath the diamond sky with one hand waving free
Silhouetted by the sea, circled by the circus sands,
With all memory and fate driven deep beneath the waves,
Let me forget about today until tomorrow.

The expression of the last line – in its anxiety *about* time, spoken from the perspective of the self *in* time – reminds us that the force of the dance is indeed only envisaged. However much the words of this lyric may predict the 'ruins of time', the lyric itself is committed in its rhyme-scheme to the pleasures of anticipation and recollection – and remains soundly structured *in* time.

The wish to suppress memory and fate touches a wish that rhyme itself – a mnemonic device grounded in the predeterminations of repetition – be suppressed. But a yearning to be 'free' is contradicted by the temporal gratifications offered at once by the rhyme with 'sea'. In this instance, as throughout, the lyric simultaneously contemplates and refuses its own ruination. The desired transcendence conflicts with the contingency of the language and form by which such transcendence is posited. It is a tension ironically caught in the rhyme that orders the image of the relationship between poetic measure and a preternatural energy: 'skipping reels of rhyme/To your tambourine in time'.

A contrast between statements concerning freedom and the boundaries of rhyme is something frequently exploited by Dylan. In 'Abandoned Love' (written 1975), for example, rhyme merely confirms the speaker's conviction of an actual, if not publicly acknowledged, entrapment:

> I march in the parade of liberty
> But as long as I love you I'm not free.

Again, in 'Jokerman' (1983), the halting fear of the natural self that it may not be ready for ultimate release is endorsed in a rhyme that forestalls escape from form:

> Freedom just around the corner for you
> But with truth so far off what good will it do?

'Subterranean Homesick Blues' (recorded January 1965) voices a characteristic American dread that in the land of the free, individual freedom has been misplaced. The nervously abbreviated metrics and the overinsistencies of alliteration and rhyme in this lyric register the sense of a culture's stunting of the possibilities of individual growth. In the second verse, even the life of the underground remains oppressively patterned, imprisoned in its paranoia about authority:

> Maggie comes fleet foot
> Face full of black soot
> Talkin' that the heat put
> Plants in the bed but
> The phone's tapped anyway
> Maggie says that many say
> They must bust in early May
> Orders from the DA
> Look out kid . . .

> Watch the plain clothes
> You don't need a weather man
> To know which way the wind blows.

A love-song such as 'You're Gonna Make Me Lonesome When You Go' (1974) shows its speaker acutely conscious of past, present and future:

> Situations have ended sad
> Relationships have all been bad
> Mine have been like Verlaine's and Rimbaud
> But there's no way I can compare
> All those scenes to this affair
> You're gonna make me lonesome when you go.

And when in this song a claim is made, true to the rhetoric of love, that it is possible to rise above a sense of time passing, it is a claim playfully undercut by a rhyme on time: 'Crickets talkin' back and forth in rhyme/. . . I could stay with you forever/And never realise the time'.

The boundaries of the time-defined, conscious self are not easily transgressed. In 'Mr Tambourine Man' the sense of strain in the image of a repression of memory and fate ('driven deep beneath the waves') hints at the sense in which the conscious will may co-operate only anxiously in a yearning for its own suspension.

But yearning can itself be part of a process of preparation, and 'Mr Tambourine Man' says a great deal about the nature of the preparation that is needed if the imaginative moment is to come. Just as, in Yeats' 'Byzantium', the 'Mummy-cloth' of mortal experience must be unwound from the 'bobbin' of the soul before Byzantium can be reached, so Dylan's lyric envisages a purgation of the ordinary self as the necessary prelude to hearing the music of the tambourine. The second verse describes the conditionless state that is yet the condition of being able to hear the music and to dance the dance:

> My senses have been stripped, my hands can't feel to grip,
> My toes too numb to step . . .

I'm ready to go anywhere, I'm ready for to fade
Into my own parade, cast your dancing spell my way

It is a state, as the first verse suggests, distinguishable from
the dominion of worldly things – a dominion whose transience
is measured in the hourglass: 'I know that evenin's empire has
returned into sand/Vanished from my hand' – a state of spiritual endazzlement transcending literal sight and natural inclination to rest; the condition of a solitary vision more intense than
the dreams of the mortal sleeper:

> Left . . . blindly here to stand but still not sleeping.
> My weariness amazes me, I'm branded on my feet,
> I have no-one to meet
> And the ancient empty street's too dead for dreaming.

All this aching, however, only directs us to the paradox upon
which 'Mr Tambourine Man' is built. As a lyric, the work itself
evidences an attainment of the creative moment which its
speaker spends so much time anticipating.

In this sense, the lyric-speaker's pursuit of an energy located
in the future turns out to be a pursuit of the lyric's own origin.
That which is desired has, in the writing out of the desire in
poetic language, already been achieved. The desire is fulfilled in
the writing of the lyric. For the speaker to stop speaking would
be to fail in the realization of his desire. But this also means,
paradoxically, that there is a sense in which it becomes impossible to conceive of a complete fulfilment, a fulfilment to end all
fulfilments. The dance is in the writing and the writing is in the
dance, but precisely because that is the case there is never a
final word, never a place (except in death) where it would be
possible to leave off writing. Writing could be phrased as a
looking for a final or an ultimate word. But that would be pure
word, the Word before words. Such a Word shadows writing, it
is writing's inspiration. But while it both energizes and is
pursued by writing, the Word is never simply contained by
words. It is, as it were, a ghost in the machine, at once
seductively beckoning and mockingly elusive.

A haunting image in the third verse of 'Mr Tambourine Man'
is committed to exploring the sense in which the mystery of

inspiration is the mystery of language. The speaker is attempting, on this occasion, to reassure the Tambourine Man:

> And if you hear vague traces of skippin' reels of rhyme
> To your tambourine in time, it's just a ragged clown behind,
> I wouldn't pay it any mind, it's just a shadow you're
> Seein' that he's chasing.

If Tambourine Man is a figure of the energy of inspiration, the lyric-speaker here finds, in the persona of the 'ragged clown', a figure for the self that has been inspired – the self that produces aesthetic form.

It is a self constituted in its very productions, as is suggested in the way the construction of the verse insists upon an identification of 'reels of rhyme' with 'clown'. Both rhyme and clown undergo a similar identification with the 'shadow' in the third line of the passage.

Yet the clown is almost simultaneously pictured at a remove from – as, indeed, 'chasing' – the shadow. The shadow might be read as that of Tambourine Man, but it might just as well be read as the clown's own shadow. Tambourine Man and clown, sharing one shadow, are as distinguisable and yet inseparable as inspiration and the inspired self might be expected to be. And just as Tambourine Man is implied in the shadow and the clown, so he is implied in the 'rhyme', the inspired language, that is interchangeable with the clown and the shadow.

The drama of this image which reflects upon itself enacts the way in which the Word and the word, inspirational energy and the poetic self and its creations, imply each other, without ever being literally one and the same thing. Poetic language, and poetic power chase each other in a circle of mutual implication, an incessant shadow-play. Poetic language, and the self that makes and is made by that language, trace an energy represented by the Tambourine Man and his music. But it is a tracing that, like all tracing, neither completely defines nor is utterly divorced from what it traces. Tambourine Man himself is inscribed in the language of 'Mr Tambourine Man', but being the essential Word he is not held once and for all time by these particular words.

Dylan's image conveys a sense of poetry as generated in a compulsive and never-to-be-literally-fulfilled cycle of desire for a meeting between language and essence, conscious and unconscious, word and Word. The logical absurdity of the compulsion directs the casting of the poetic self in the figure of a clown.

Yet for all his raggedness the clown is by no means to be pitied. The speaker's attempts to reassure Tambourine Man have the odd and lovely effect of celebrating the dignity of the tracing, the 'reels of rhyme' themselves, the achieved art-form.

Such celebration is an integral part of the lyric's self-celebration – a self-celebration that is one of the prime functions of the third verse. The opening lines of this verse characterize the state of dæmonic possession as a joyful emancipation from constraint, including even the constraint of responsibility to an audience. As the speaker addresses Tambourine Man, a disorientation of ordinary perceptual and sensory terms of reference is suggested through an image of motion – spinning and swinging – along two different axes simultaneously:

> Though you might hear laughin', spinnin', swingin' madly
> across the sun,
> It's not aimed at anyone, it's just escapin' on the run
> And but for the sky there are no fences facin'.

What is distinctive here is that the speaker does not, as in the first two and the last verses, simply look forward, insisting on his own preparedness.

The possibility of Tambourine Man hearing the music might be read as a future possibility. But there follows a striking use of present and present continuous tenses. Not 'it *would* not *be* aimed' but 'it *is* not aimed'. Similarly, in the passage that concludes the verse, it *is* a ragged clown *chasing* a shadow.

The shift in this stanza out of the temporal logic of the rest of the lyric on the one hand enhances the universalization of the reflection on poetry contained in the image of rhyme, clown, shadow and Tambourine Man. On the other hand, the placing of an image in a kind of perpetual present enables it to reflect directly on the lyric in which it occurs. The laughing, the spinning, the swinging and the chasing are what is happening as this lyric is being written.

54

The return to a future-oriented perspective in the last verse allows the work once again to look outward beyond itself to other creative moments, to lyrics yet to be written.

The sense of an endlessly repeatable pattern of beginning anew with Tambourine Man, of endless possibilities of writing and re-writing the Word, is conveyed in the open-endedness of a refrain that is reiterated without variation five times in the course of the lyric:

> Hey! Mr Tambourine Man, play a song for me
> I'm not sleepy and there is no place I'm going to.
> Hey! Mr Tambourine Man, play a song for me
> In the jingle jangle morning I'll come followin' you.

In the Factory: Dylan and Warhol's World

Patrick J. Webster

Both the major biographies of Bob Dylan published so far make no more than a passing reference to Andy Warhol, and imply no real connection between these two major twentieth century artists. Recently, Robert Shelton observed obscurely that Warhol 'became a Dylan freak', but implied that the singer wanted nothing to do with the artist. Scaduto commented briefly that Warhol wanted Dylan to 'decorate' his parties, nothing more. In fact, there was much more connection between Dylan's and Warhol's world than either biographer suggests.

Bob Dylan seems to have first come into contact with Andy Warhol in the summer of 1965, presumably shortly after Dylan's return from Europe. Warhol described it thus:

I'd met Dylan through the MacDougal Street/Kettle of Fish/Cafe Rienzl/Hip Bagel/Cafe Figaro scene. He was around twenty-four then and the kids were all just starting to talk & act & dress & swagger like he did. But not so many people except Dylan could ever pull off this anti-act, and if he wasn't in the right mood, he couldn't either. He was already slightly flashy when I met him, definitely not folksy any more; I mean he was wearing satin polka-dot shirts.[6]

Warhol's introduction was probably via Barbara Rubin, a film-maker on the fringes of the Factory scene – the Factory being the large warehouse-like building on 47th Street used by Warhol as an open-house studio. Rubin, pictured on the rear of the *Bringing It All Back Home* sleeve massaging Dylan's head, is known to have brought the Byrds and Donovan – among others – to the Factory, and has been described thus:

> . . . a boyishly attractive, precocious 21-year-old art groupie . . . an intimate of, among others, Allen Ginsberg, William Burroughs, Bob Dylan . . . who according to Ginsberg 'dedicated her life to introducing geniuses to each other in the hope that they would collaborate to make great art that would change the world.'[7]

By 1965 Warhol was one of the leading painters in the pop art movement. His film-making experiments must have been of interest to Dylan, who was already talking about making movies of his own. Dylan was to acknowledge this later, on more than one occasion:

> You know who understood this [the possibility of making films outside the commercial Hollywood formula]? Andy Warhol. Warhol did a lot for American cinema. He was before his time. Warhol was important to me.[8]

> Warhol was more than just a director. He busted through new territory.[9]

> I like Warhol a lot. I think his *Empire State Building* is more exciting than Bergman.[10]

(Incidentally, one *song* of Dylan's which may show the influence of Warhol's style is 'All the Tired Horses' on *Self Portrait*. I have in mind the similarity between the continuous repetition of the song's two lines and Warhol's paintings of rows and rows of Coca-Cola bottles, hours of filmed sleeping, the 24-hour movie of the Empire State building and more.)

Warhol actually made two films concerning Dylan – one was *about* him, and was described by the Velvet Underground's Sterling Morrison:

Dylan was always lurking around. There was one film Andy made with Paul Caruso, *The Bob Dylan Story*. I don't think Andy has ever shown it. It was hysterical. They got Marlowe Dupont to play Al Grossman. Paul Caruso not only looks like Dylan but as a super-caricature he makes even Hendrix look pale by comparison. This was around 1966 when the film was made and his hair was way out here. When he was walking down the street you had to step out of his way. On the eve of filming, Paul had a change of heart and got his hair cut off – close to his head – and he must have removed about a foot, so everyone was upset about that! Then Dylan had his accident, and that was why the film was never shown.[11]

The second film featured Dylan as himself, and was recalled by Robert Heide, writing in the *Village Voice* in July 1982:

Dylan turned up at the silver factory that week for a filmed portrait by Andy – a 15-minute study in stillness, silence and emptiness. Dylan decided his payment would be a giant Warhol silk-screen canvas of Elvis in cowboy attire firing a revolver. Andy was livid when he saw Dylan taking his 'payment', though he opted for cool silence. Mr Tambourine Man did not sit for nothing.

Warhol, however, gives a rather different account both of the film and of the Elvis picture involved:

Brian Jones was a good friend of Nico's and he and Dylan came to the Factory together one afternoon when the Velvets were rehears-ing and I was working . . . Then Allen Ginsberg and Peter Orlovsky dropped by. We did screen tests of Brian and Dylan while Gerard [Malanga] fought with Ingrid Superstar over whose turn it was to pay for the malteds. I liked Dylan, the way he'd created a brilliant new style. He didn't spend his career doing homage to the past; he had to do things his own way, and that was just what I respected. I even gave him one of my silver Elvis paintings in the days when he was first around. Later on, though, I got paranoid when I heard a rumour that he had used the Elvis as a dart board up in the country.

I did eventually find out what Dylan did with that silver Elvis painting. More than ten years later, at a time when similar paintings of mine were estimated at five or six figures, I ran into Dylan at a party in London. He was really nice to me, he was a much friendlier person all round. He admitted that he'd given the painting away to his manager Al Grossman, but then he shook his head regretfully and said, 'But if you ever give me another one, Andy, I wouldn't make that same mistake again.' I thought the story was finished then but it wasn't. Shortly afterwards, I happened to be talking to Robbie Robertson, the guitarist in The Band, and he started to smile when I told him what Dylan had told me. 'Yeah,' Robbie laughed, 'only he didn't exactly give Grossman the painting, he traded it – for a sofa!'[12]

At the same time as he came into contact with Andy Warhol, Dylan's path also crossed that of Edith Mintburn Sedgwick – 'a charming, well-born débutante from Boston' Truman Capote called her. She had had a brief career as a top model, but set herself to become a movie actress and was taken up by Warhol.

Dylan's long-time friend Bobby Neuwirth described Dylan's and Edie's first encounter:

Bob Dylan and I occasionally ventured out into the poppy nightlife world. I think somebody who had met Edie said, 'you have to meet this terrific girl.' Dylan called her, and she chartered a limousine and came to see us. We spent an hour or two, all laughing and giggling, having a terrific time. I think we met in the bar upstairs at the Kettle of Fish on MacDougal Street, which was one of the great places of the sixties. It was just before the Christmas holidays; it was snowing, and I remember we went to look at the display on Houston Street in front of the Catholic church. I don't remember how the evening ended . . . Edie was fantastic. She was always fantastic. She believed that to sit around was to rot – an extension of the sixties pop culture, from a Bob Dylan song: 'He not busy being born is busy dying.'[13]

Dylan was to be seen hanging out with Warhol and Edie together in the early days of his acquaintanceship with them. On 29 December 1965, they made the gossip columns of the *New York Post*: 'At Arthur last night, Bob Dylan, Andy Warhol and Edie Sedgwick watched a girl in backless pyjamas and parachute boots. She stared right back at them.'

Arthur was a chic, poppy nightclub in New York, described by Warhol as 'all bright darkness'. A haunt of rock stars, film stars, astronauts and other celebrities, legend has it that Arthur was where Warhol uttered his celebrated remark: 'In the future, everyone will be world famous for fifteen minutes.'

Despite Dylan's marriage to Sara Lowndes in late November 1965, (which was a secret known only by Dylan's very closest friends, and certainly not by the Warhol crowd), Dylan and Edie began to spend time together.

Edie – now intent on becoming a singing star – began to claim that she was to have her career managed by Al Grossman, but Andy Warhol was hardly impressed by Edie's vocal gifts. He describes an incident from a banquet held in the Delmonico Hotel, New York (the hotel where, according to legend, Dylan turned The Beatles on to marijuana):

> Edie had come with Bobby Neuwirth and while the film crew arrived, and Nico sang her Dylan song, Gerard [Malanga] noticed that Edie was trying to sing too, but it was obvious even in the incredible din that she didn't have a voice.[14]

There was also talk of Dylan and Edie making a non-Warholian film together, though nothing ever came of this. What certainly happened was that Edie slowly became estranged from Warhol; she no longer starred in his films or hung out at the Factory. Viva, a new Warhol superstar, suggested that Andy felt some bitterness at what had happened:

> It must have had an effect on Andy – Edie leaving him for Dylan. He was probably in love with Edie, with all of us – a sexless kind of love – but he would take up your whole life, so that you never had time for any other man. When Edie left with Grossman and Dylan, that was a betrayal, and he was furious; a lover betrayed by his mistress.[15]

Warhol himself admitted some sadness at Edie's 'drifting away' with 'the Definitive Pop Star – possibly of all time. . .the thinking man's Elvis':

> I missed having her around, but I told myself that it was probably a good thing that he was taking care of her now, because maybe he knew how to do it better than we had.[16]

59

Edie needed someone to take care of her because she was already well strung out on drugs, and Warhol recalls people suggesting to him that Dylan's song 'Like a Rolling Stone' might include an attack on him:

> I'd get answers like 'I hear he [Dylan] feels you destroyed Edie' or 'Listen to "Like a Rolling Stone" – I think you're the diplomat on the chrome horse, man.' I didn't know exactly what they meant by that – I never listened to the words of songs – but I got the tenor of what people were saying, that Dylan didn't like me, that he blamed me for Edie's drugs.[17]

Warhol ought to have been reassured by the fact that this song had been written some weeks before Dylan had even met Edie Sedgwick.

Paul Morrisey, soon to become an important part of the Warhol film factory, had this to say about the split between Andy and Edie:

> The Dylan relationship came up one night when we saw Edie at the Ginger Man (a restaurant opposite the Lincoln Center). She told us that she didn't want Andy to show any of her films any more. By that time she'd made about eleven films with Andy in only four months. She told us that she had signed a contract with Bob Dylan's manager, Albert Grossman. Grossman used to come round to the Factory with his assistant, supposedly to listen to Nico practise, but for some reason he had lost interest in her. It was Edie Sedgwick he wanted to put under contract, so he'd ask, 'Do you have any of those old movies of Edie Sedgwick we've heard about? We'd love to see them.' They wanted to see what she looked like on the screen, but doing it very sneaky and behind our backs. Actually, Edie was all part of it, which we didn't know then. Dylan was calling her up and inviting her out, telling her not to tell Andy or anyone that she was seeing him. He invited her up to Woodstock and told her that Grossman hoped to put her together with him. She could be his leading lady. So she said to herself, 'Ah, this is my break'. She signed with Dylan at Grossman's urging. Apparently Grossman had said that he didn't think Edie should see Andy so much any more, because the publicity that came out of it wasn't that good.[18]

But Edie's relationship with Dylan, whether professional or private, was doomed too. In the first place, it was accelerating

60

her self-destruction, at least according to Malanga, who felt that 'the pressures of the life she was leading weighed heavily upon her exotically unstable character', as did a 'growing involvement with Bob Dylan's circle, where the manipulative use of acid and amphetamine did little to bolster her ego.'[19]

In the second place, (as already mentioned), Dylan had been secretly married since late November 1965 to Sara, and Edie was badly shaken by this discovery, as Paul Morrisey recalls:

> [Edie] said, 'They're going to make a film and I'm supposed to star in it with Bobby.' Suddenly it was Bobby this and Bobby that, and we realized that she had a crush on him. We thought he'd been leading her on, because just that day Andy had heard in Sy Litvinoff's office – our lawyer – that Dylan had been secretly married for a few months. . . Everything was secret those days for some reason, all phoney secrecy. So Andy couldn't resist asking: 'Did you know, Edie, that Bob Dylan had gotten married?' She just went pale. 'What? I don't believe it! What!' She was trembling. We realized that she really thought of herself as entering a relationship with Dylan, that maybe he hadn't been very truthful. So off she went and we never saw much of her after that. Probably none of it was true; Dylan never had any intention of making a movie with Edie.[20]

In early 1966, Edie's relationship with Grossman and Dylan came to an end.

How much, if any, of all this is reflected in Bob Dylan's songs is of course debatable. Nico heard something of Edie in 'Leopard-Skin Pill-Box Hat'; there's mention of 'your débutante' in 'Memphis Blues Again', but 'Just Like A Woman' in particular seems to have been thought to be about Edie by several people in the Warhol circle. Jonathan Taplin – then Dylan's road manager – commented on this, and upon one of the main reasons for Dylan's being attracted to Edie:

> Dylan liked Edie because she was one of the few people who could stand up against his weird little numbers; she was much stronger than the sycophants who were hanging around him at the time. He was always in an adversary relationship with women. He tested people, perhaps to find out about himself. His transition from folk

purity to rock insanity was overwhelming him. He needed to know: who was he? Dylan respected Edie's spirit and her strength in being able to deal with him, and that she didn't wither. You know that song 'Just Like A Woman'? They say he wrote it about Edie.[21]

Edie's strength and vulnerability may well be reflected in the song's subject, 'with her fog, her amphetamine and her pearls'. Andy Warhol said of her: 'She had a poignantly vacant, vulnerable quality that made her a reflection of everybody's private fantasies. She could be anything you wanted her to be: a little girl, a woman.'[22]

Ciao Manhattan, the Robert Margoulef film about Edie's life – which starred Edie herself – had 'Just Like A Woman' as part of its soundtrack, perhaps suggesting that Edie too felt it to be her song. Dylan had her pictured on the inner sleeve of *Blonde On Blonde*, and in a poem called 'Edie Sedgwick (1943–1971)', Patti Smith wrote explicitly:

> Everyone
> knew she was the real heroine of
> Blonde on Blonde
> oh it isn't fair
> oh it isn't fair
> how her ermine hair
> turned men around
> she was white on white
> so blonde on blonde . . .

Edie Sedgwick became a classic casualty of the '60s. After repeated spells in mental clinics, she moved to California; she died in bed on 16 November 1971 of acute barbiturate poisoning.

Andy Warhol survived being shot and critically wounded in June 1968 by Valerie Solanis, the founder and only member of SCUM (the Society for Cutting Up Men). He died, of a massive heart attack following a gall bladder operation, on 21 February 1987.

1966 and All That: D.A. Pennebaker, Film-maker

Interview by Shelly Livson, New York City, Spring 1984

How did filming Dylan's 1966 tour come about, after you'd already made your film of his '65 tour, Don't Look Back?

Pennebaker: Dylan wanted to make a film of his tour with the band [later The Band], and he wanted to direct it and he asked me if I would help him film it.

Making the film was his idea?

Yeah. . . .It was to be a TV show, that's what I was told, and later on I did have some talks with ABC about it. I wasn't supposed to be the producer . . . and I wasn't supposed to be the editor necessarily, though it was unclear. We were going to do it as we went along.

[In the event, the ABC-TV deadline was one of the things blown out by Dylan's motorcycle crash. When it came to editing, the film material effectively split into two potential projects.

Dylan worked on editing the mainly non-concert footage with Howard Alk, who had been Pennebaker's assistant on *Don't Look Back* the year before. The resulting film, never widely shown, was *Eat The Document*.

The other potential project, the film Pennebaker might like to have made, using mostly the still-unshown concert footage, never was put together, since this time around, unlike with *Don't Look Back*, Pennebaker had merely been hired to help shoot whatever film Dylan wanted.]

When did you join the tour? You didn't go on the Australian leg?

I was doing something else. I don't remember what it was now. I met him in Stockholm.

And then from Stockholm [29/30 April 1966] you stayed with the tour till London [26/27 May]?

Yeah. Through the Albert Hall.

How many cameramen were there?

Just Howard Alk and myself.

And did you have a sound man?

Yeah. We had a sound man. And Dylan had a sound man, Bob Alderman, who was supposed to be recording all the concerts on a sync tape. We later found out that for some reason it was breaking down – that it hadn't worked and that none of the concerts had any sync track on them; so one of the problems we had was trying to sync those concerts up. I had one sound person with me – well, I guess I used Jones Alk, Howard's wife . . . My recollection is that it was Howard and I and Jones. Pretty much the three of us were doing it.

Were all the concerts recorded?

We recorded every concert from beginning to end, on audio tape.

And did you film all the concerts as well?

Parts of concerts. Some concerts were filmed. Some concerts Howard Alk filmed and I wasn't even there. I went to Cannes for two or three days and so there is some material that I never saw that Howard shot. But most of the stuff, I shot. As I recall, most of the filming, I did.

. . .Again, it was Bob's film, and he wasn't really interested in making a concert film. He was interested in making a film for television. He wasn't even interested in a theatrical film. He was interested primarily in directing material off the stage. Stage material did not interest him, and in fact I shot a lot of it kind of on my own . . . The time that I got on the stage with him . . . I filmed the whole concert from on-stage . . . he didn't know that I was going to do that. He was kind of surprised to see me there.

Which concert was that?

I think it was Glasgow. But it might have been Edinburgh . . . my recollection is that it was in Scotland . . . I filmed two or three concerts very hard and then I filmed in France and [at the] Albert Hall. I missed three concerts . . . I missed Cardiff, Birmingham and Liverpool. Or maybe it was Cardiff, Bristol and Birmingham.

Did Howard Alk film those?

Yeah. But again, I've never actually seen what he filmed.

He gave it to Bob?

Bob has all that footage as far as I know.

The press reports at the time indicated that the audience reaction was pretty negative to the electric half of the concerts. Was that your impression?

No. Some places it was, some places it wasn't. It varied. It didn't bother him that much . . . in general he was having so much better a time with the band than he was by himself that you could see right away that the difference was night and day in terms of his performance.

So he actually enjoyed the tour?

Well, he liked playing with the band a lot.

We were led to believe he was on some kind of death trip.

Oh, there was a lot of weird behaviour on the trip. I don't think it was a death trip. The pressures were enormous . . . he did behave weirdly sometimes, but the one thing that I was really sure of was that he really liked playing with Robbie and having that electric music all around him. It was a really big incentive to him musically and I saw him do a lot of work. He wrote a lot of music on that trip, some of which we filmed. I think there's snatches of it in the film that he made.

About Paris: the reports were that there was particularly negative reaction by the audience there, and that Dylan was supposedly tuning up for ten minutes between each song . . . and that he said if you don't like it, go read a newspaper, or something like that . . .

Yeah, he did long tune-ups . . . well, the French were very freaked out by Dylan. I think he couldn't be too outrageous for the French. I think no matter how outrageous he was, they were ready to – despite the screaming and yelling I think they took it as some kind of monumental manifestation of some sort . . .

there were people who were outraged in the audience but I never got the feeling that any audience was really totally hostile.

But that may be just my memory. You gotta understand, when you're making a film, you're really underwater. And you don't have time for a lot of the niceties of social gatherings, and you tend to be really preoccupied with what you're doing, and sometimes it's backstage and sometimes it's onstage and sometimes it's audience. Sometimes you miss what later everybody remembers as the same occasion. You were just somewhere else . . . or else you're just absolutely out of it.

It's a really hard process to follow a concert-tour, because you're unlike anybody else. They can knock off at five in the morning and sleep for eight hours. You're processing film and getting your batteries charged practically round the clock. So you're never off, you're always doing something.

In this instance I felt that there would be more people helping us but the people were not much use to us . . . It just came down to Dylan and me, and sometimes I had somebody else doing the sound. I think he had some actress there – Zuzu [a French actress] was doing sound at one point and at another point I think I had . . . Marianne Faithfull. I mean people like that were always in very good control of themselves because they had to go out and do concerts and stuff – they didn't mess around and get drunk and stuff. So you could always count on them to be alert and capable for periods of time. A lot of the people who just hung around, who were supposed to be helpers, got really into the process of knocking themselves out and became useless. And that's a problem you get used to, but it still makes it difficult.

Who were the people hanging around Dylan on that tour?

I don't remember. They used to change overnight . . . I do remember the two Canadian girls that came in. Later, Robbie married one of them . . . we were looking for somebody to help us do something and we found them out on the street. They were hanging around outside the Embassy, or something. We brought them along . . . They were friends, and they went to England with us and they were very helpful and Robbie fell in love with one of them and married her.

You really get cut off. You don't have access to normal – I mean, you're not going to go out and hire a union camera person . . . They're not going to work under those conditions. So you look for people who are already there, who look like they're going to hang in and be useful to you.

There was an endless succession of people, many of whom I never knew. Some of them I did: people whose names were familiar to me appeared and disappeared. It was constantly going like a big New Year's Eve party. It's hard to be part of that, because you can't totally sit there and stare at everybody soberly, you know, while they're jumping around, so you kind of have to go along with it to some degree, but you can't get into it or you'll never film it. It's one of the problems with filming: it requires an enormous kind of concentration that most people never have to do in their lives.

How many hours would you say you shot each day?

Some days I wouldn't shoot any. You don't go at it like picking potatoes . . . if you did, you'd never get anything. But in this case it was a little complicated, in that I was kind of trying to do two different films.

In the beginning I was only trying to respond to Dylan, what Dylan wanted. Dylan said, 'I'm going to direct you. Get the camera and we'll decide what to do.' He would direct people and say, 'Can you film it this way?' 'Did you get that?'

Would this be on the street, in the hotel room?

Everywhere. He'd put little scenes together. I believe there was one up in my room in the hotel. We were at the Georges V [in Paris]. There was this huge mirrored clothes cabinet, and he had people going in, closing the doors and coming out. There would be a succession of people – I don't know where they came from, people would find them for him. There would be strange women and guys and I would just film these little scenes and then he would set up things. Sometimes he wouldn't do anything: he was just totally into something else and we would be sitting around. And sometimes I would film the way I felt. I would film things as I saw them, and I would decide what to film. I'd film concerts.

So really I was trying to make two different films, and I don't know why I made the last film because I never expected to release a film or anything of it. It's just that I didn't know what else to do ... Making home movies – well, it's simply that it doesn't interest me very much, as a rule ... to make other people's home movies for them – I'm not sure how to do it. It's not that I put them down at all, I don't: [but] as soon as you're looking through a camera trying to figure out what someone else wants to get, it's very hard ... my sense is to give them the camera, let them shoot whatever they want. And in a way we were doing that. Howard was doing some of that himself. But since I was really responsible for most of the camera-work, I felt very ambivalent as to what I should be doing: and I never did sort it out. In fact, since then I've never – I would never do a film like that again, under those conditions. It's just simply too hard.

Are there any special incidents in dealing with Dylan on the tour that come to mind?

One thing I remember. We were in Stockholm, or in Denmark, I don't remember which; and Dylan wanted to do some scene. But we had been up all night, shooting all over the place, and everybody was really gone, and we were down by the docks and it was dawn. And ... he was shooting film at a tremendous rate, and I had only brought a certain amount of film to Stockholm; we had the rest in London.

And we were out on this dock, and there was this big American destroyer sitting alongside the dock – have you heard this story?

No.

I'm surprised [this story has] never surfaced because there must have been twenty people there. We were filming in a little cluster, about fifty yards away from where the boat was, and on the boat – I had spent some time in the Navy so I knew – they had blown the whistle and everybody was coming out in the morning for assembly. So there were all these sailors assembling all over the deck, and they started to notice us, because Dylan had this huge – his hair all over the place, and we were really quite motley, and I was there with a camera, and we must have looked really peculiar.

So pretty soon all these guys began watching us, and we figured we better get out of here – we got some problems. And [Bob] Neuwirth tried to get Dylan, but Dylan wouldn't leave. So pretty soon there's a big announcement, and the gangway comes down, and this guy, the captain of the ship, comes down the gangway and comes over to see us. And I don't know if they're going to arrest us or not – who knows? Maybe there's some drugs around me or something . . . Just something told me that we shouldn't be there.

But there was no way to escape. The guy came over and he stood there. Dylan barely noticed him – and then suddenly caught sight of him and twitched a little bit. And the rest of us were covering our faces and everybody, 500 sailors, were all lined up watching. And he says: 'Are you Bob Dylan?'

Dylan says something just totally ridiculous. I mean, he was not responding to anybody on the same level, and so he said something like 'No, I'm Mother Hubbard,' or something like that. And the guy says: 'Didn't you write a song called "One Too Many Mornings"?'

And of course he was singing that song on the tour, and Dylan said yeah. And the guy said: 'When I was a freshman in college, I wrote a novel, and that was the title,' and he shook hands with Dylan and walked back on the ship. And Dylan was really touched. He stood there for a minute and he just – he couldn't absorb all the connections that were going together – that he was in this foreign land, thinking he was totally a stranger – like . . . on a battlefield on which he was walking around the edges and nobody knew who he was, and suddenly this entire destroyer comes up and – it was really an amazing moment. He was totally caught off guard, and quite caught up in it. And I never again saw him respond in that way to a peculiar situation.

When the tour was over, and it came to editing the material, did you start work on the film as soon as you got back to the States after the tour?

Well, we got it processed first. Then we had to sync material up, so two or three people were put to work syncing it up . . . it took maybe a month to sync it up.

Were you working on your film or did you turn over the footage to Dylan?

We had all the film in the studio. Dylan came in . . . sometime in

July. He drove down and we looked at stuff – he spent two or three days looking at stuff in the studio and then he said, 'Well, I want you guys to go ahead and make some sort of rough edit to get an idea of what you did,' because ABC was coming after it. . . .So [Bob] Neuwirth and I started to edit something together – we did a twenty to thirty minute thing, just a rough idea. Then Dylan had his accident and [his manager] Albert [Grossman] got pissed at me because he said I wasn't helping him edit enough. And I explained to him that I was never supposed to be editing it: I had another film to make.

You weren't helping Dylan edit?

Yeah, well: we started something and then Dylan didn't know what he wanted to do. Then he wanted us to come up and work up at Bearsville. I couldn't do that. So we sent an editor up there to work with him – but then Dylan and Howard Alk started editing film . . .

I think this was before the accident. I heard about the accident when I was in California, and then I came and I saw him a couple of days later, walking round with a brace. He didn't appear very knocked out by the accident so I never quite knew what happened or talked to him about it.

But he was very pissed at everybody and I don't know whether it was because they were putting pressure on him to get the film ready for TV and he didn't want to do it, or whether he felt he was in some kind of film competition with me: which I certainly never wanted to get into. And I don't know, he was just very pissed about it all, and I could see nothing positive coming out of trying to make the film.

I didn't – I certainly wasn't going to grab the film away from him: it was not my film. I had made my film [*Don't Look Back*] the year before: that's the way I felt about it. So this one was basically his, and if he didn't want to make it, that was fine too. I didn't care. So we just tucked away the film that Neuwirth and I had worked on. We just buried it, and they went on and made a film.

. . . It's an interesting film. I've always felt that he made it out of our outs [out-takes]: which was like he was trying to prove something.

It's interesting because he was involved and he set out to

70

make his own film. How much of it is his film and how much was Howard Alk's film I don't know. I think that he [Dylan] was, at the time, not in his highest creative powers. That was the feeling I got, so I didn't spend a lot of time trying to coerce him or coax him to make a film . . . But I think he was very influenced by Howard's film ideas, which didn't interest me much, frankly, at the time, and they still don't. I think they tend to be sort of intellectual ideas . . . but I don't think they are very interesting visual ideas, for me.

So, personally, *Eat The Document* was not that interesting. It's only interesting because he did it, because he was involved in it. It's like if Abraham Lincoln or Nixon did a film: you'd have to be interested in it.

Well, the film that you made. . . ?

We didn't even make a film. You gotta understand it's a sketch: it's like a rough thing you do on a piece of paper – not a finished film. It was just a work print and the original was taken away when they cut *Eat The Document*. And they cut the original . . . so, at this point, no original even exists to make that film. That film is lost irrevocably to the process. Because when you take the film, the original roll: if you cut it up and use the original in one film, you probably can't use it for another.

Are you saying that they took all the original film?

They cut a final release print of *Eat The Document*, and to do so they took the original – when they did that I asked Howard to go through and not cut that original. I said someday some-body's going to want to look at that. This is the inevitable second film to *Don't Look Back*, because it's what happens if, you know, you don't look back . . . I said you don't have to cut the original: go in optically and make an optical dupe and for the purposes of that film it would be fine.

But they chose not to. They actually cut. I think Howard was feeling very protective of the film and he felt that *Eat The Document* was in some sense his film, his and Dylan's, and that he wanted to make that film have some plausibility. And I can understand that, as a film-maker. It's just that it never interested me that much and I don't think the film interested the audience that much.

71

I think it just mystified people. This is always a question you get into with people like Dylan . . . can that fantastic kind of sovereignty that surrounds a name that gets emblazoned on the public mind – can you do anything off it? And always the answer is, no you can't. Whoever's the greatest movie actor of all time can't just walk out and make a hit record . . . it took Barbra Streisand a long time to be able to conquer two worlds, and she had to work her way up, even though she was tops in the other. And I think that's the same with anybody.

And I think Dylan found that out with his other film, *Renaldo & Clara*. No matter how interested people were in Dylan, and the myth of Dylan, you can't just deal off of that.

I mean, I happen to think that Dylan at his best is a first-rate poet. But you know that if you take the half-dozen first-rate poets . . . Ezra Pound, whoever – and you put all their total incomes for their lives together, you aren't going to make one big concert date. So you have to figure that being a first-rate poet is not a very productive line of work if you're looking for a return. So he never really went at it in that way . . . He could do that if he wanted to. You could take fifty lines of Dylan that are as good as anybody's ever written in this century, as far as I'm concerned. But there are thousands of lines he's written that are terrible and deserve to be lost. In music that's easy to do, so that works for him fine. It doesn't mean he's less of a poet. It's the way he goes at it, that's all. So you don't try to be Lowell at the same time as you're Dylan. And there's no reason why you should be.

And the film thing. I guess I had somehow hoped, and I've always had this feeling – I had it about Dylan, I had it about Mailer. . .I mean, in addition to being artists, really good artists, there was some kind of sense of film and what made film work. They responded to film. But it still left them a long way from being able to turn out a film that was going to be successful – and I don't mean necessarily critically successful in the Hollywood sense of it.

Did you see any of Renaldo & Clara's *ideas as things he wanted to do back in '66?*

I have to tell you something. I haven't seen *Renaldo & Clara* . . . I want to see the long version . . . but there's lots of things you just can't get to do.

That film was also called confusing by the critics.

Critics – I don't worry about critics . . . in any kind of interesting work, critics can sometimes help you but mostly they can't. They can really only help you with work that's right today. Anything that's got any kind of lead-time to it, they're always looking for the wrong thing. They're being dressed by last year's style . . . That's not my business, to please critics. So I never really worry about critics and what they say.

What I do respond to is [with *Renaldo & Clara*] . . . that there was a lot of ambivalence – not in the film itself but in the making of the film. Dylan couldn't decide whether it should be long or short. If you make a four-hour film, then that's the film you want. You don't cut it no matter what. I mean, you just finally make life come to that. If you do cut it, it means that maybe you weren't sure and you're prepared to try different ways . . .

It's like, we had a two-hour *Don't Look Back* originally – I always have a longer version of the films – but we never released that. We made it, edited it, mixed it, had a release print and I sat and looked at it maybe two weeks in different situations, and showed it to different audiences, and then I knew that it had to be cut and I knew where to cut it, and I knew that it had to be about ninety minutes long . . .

People don't pay for film by the length – really what they're paying for is somebody's taste: somebody's judgement of what a film is all about; when it's told you all it's going to tell you. If it starts to go over old ground, nobody's got time for it. They've got other things to do. You can't have it cut off and say 'you can leave here if you want to'. It's still tied to the novel: it has the same kind of form as the novel, and you want to finish a novel, you don't want to stop wherever it's convenient. And so the dramatic sense of it is, it has to be a story – it has to be one story.

You have to plot it out, figure out what the story is and go for it. And I sensed that all the way through [*Renaldo & Clara*] . . . what he had was this wonderful idea happening, and the [Rolling Thunder] tour itself – full of all kinds of dramatic possibilities in his own life, and the idea of using fictional people: I think all of that is terrific. What he never had a sense of is what the story was going to be about. In other words, what he was going to settle for to release.

73

I don't think he should have released two lengths. Those are just as important decisions, maybe more important, than decisions made within the film of what to shoot, what kind of camera-work or anything else. What you finally put out there is just like his songs: the song is the song. . . .but in film he's not bringing that kind of spiritual solvency, that determination of what he knows is right. He's not bringing that to the film, and . . . it's hard on the film. People don't know whether to accept it seriously or not.

And I think that makes it hard to distribute. Film distribution in the real world, for independent film-makers, for people who make their own films – I don't know what it is equivalent to, but it's as crucial to the life of the film as anything you do within it.

Going back to the '66 material – not Eat The Document *but what you called the inevitable* Don't Look Back *part 2: the film you wanted to make . . .*

What was clear by the end of the first filming [i.e. of the solo tour of 1965 that made up *Don't Look Back*] was that it was a drag for Dylan to go out and support that whole kind of myth – the acoustical concert and doing the talking Bob Dylan concert, which in a sense was Guthrie's, or other people's. He refined it and brought it to an extraordinary level and he didn't want to have to deal with it any more. I understand that. God, I can't think of anything in the world more difficult than having to be perfect every night.

Perfect in what way?

. . .You gotta be some kind of sacred image and you gotta be perfect in every way. You can't just have a hall full of people, it's got to be overfull: there's got to be turnaways . . . if the place is full of people and they're all screaming and yelling at you, that's OK, but it's gotta be full of people . . . So he's got to do that every night and it's all on his head, and musically it's not that interesting.

But when he got the band together and all of them – Garth and Robbie and the whole batch of them – they are playing so fantastically, even Mickey Jones. Nobody understood what Mickey Jones was up to, collecting his Nazi paraphernalia all over the place. He was from the Johnny Rivers band. I got to really like Mickey. He was the drummer, he filled in for what's his name: Levon Helm. He had, you know, no idea – the rest of those guys were from a different part of the world . . .

The music was so fantastic and they were all so into it, and Dylan's role in it . . . Dylan was so happy, he was jumping around like a cricket in the middle of the thing. That's when I realized that the only way I could film those concerts, instead of doing them the way we had done the other [solo] ones (which was from a distance, with a long lens watching him as the audience did) was to get down there in the middle of it – be right on top of him with a wide-angle lens, which is hard to do. You gotta be in the concert, you can't hide.

And when I realized that, I knew that this had nothing to do with what he was doing. He didn't care about that. He didn't want to think about that. He was much less interested in how he looked than in what kind of film he could make.

I think he felt in some sense that he was going to be Ingmar Bergman or something, and make some new kind of film. Which was terrific: I didn't want to discourage him from doing that. But what I saw, what really knocked me out, was that it was the first time that I had ever seen him really happy in the middle of music. And the music was incredible. It was a great band. The sound of that band was the best sound I ever heard. People would listen to that stuff and it would just blow the life out of them. I've never heard a concert like that since. Never.

So I knew that that was something extraordinary and in order to film that, you couldn't do it by filming these goofy little scenes in rooms with nutty people . . . What was interesting had nothing to do with that – and I think that they later edited some kind of mystical film to put people off: you know, in a way it was like they were saying no, nothing went on on-stage. My feeling was the opposite. Unlike *Don't Look Back*, which you couldn't centre on the stage because what went on on-stage really wasn't that important to his life, *this* film centred on the stage: he came to life in the middle of that stage . . . that was really the kind of film we started to make, but it wasn't for us to make it; and I didn't feel called on to make a film or die. But I always felt that that film was there and it made me sad that it was never found and never will be found.

Just to clarify the position with the film and the tapes. Where are they now? Do you have any film in your vaults?

I don't think I've got any of that original film. I think that it all had to be turned over to Howard Alk, because they had to cut that original. To my knowledge, he took all the original and it all went someplace, probably embalmed it or something . . . The original film is gone; now we might have some work print kicking around I don't know. Because we re-duped a lot of material and to keep it from getting confused you keep it separate. As for the tapes, I'm not totally clear . . . we had to have copies of the quarter-inch tapes that Dylan's sound-man Bob Alderman made because of the sync problem. Whether we gave Dylan the originals and the copies, or whether we kept the originals in our vault I simply don't know . . . As for the tapes we made with our separate recorders, we probably have those. But those wouldn't be concert tapes necessarily. There might occasionally be bits of concerts but basically they're non-concert tapes. They were all transferred to 16 Mag, which was given to Dylan, but we'd usually keep the original. So those would be in vaults too.

Are you free to make a movie from any film you do retain?

No.

You'd have to get Dylan's permission?

Yes. Sure . . . well, it's complicated . . . usually you specify when you make your contract, you say who the outs are going to belong to mechanically. Whether or not that confers licence to use them is a different matter. It's just like we could have Dylan singing a song of somebody else's and if we didn't have a release for the music, we still couldn't use the footage. For any creative work that's within your film, you have to have licence to use it from whoever owns that work. But we may well own the film and I almost always take the position that I own the material I shoot. But in this case it was a little different. The film itself was clearly Dylan's. We made it for Dylan. I was really doing something for him. He asked me to do it and I was filming – in effect he was going to be paying me to film for him.

I still take the position really that outtakes of that film which didn't involve the production I would own, if only because I hate to see the stuff get strewn around and lost. I would usually take responsibility for seeing that it's archived and protected, and we would never let it go out of here to let anybody use it, or use it ourselves, without Dylan's permission. On that film it was a little grey because it wasn't like most of our films.

On *Don't Look Back* I would take the position that all the outtakes were mine. I still can't use them without his permission. I can't use them without the music clearance. I have no rights to them. But I own them mechanically and I'm responsible for seeing them preserved and kept in a safe place and that they don't get ripped off or destroyed by fire or something else. That's basically what my responsibility is as a film-maker, and I take that very seriously.

. . .We store them [the *Don't Look Back* outs] because film is very vulnerable. People don't tend to store that kind of tape – they throw them out . . . they put them in a big box and they're stuck someplace and then they move or forget where they are, and since nobody's using them they can get lost. And when they're lost, nobody ever knows what they are, and they just look like rolls of film somewhere. So it's really crucial that some effort be made in the very beginning to make sure that they are protected.

Particularly because most of the films that I've done are about people who, it seems to me, will have some kind of historic interest. So we always make that the criteria, whether it's Dylan or Janis Joplin or whoever. We keep that material for some kind of long-range use, if only for study.

I'm sure Dylan fans will be happy to hear that.

We've never lost a foot of film, and as far as I know none of the tapes that we have – and we've got a lot of musical tapes of his – none of them have ever hit the streets . . . unless we set it up to do it with Dylan's concurrence.

And those tapes are in your vaults?

Yeah. I know Dylan's very paranoid about his material . . . He hates the idea of it floating around. People getting access to it that he doesn't know about; and the fact that he feels that way probably puts a big incentive on people to try to get it. So the thing feeds on its own problem. As far as I know, we never released anything, because from our point of view there's no return to us . . . we're not a record-company . . . we don't make any money from records. The only way we would ever use sound would be with a film.

There was a rumour a while back that a Cable-TV Special was being planned and that Dylan's people were looking for material.

Yes. They called me and asked me if we had the concert stuff from *Don't Look Back*. I said sure, we have all that. But as for the 1966 stuff, I'm not sure, for the reasons I've explained.

I know a lot of people who would love to listen to it . . .

It's very interesting material. Well, I always felt that someday Dylan will have to deal with it. Whether I'm around and involved in it, who knows? I think what happened there on that tour was very essential to where music was. As with Bowie: the Ziggy Stardust tour was central. This is what David and I realized when we decided to re-release *Ziggy Stardust*. That will always be interesting to people. I think that Dylan's stuff is the same way. That tour [1966], musically, was the most interesting that happened anywhere in the world at that period.

And he was at the peak of his career.

It isn't just that, but that that music was generating all music everywhere. People who didn't even see those concerts were getting something from it indirectly, in many ways. And, ultimately, everybody wants to see what the centres of things are.

We happened to do it a few times in our life – I did it at Monterey. We happened to be at the centre of something. So what we filmed [for *Monterey Pop*] became absolutely crucial: people will want to see that forever. A far better film in many ways is *Keep on Rocking*, which is Chuck Berry. But musically nothing was starting there. They were doing the same thing they had done . . . so everybody knew it was old news. So while that's interesting, it doesn't have anything like the charismatic attraction that the centre of the storm will always hold.

So someday Dylan's going to have to deal with that material

in some other way than *Eat The Document* . . . And if it's not Dylan, it's going to be his heirs; somebody.

So it's always been my contention that that material should be kept, really as archively as possible. But it's Dylan's responsibility . . .

Is it your feeling that he has kept that material?

I hope so. I don't know. I don't know what he does. But I know if we had it, we would have kept it . . . that material will live forever, as long as people don't lose it.

And it's so frustrating to the fans who never get a chance to see it.

It is frustrating, but in a way that keeps fans alive. That constant pressure of the myth against the reality . . . it keeps them all tuned up . . . I don't think you can set that in motion or build up any kind of appetite . . . if it isn't really there. All you have to do – you don't have to even try to sell it or get an interest in it; you just have to make sure you're protected: and that's what the business ought to be able to do . . .

I don't know: I assume Columbia Records protects its music, but I don't know how well. I wouldn't trust Columbia Records. I wouldn't trust any record company because every time they have a turnover in vault workers, you have to assume the old workers took home everything that had any value; so you have to assume in the end that what's left is what nobody ever wanted. So I would assume that that is not a good way to keep valuable material – under large corporate protection. You take a chance with this stuff.

I mean, in the end, some way or other, people like yourself, who really have a strong interest in it, are getting hold of little bits of it and hanging on.

It's amazing how you can find film. We're looking at old footage of Billie Holiday: it's amazing how much stuff was kept. You don't expect to find it, but people just knew, somehow, this stuff is valuable. Even though not much had been filmed, what there was, somehow or other, sooner or later, always surfaces.

The Mailbox Unlocked, Part 2

Dear *Telegraph*

I'm going to come right out and say it, just so you know what you're dealing with here. I think that the '66 Albert Hall electric set is terrible. There. Slips out easily enough. No thunderbolts from above. No earth tremors.

You see, I have this theory that a lot of people who discovered Dylan in the seventies have been conned into 'appreciation' of this famous tape by the reverence in which it is held. You start off with the official albums and some of the books, and you read about these nefarious *other* recordings that you might be able to get if you try hard enough. So you obtain a bootleg or two and everyone says, 'Royal Albert Hall. That's the one. That's the essential Dylan.'

As far as I can tell, it's the 'intensity' on the performance that gives it such popular appeal. Well, it can't be denied that the music seethes with vituperation but, to my ears at least, this does nothing but blanket over every other more subtle emotion the songs may have contained. The melodies, meanwhile, are destroyed by the rough, raucous delivery, and we're left with a lot of, well, noisy rubbish. Paul Cable's appraisal of this tape as 'perfection' makes me wonder if we've listened to the same thing.

Maybe the old-stagers who actually *saw* the '66 show(s) have special memories of the magic being worked back then, which lends the recording a certain something denied to the rest of us. All that hate, plus a touch of subversion, makes a heady mixture, after all. Maybe it's the fact that it was among the earliest unofficial material to get out, which would again lend it a piquancy all its own. But put aside the memories and accolades and get the record on the turntable and – I can't help it, it's awful.

In the studio at this time Dylan dealt admirably with his angst to produce 'Like a Rolling Stone' and 'Positively 4th Street' – both excellent. In the concert hall, however, it seems to me that it all got totally out of control, to the detriment of all concerned. Give me *Self Portrait* any day. 'Early Morning Rain' is a good song. Even the LP *Dylan* has 'Lily Of The West'. As for Royal Albert Hall '66, you can keep it.

Jim Dring
Colchester
Essex

1966 and All That: Levon Helm, Drummer

How many of you subscribe to Modern Drummer *magazine? Quite. Well* Modern Drummer *is 'The International Magazine Exclusively For Drummers'. In August 1984 writer Robyn Flans offered readers an interview with Levon Helm. Here is the relevant extract. Keep the beat . . .*

How long did you play as The Hawks before Bob Dylan entered the picture?

Helm: I guess we were around for a year or two like that. We had a couple of different aliases that we went by, but it didn't seem to help. [*Laughs*] We would try something new, but business wouldn't noticeably pick up a whole lot. We ran across Bob at that particular time and that was just some real good God-given timing for us, as it turned out. That opened it up for us to finally get a recording contract.

We signed to Capitol Records as The Crackers. The first record didn't have a name on it because Capitol wasn't crazy about putting 'by The Crackers' on it. So on the back of it they put our family pictures, and then 'The Band', along with the names of our band members. When the second record came out, they still didn't like The Crackers and that's when we started to be called The Band. I voted to call it The Crackers. I'm no fool.

The story goes that Dylan saw you playing in some club somewhere.

We had a mutual friend, Mary Martin from Toronto, who introduced us. Bob needed a group, and we needed a break, so lo and behold, the two things coincided.

Were you very familiar with his music?

No, I wasn't. I was into B.B. King, Muddy Waters, and I still felt Ray Charles had the best band.

Why did only you and Robertson play the first [Dylan] gig at Forest Hills? Many accounts suggest that it was because the band was initially sceptical about playing with Dylan.

No, no. There were other musicians involved at the time and there was no room for any of us. Then some room appeared for Robbie and me to play with them, so the two of us ended up playing it. Altogether there were five pieces. We got together and had a couple of rehearsals to go over the tunes. It sounded like country music to me. I thought the songs were a little bit long. But that's alright with me.

After you did the Forest Hills gig, technically The Band – or The Crackers, alias The Hawks – joined Dylan. Why didn't you go on the '65–'66 tour?

I did some of the American part, but I stayed in the Memphis area when the show moved to Sydney, Melbourne and London.

Was it because you weren't ready?

I just didn't want to go. We had played the American part and that part was pretty good. But back in those days when you played for some of the folk-purist crowds, the electric portion, which was us, would get all the booing and the hissing and stuff. After a while it wasn't a whole lot of fun.

It wasn't like I was ready to go into a hospital and give up or anything like that, but I figured maybe we should practise or something.

Why did you decide to do the rest of it?

Times change, people change, and music changes a little. People's ears change. We just continued along, the same as always. It was just a shorter tour for me – a shorter dose.

What were some of the highlights about playing with Dylan?

We certainly owe a lot to our relationship. It's done a lot for us in everything from trying to construct a song to being able to catch the attention of a recording concern. It's going to take me a while longer to even understand it all.

It was certainly one of the highlights of my musical career to play with Bob, tour with him, and go through some of the times we had a chance to go through together. He's a great musician and a lot of fun to make music with. He can sit down and make music any time he wants to. Most of the times we played together, it just really suited my style, because I like walking on the edge.

From what I understand, Dylan's show is pretty improvisational.

Yeah, boy! Nice and loose. Let's not over-prepare. My man Bob. I'm with you Bobby! You could just about throw away the game plan for a show – which makes a lot of people nervous, but it tickles me.

Isn't that harder, almost?

Hell no! He does it right.

You mentioned that working with Dylan helped the members of The Band with their writing.

It sure did. We learned a whole lot from him. We never had done a lot of recording, songwriting, playing shows or anything before we worked with him. All we had really done was try to practise our craft by playing honky-tonks and dance halls.

Did the writing actually start during the time with Dylan?

That's when it started coming together. That's when Richard and Robbie, and even the rest of us, got the opportunity to see it that way. All of a sudden it was a new game, so I'm sure that we profited more than Bob. But I know that we had a good time, and I would like to think that we rubbed off a few good things onto him.

Do you feel that you had to change your style when you played with Dylan?

Yeah. I think that we started playing more of ourselves, instead of copying something that we liked and respected, or something we knew the crowd wanted to hear. By then we were getting to the age where we would have a little more personal input. So I think that the time and Bob's influence certainly helped us and encouraged us to play with a more personal style, and to play as well as we could. We learned a lot through that period. Having the opportunity to work with somebody who knows as much as Bob knows about music sure didn't hurt us a bit.

Then when you began to work exclusively in The Band context, did you find that you were even freer to give your input?

Playing with Bob encouraged that kind of growth because there were no rules, other than that the song should sound good and be fun to play.

He never really suggested how he wanted a song to be played?

Not really. He liked to throw the game plan away and just play. It was different every night, and as long as there was a key established that we were going to play in, the tempo and melody could change according to the mood. If it was later in the show we might have backed the tempo down a little bit or whatever.

Being the drummer, you probably established the tempo.

Once we got started, I took it wherever I wanted to go. I wish I could play like I've heard some of the great studio musicians play over the years, but I just get so excited and carried away with it at times that I can feel my tempo rising. Sometimes I can hear myself laying back too much, but back when we played with Bob a lot of tunes had really not been played yet, so there were no established arrangements for some of the stuff.

Take me to a Dylan recording session. How did you guys work? Was there much overdubbing?

I've never recorded a whole lot with Bob. I've had the pleasure a few times, and it was always pretty much the same as the way we played a show. We'd go over the tune and, without beating it to death, try to do it as well as we could. We'd do it once or twice and then go on to the next one. I've never been involved in any overdubs and all that. I don't think he enjoys that. I'm not real fond of it myself.

The Motorcycle Crash and the Woodstock Seclusion: July 1966 to October 1967

John Bauldie

Part 1: The Crash

We see several risky periods during the next twelve months when it will be in Bob's interest to remain fully alert and to exercise all due precaution.

[Bob Dylan's horoscope, Hit Parader *magazine, June 1966]*

On 29 July 1966, Bob Dylan was riding his Triumph motorcycle along Striebel Road in Woodstock, New York State, when he fell off and cracked a small bone in his neck. He wasn't on his way to any particular destination; he was just riding around at the back of the estate where manager Albert Grossman had made his home, and where Dylan and, subsequently, members of The Band were also to move: a setting of forests and mountains and winding back-roads.

Dylan was taken up to Middletown Hospital suffering concussion, lacerations to the upper forehead and, as X-rays revealed, that cracked vertebra. He was shaken, and physically not in good shape anyway. The road had already begun to take its toll of Bob Dylan before the fall: he had been touring with his band since November 1965, travelling through the USA, Hawaii, Australia, Scandinavia, Britain and France – getting booed and jeered on-stage, hounded and hassled off-stage, hardly sleeping and hardly eating. And the Bob Dylan of mid-1966 was not in good shape because aside from everything else, what had really been happening on the '66 tour was drugs.

In the midst of it all, Dylan was on the crest of a huge creative wave – but one that was carrying him forward with such momentum that, as far as many observers were concerned, wipe-out time seemed imminent. Indeed the importance the motorcycle crash has always enjoyed in Bob Dylan mythology is precisely because it has been assumed to have rescued him from that far more lethal wipe-out.

The road for Dylan and The Band (at that time referred to as 'the group') had not reached its end at the Royal Albert Hall. Albert Grossman had already negotiated sixty-four further dates: Yale Bowl, New Haven for the first week in August, Shea Stadium for 13 August, and then concerts right through to the end of the year.

There were also three important deadlines to face. Most pressing was a deal for the production of a film of the 1966 tour – contracted between Grossman and ABC-TV for their fall series, *Stage 66*, for which ABC had already advanced $100,000, subject to the film's delivery by September. There was also *Tarantula*, Dylan's 'spider-book' from 1965. Again, contracts had been exchanged and big money advanced. Macmillan had advertised the book and were expecting Dylan's final adjustments to the galleys, which were waiting for him in Woodstock on his return from Europe at the end of May. Finally, Dylan's record contract with Columbia had run its five-year course and was about to expire; but Dylan was obliged to fulfil what remained on it by recording fourteen tracks for an LP release.

It was simply too much. The responsibility seems to have been Grossman's. He had complete control of the singer's affairs and seems to have been accepting every big offer that came his way: book publication, film for TV, bigger and bigger stadium concerts – there was even talk of Broadway for Bob: a show called 'The Pied Piper' had been written for him, and in the New York entertainments columns a musical about James Dean was touted with Dylan as lead. So the singer found himself with too much to do. His interest in *Tarantula* had already waned – it was an out-of-date project to him by this time; the tour film was proving impossible to organize; and he had used up a lot of new songs on the double-album *Blonde On Blonde*.

Grossman knew well enough that for Dylan to duck out of contractual obligations would be very costly indeed – both financially and in terms of reputation. The motorcycle crash was perfect.

Of course, Dylan did crack that bone in his neck. He had to wear a neck-brace for a while. He needed peace and quiet. But if the public and the pressing corporations (ABC, Columbia, Macmillan: all companies with real clout) could be convinced that Bob Dylan was *seriously* injured – too ill to be bothered or

86

pressured or threatened or summonsed – then he could recuperate without damage to his (or Grossman's) bank-balance and reputation.

Motorcycle accidents always sound serious. Richard Farina had been killed in one only months before. Perhaps Richard (or 'Homer', as he was nicknamed by friends) opened this idea for a door out for Bob Dylan.

Grossman issued the press release: Dylan was to be laid up (and laid off) for at least two months. The story was manufactured, even down to the implication that the motorbike was faulty. Dylan had been 'taking his motorcycle to be repaired'; the machine 'spun out of control'. The unfortunate victim got lucky in that 'a friend who was following Dylan in a car picked him up and drove him to a local doctor'. The singer didn't have to lie in agony for too long, then. Grossman's bottom line, 'He needs rest,' meant *please lay off*.

And Dylan did need rest. The period of what turned out to be spiritual as well as physical regeneration was so necessary and important that the accident story was certainly justified; but half-truths bloom into untruths, especially when they're told to the papers.

'Dylan Hurt In Motorcycle Mishap' grew in the telling. *Time* magazine (12 August 1966) emphasized that Dylan 'wasn't wearing a helmet' and that he had sustained 'severe face and back cuts'. Gossip columns like Charles McHarry's 'On The Town' in the *Daily News* stretched it further: 'Some say his accident so disfigured him that he won't perform again'. There was plenty more where that came from.

Grossman found that his tale had grown *too* tall; concerned to reassure anxious teenage fans (Dylan, back then, was a real teen-magazine idol) that they didn't have a vegetable as a hero, he told the press that Dylan was in 'fair shape'. *Broadside* reported in its August edition that 'the injuries were slight and he is recovering satisfactorily', while Ed Sullivan's column had the subtlest of hints in an exclamation-mark: 'Bob Dylan's broken neck mending. Motorcycle crash!'

Some people had been unimpressed all along. Dylan's Greenwich Village companion, the actor David Blue, ever pithy, sent a note up to Woodstock when he first heard about the 'crash'. It read: 'It's been done already'.

Grossman had asked for a two-month truce for Dylan's recuperation, and got it; but when August and September passed and Dylan still did not emerge, the newspapers began to get restless. *World Journal Tribune* staff-writer Mike Pearl began to ask questions. Macmillan told him that publication of *Tarantula*, originally planned for that autumn, had been 'indefinitely postponed'. Dylan's editor there, Robert Markel, spoke of necessary revisions but admitted he had no idea when these might be completed. ABC-TV told Pearl a similar story about their already-advertised tour-film. The November date had been abandoned and there was no speculation about later alternative dates.

Pearl wrote of the 'morbid game of speculation and rumour' that had been encouraged by such a lack of news: 'Persistent stories that his career is finished have cropped up from Newport to Greenwich Village.' This time Albert Grossman's office would only offer that Dylan was 'not seriously hurt' and that he was still convalescing. All rumours and speculation were dismissed as 'gossip'. Exactly where *was* Dylan? At a secret location.

The persistent Mike Pearl became the first journalist to find Dylan, possibly because of a moment's indiscretion by the poet Allen Ginsberg, who had been to visit Dylan at the end of September. Ginsberg had taken 'a box full of books of all kinds' to Dylan – 'all the modern poets I knew, some ancient poets like Sir Thomas Wyatt, Campion; Dickinson, Rimbaud, Lorca, Apollinaire, Blake, Whitman and so forth' – and who subsequently told Pearl that he thought the accident 'may have been a a good thing. It's forced him to slow down.'

Whether or not it was Ginsberg who pointed Mike Pearl towards Dylan's dark brown cedarwood house in Woodstock, the intrepid reporter found his way there and on 14 October, though he had failed to get beyond the front door, he told the tale of what he found in his newspaper:

Ten cats and two dogs romped about the grounds. An electrician from a nearby village was hooking up a hi-fi speaker. A young woman came to the door and at first denied that Dylan was there: 'We are afraid of all kinds of nuts coming around and bothering him,' she explained . . . 'It gets very lonely here,' she said. 'Very few friends have come up, and we never go into town.'

Part 2: The House

Dylan's house was a so-called 'Byrdcliffe house', named after a colony of writers and artists founded in 1902 by Ralph Radcliffe Whitehead, the heir to a Yorkshire textile fortune. The house that Dylan bought had been built in 1910 for an architect and stage director called Ben Webster, on a four-acre site along a hillside. It had twelve rooms, five fireplaces and five bathrooms. The huge living room had a high, wood-panelled ceiling while upstairs long, somewhat gloomy corridors with wooden floors and red carpet led to the many children's and guests' rooms. Outside, at the back, was a swimming pool fed by mountain streams, and two cabins which could be occupied separately.

The overall impression was of 'a vast, mahogany-stained ski lodge'; at least, that's how it seemed to the reporter who first crossed its threshold.

In January 1967, Barry Cunningham was sent out to find Dylan by the *New York Post*. Cunningham trudged through the snows, risking attack from the Dylan St Bernard guard-dog, and found the house with its garage door open and Bob's vintage black Cadillac limousine inside, complete with running-boards and non-vintage TV.

Bold as brass and twice as cold, the newsman walked right in through the house's unlocked front door, and found himself in the living room. He just had time to note the picture-window with its panoramic view out from Mount Mead, admire an oriental rug and run his eye over 'sundry *objet d'arts*' before an outraged Mrs Dylan caught him frozen-footed:

'You're trespassing! You're trespassing!' Mrs Dylan, in black leotard stockings and high button shoes glowers over the rims of her granny specs. 'Get out of here or I'll call the police,' she demands. To emphasize the unwelcome, she tucks her dark braids under a shawl and slams the door. Abruptly, two grizzly bears masquerading as watchdogs drag the intruder away to his car by the coat tails. He . . . trips over a tricycle and makes an escape back down the valley. There he is roadblocked by Woodstock Town constable Paul Senecal, a good-natured cop who says he doesn't listen to Dylan's songs, but that he has liked the couple since the time they tried to unload fourteen kittens on him. 'By the way,' he adds, spitting tobacco, 'let's see your driver's licence. The Dylans say you stole the dog's collar.'

It was perhaps after this incredible invasion of privacy that Dylan had an escape hatch constructed – according to subsequent owner Sy Gottlieb, proprietor of the Donna Jewellery Shop on Woodstock's 8th Street – leading from the master bedroom to another room, from which a trap-door gave quick access to the basement.

Dylan's reclusiveness had become almost habitual. The *Village Voice* gossiped that his mother had sent him a postcard asking plaintively: 'How many times must one mother write before her son answers his mail?' There was, of course, still no *Tarantula*.

Part 3: The Book and The Film

Dylan seems to have been tapping away at what was supposed to have become *Tarantula* since the autumn of 1965. (I have established that what Dylan is seen typing on tour in England earlier that year in *Don't Look Back*, was the short piece 'Alternatives To College', finally published in *Lyrics 1962–1985*.)

Publication of *Tarantula* had been fixed initially for August 1966. Five excerpts were to appear in *Atlantic Monthly* and the possibility was mooted of Dylan's appearing at the American Booksellers' Association convention that year. Macmillan's promotional plans were well advanced: ten thousand shopping-bags had been printed up with the Jerry Schatzberg shadow-and-light portrait and, in large letters, the inscription 'TARANTULA BY BOB DYLAN?' There had been ads in the trade papers, bookshop window stickers and even TARANTULA! badges.

Dylan had been working on the galleys in the weeks before the accident, after carrying the book with him all through his world tour. The planned date for the final go-ahead was fixed for early August, and editor Bob Markel was looking forward hopefully to duplicating the success attained by John Lennon's book *In His Own Write*. The accident put paid to these hopes once and for all, as Markel later recalled:

We brought a set of galleys to him so he could take one last good look at it before we printed it and bound it and started to fill all the orders that had come in. Bob took a break from some film-editing he was doing. We talked a little about the book and about Rameau and Rimbaud and Bob promised to finish 'making a few changes' in two weeks. A few days after that, Bob stopped working . . .

Markel would not hear from Dylan again until seventeen months later.

There was also no *Eat The Document*. The interview with D.A. Pennebaker elsewhere in this volume gives some glimpses of the trials and tribulations in the film's making. Shot by Pennebaker with help from Howard Alk, but shot mainly in accordance with Dylan's and Alk's direction, the footage was proving impossible to edit. Pennebaker wanted no part of it. Bobby Neuwirth had tried to help, and later Robbie Robertson would apparently contribute significantly to the production of the final version, but at the time Dylan and Alk weren't getting far with it.

In the spring of 1967 ABC-TV announced the final cancellation of the project as far as they were concerned. 'There was some disagreement over the format of the show,' a spokesman explained.

Dylan, however, was filming away around the Woodstock estate in March of 1967, using equipment given to him by Pennebaker. Paul Stookey, of Peter, Paul & Mary, visited Dylan at this time and was pressed into work as an actor: 'I'm a seeker in monk's clothing, cavorting with Tiny Tim and Howard Alk, and a winterscape [*sic*]. I end up on the cutting-room floor.'

Stookey was advised by Dylan to 'do some Bible reading', and Dylan himself seems to have been immersed in study – or, as he put it at the time, 'porin' over books by people you never heard of'.

These words are quoted from a famous interview – headlined as 'Scarred Bob Dylan Is Coming Back!' – Dylan's first since his accident, and given in May '67. It was with Michael Iachetta of the *New York Daily News*, a writer who had spoken to (and impressed) Dylan three years earlier.

One section of the new interview was curious and striking; he told the writer:

Songs are in my head like they always are, and they're not goin' to get written down until some things are evened up. Not until some

91

people come forth and make up for some of the things that have happened . . . somethin' has got to be evened up is all I'm going to say . . .

Dylan told Iachetta that he had been thinking about 'what am I givin' and what am I takin' ', and he'd clearly been considering the price put on his soul by Albert Grossman. Many years later Dylan told Ben Fong-Torres, of *Rolling Stone* magazine, about a 'turning point . . . back in Woodstock, a little after the accident':

Sitting around one night under a full moon, I looked out into the bleak woods and I said: 'Something's gotta change'. There was some business that had to be taken care of . . .

But the most immediately pressing business in the early months of 1967 for Grossman himself, on Bob Dylan's behalf, was the negotiation of a new recording contract.

Part 4: The Record Deal

Dylan's contract with Columbia was five years old in late summer 1966. It had been signed with John Hammond and Dylan's royalty rate was standard – five per cent. The first LP had sold poorly and Dylan had thus acquired the unkind 'Hammond's folly' tag from sceptical record executives. Even as his fame and modishness increased, the sales of his records were always far less than anyone outside of Columbia may have suspected. The albums went straight into the charts on release, but were not consistently good sellers. (This is still true today.) The unlikely consequence was that even while Dylan was riding the crest of his wave of success, his albums were failing to reach the gold-record shoreline of 500,000 units.

Only Columbia knew this, and the knowledge was later to prove a useful weapon in the struggle to retain Dylan on their label. In their ignorance, rival companies considered Bob Dylan to be a very hot commercial property. Clive Davis, then president of Columbia, knew he was not, but valued Dylan as an innovative artist: one whose presence on the label would attract others to sign; and he saw in Dylan a figure of lasting significance, and therefore a long-term investment.

So Clive Davis wanted Dylan to remain 'his' artist, while predatory rivals were aware that he was available at the right price.

Variety revealed, in October 1966, that Dylan was demanding a five-year deal worth one and a half million dollars. Columbia had offered only half a million and their regular five per cent royalty. Capitol Records were in the running to top this, but the big offer came from Mort Nasatir, then president of the records division of MGM, who spent several days talking with Dylan over Christmas 1966.

In February 1967, Dylan's attorney, David Braun, told an eager press that contracts had been drawn up and a deal agreed with MGM. Nasatir, it would be revealed later, had not only met the demand for a million and a half dollars, but had also offered a then unprecedented twelve per cent royalty, and had suggested that there would be opportunities, through Metro-Goldwyn-Mayer, for Dylan to go into movies. Clive Davis, knowing that he couldn't hope to compete in this marketplace, was downhearted, though not ready to concede to MGM without something of a fight.

Unexpectedly, his next tactic, announced for 25 April 1967, made headlines in the *New York Times*: BOB DYLAN SUSPENDED. Columbia were demanding that Dylan complete his contract with them, by recording fourteen new tracks for a last album (the release, just eight days earlier, of the *Bob Dylan's Greatest Hits* LP did not satisfy this requirement) before he could take up any MGM offer. Dylan had no choice; he accepted his obligation, Mort Nasatir agreed to be patient, and Columbia dropped their 'suspension' within hours of having publicized it.

The ensuing period seems to have given Clive Davis the breathing-space he needed to discourage MGM. With some timely good luck, he succeeded. The next contractual announcement about Dylan came on 21 August, in Columbia's own *Record News* publication: BOB DYLAN INKS LONG-TERM PACT WITH COLUMBIA RECORDS. So what happened?

Clive Davis explained (in *Clive: Inside The Record Business*, Ballantine Books, USA, 1974) that actually Dylan himself had already signed the MGM contract, and that it was the signature of MGM's corporate management that was missing. The Records Division had no authority to operate without the approval of the board, and the board – primarily a movie-oriented management board – was dominated by the controversial figure of Allen Klein, who was later to gain and lose the Beatles and much of their money.

Incredibly, though Mort Nasatir had worked long and hard to get Dylan for MGM Records, Klein now sought the advice of Clive Davis about the wisdom of the deal!

Clive Davis played his ace: he gave Klein Dylan's sales figures.

As Davis acknowledges, though Nasatir had been wrong all along in his assumptions about Dylan's sales, he at least *did* know that Dylan's worth was not to be measured in short-term sales alone, and that his special value to MGM would have been in giving their ailing label new prestige and so new force in the marketplace. But Klein did not understand this. Klein saw the disaster of unbalanced books, and nothing of Dylan's value as an artist. It was he who therefore turned the board of MGM against Nasatir and against the contract which lay waiting in MGM's offices for the corporate counter-signature.

It must have been some time that August that Albert Grossman realized that MGM were about to pull out – that they were taking too long to seal the deal. So he realized that his strongest bargaining position was to approach Columbia *immediately* on Dylan's behalf, offering *them* a deal before MGM's turn-down became well-known.

The proposition with which Grossman approached Clive Davis was unorthodox: a then huge royalty rate of ten per cent (twice the Columbia 'standard') but no guaranteed payments and no stipulations about minimum 'product'. For the record company, this meant no commitments and therefore no risks. Dylan would be contracted to them for five more years, in which if he chose not to record, they would have no expenses; and if he recorded and had success, he would earn a great deal of money, but then, so would they. Columbia couldn't lose, while Grossman was able to snatch success of a sort for Bob Dylan out of the jaws of contractual defeat – not least in achieving a deal that didn't put his artist straight back under pressure to deliver to deadlines.

Part 5: The Band, Big Pink and The Basement Tapes

The band moved to Woodstock in the spring of 1967. Dylan had asked Robbie Robertson to help him edit the 1966 tour footage, and Robertson certainly ended up having some influence on the production of *Eat The Document*. The other musicians moved into what writer and friend Tony Glover described as 'a large, ugly, pink-shingled house' in nearby West Saugerties on Overlook Mountain. Big Pink, as the house was known, gave its name to the band's brilliant début LP. The music on the record was the product of months of co-operation between Dylan and his friends.

The work towards this album and towards The Basement Tapes became an everyday business. As Robertson explained in a 1970 interview with Roelof Kiers, VPRO-TV, Holland: 'We used to get together every day at one o'clock in the basement of Big Pink. And it was just a routine. We would get there and to keep one of us from going crazy, we would play music every day. And [Dylan] wrote a bunch of songs out of that, and we wrote a bunch of songs out of that.'

One Dylan composition and two co-written songs (one with Rick Danko, the other with the late Richard Manuel) would be included on *Music From Big Pink*. And, said Robertson, 'Bob offered to help us out in any way we wanted – play harp or piano or sing harmony. We thought it over and decided it wasn't right to trade on the name of a famous man, so, instead, he painted the cover for us. A very warm, neighbourly gift.'

The sessions which produced The Basement Tapes took place between June and October 1967, and the most immediately striking thing about the songs is that they are clearly the product of much improvisation, of Dylan and The Band interacting, trading musical ideas, and using music to prompt words. You can hear Dylan mouthing sounds and trying out words on tracks such as 'Apple Suckling Tree', 'Get Your Rocks Off' and the marvellous 'I'm Not There (1956)'.

Sometimes they worked a quite different way, so that songs weren't improvised at all – including the co-written 'Tears Of Rage' and 'This Wheel's On Fire'. Of Dylan and the former song, Richard Manuel explained:

> He came down to the basement with a piece of typewritten paper
> . . . it was typed out – in line form – and he just said 'Have you got
> any music for this?' I had a couple of musical movements that fit,
> that seemed to fit, so I just elaborated a little bit, because I wasn't
> sure what the lyrics meant. I couldn't run upstairs and say, 'What's
> this mean, Bob: "Now the heart is filled with gold as if it was a
> purse"?'
>
> [to Ruth Albert Spencer, *Woodstock Times*, March 1985]

Likewise Rick Danko recalled that Dylan gave him 'typewritten
lyrics to "Wheel's on Fire". At that time I was teaching myself to
play piano. Some music I had written on the piano the day
before just seemed to fit with Dylan's lyrics. I worked on the
phrasing and the melody. Then Dylan and I wrote the chorus
together.'

The first the world knew of these basement tapes came in the
form of an acetate disc which was distributed by Dylan's music
publisher as a selection of demos of songs. There were fourteen
tracks, and three of them became hit records: for Julie Driscoll,
Manfred Mann and The Byrds.

The acetate wasn't widely circulating until early summer
1968, although most – not all – of the tracks had been recorded
between June and August 1967. Four of them – 'Tears of Rage',
'Quinn The Eskimo' (then usually known as 'The Mighty
Quinn'), 'Nothing Was Delivered' and 'Open The Door, Homer'
– must have been recorded later, presumably in September or
October, for they were not copyrighted until 16 January 1968,
the other ten having been copyrighted on 9 October 1967.

Clearly Dylan and the band must have recorded several
versions of each song, and other songs have emerged which
were not included on the original acetate: namely, 'Goin' To
Acapulco' (released officially in 1975); 'I'm Not There (1956)' and
'Clothes Line Saga' (still unreleased – as indeed, surprisingly, is
the widely-known original acetate version of 'I Shall Be Released', the title notwithstanding); 'Odds and Ends' and 'Apple
Suckling Tree'. Four of these were only copyrighted in the first
week of January 1970, and their superior sound-quality suggests
that they may not be 'basement' tapes at all, but studio
recordings from around the same time. Two further songs,
'Don't Ya Tell Henry' and 'Sign On The Cross', have a strange
and crude stereo effect, quite unlike anything so far heard

elsewhere among the basement recordings. Without further evidence it's impossible to determine recording dates for these, though October or November '67 seems the appropriate guess.

Rick Danko spoke of 'about 150 songs', however, and a taste of what he was alluding to came to collectors in the last months of 1986 with the emergence of a three-hour tape of band and Dylan material also from 1967.

Here were all kinds of undreamt-of extra songs: the Chicago-type blues of 'Don't You Try Me Now'; folk songs – 'Young But Daily Growing', which Dylan had sung at his first solo concert in 1961, and 'The Hills Of Mexico', a variant of 'On The Trail Of The Buffalo' (which again we have a recorded performance of from back in 1961) and 'Bonnie Ship The Diamond'; the gospelly 'People Get Ready' (later re-done in 1975's *Renaldo & Clara*), the pop-song 'A Fool Such As I' (re-done in 1969, issued on the LP *Dylan*); much striking country material, including 'One Single River', 'I Don't Hurt Anymore' (anticipating the melody of *Self Portrait*'s 'Living The Blues'[23]) and the remarkable 'Be Careful Of Stones That You Throw', a song credited to 'Dodd' and recorded both by Hank Williams (as Luke The Drifter) in 1952 and on an early Staples Singers LP, 'Amen'. And we can still conclude that we've heard nothing yet.

Postscript

What, beyond that, remains of 1967? The recording of *John Wesley Harding*, of course, but that's another set of stories. But remember Robert Markel, long-suffering editor at Macmillan, sitting alone in his office far into the night, waiting for a call from Dylan? He was invited up to Woodstock at the year's turning, and, as he told Michael Gross for *Bob Dylan: An Illustrated History*:

> The two of us sat and talked for about an hour. He drove a car. He looked fine: older, serious. He was far more friendly, far less distracted. He was more grown up and professional, easier to be with. He said he didn't know if he wanted the book published at all. It wasn't something he wanted to improve; it didn't interest him any more. He'd gone past it. He wasn't sure if he wanted it published as a 'relic' or an unfinished work. I harboured the hope

97

that he'd want this youthful work shown to the public, but left feeling ambiguous about his intentions.

He drove a car ... and what of the motorcycle? A last word from the *Village Voice*, 22 August 1968:

> Down from Woodstock drifts this latest piece of Dylan memorabilia – last summer, in a fit of Diggerism, the poet laid his Triumph motorcycle (on which he had his near-fatal accident) on manager Albert Grossman's young gardener. The lucky gardener has been happily barrelling round the countryside often accompanied by lady Dylan fans who he says were 'anxious to straddle the seat that once bore their favourite man' ... the gardener, Tony Raosto, is now in town, monstrously broke, and wants to sell the machine, which he says is in dynamite condition. Best offer takes it; call GR7–9126.

Dynamite condition ...

Bob Dylan and the Search for the Past

David Pichaske

Social transformations, political revolutions and religious reforms are almost always cast in terms of the past. 'When Adam delved and Eve span, who was then the gentleman?' 'Some of the earliest societies, you know, were matriarchal.' 'It is time to recapture the purity of the early Church, the true religion of the Fathers.' 'Back in the days of the good King Arthur ...' The New Thing which is being done always turns out to be an Old Thing – or it is consciously or unconsciously advertised as a return to the past, perhaps to make the revolution seem less revolutionary, perhaps to shift the burden of proof, perhaps to cloak the unknown in the comfortable and respectable garb of recovered tradition. It's easier to promote a return to the Golden Age than a Brave New World.

The dream of a Golden Age is a human dream, of course, but in America it has special power because Americans seem to be living so close to their particular Golden Age and because America perceives itself as having a peculiar and messianic mission, stemming either from its covenanted relationship with God (the theocratic vision of the northern colonies, of the Puritans) or its role as the great experiment in participatory democracy upon which the eyes of the world are fixed (the enlightenment dream of Jefferson and Franklin). Every American understands that the founding fathers were more heroic, stronger, more generous and large-minded than the present generation of fumbling money-grubbers. The founders were statesmen; today we have politicians. The founders were yeomen pioneers; today we have middle managers and bureaucrats. The founders were cowboys and outlaws and individuals; today we have become a nation of sheep. Americans on the East Coast live not 200 years separated from the founders; those of us living in the Upper Midwest and on the Great Plains are not much more than a century from the taking of the land by 'Giants in the Earth'.

What makes Americans feel especially guilty, however, is what they perceive as the precipitous fall from grace these last 100 or 200 years. How have we descended so far so fast? More importantly, what is to become of our special relationship with God, of our status as the great experiment, if we can't recapture, immediately, the purity and the greatness – the state of grace – which was ours only yesterday?

I do not think I exaggerate here, although it may be difficult for a foreigner to understand this obsession with being right, with a moral vision that has been projected upon the past so that it can be realized in the future. The obsessiveness stems from the basically Protestant nature of the country (and the Middle West is, as Minnesotan Sinclair Lewis observed in *Main Street* – a book which happens to be about Sauk Center, Minnesota, although it could easily have been about Bob Dylan's home town of Hibbing – 'double Puritan: prairie Puritan on top of New England Puritan'). This Protestantism is imposed on all Americans, Catholics and Jews and agnostics, native-born and newly come. Dylan could no more escape it in Hibbing than could the Swedish-American Lutherans of

Minneapolis or the Italian-American Roman Catholics of St Paul.

The obsessive search for a past which embodies, as the present does not, 'the virtues', is a source of American strength as well as American weakness. It is clearly a quest after the ideal, out of which grow America's most generous impulses; but it is a quest after an impossible ideal, an ideal which probably never existed even 100 or 200 years ago, and frustration probably accounts for the American neuroses and insanities too well-known to the rest of the world. Ultimately the dream is both beautiful and impossible, both heroic and self-destructive, as Dylan's fellow Minnesotan F. Scott Fitzgerald understood when he wrote the magnificent and absolutely accurate conclusion to his own analysis of the American Dream, *The Great Gatsby*:

> Gatsby believed in the green light, the orgiastic future that year by year recedes before us. It eluded us then, but that's no matter – tomorrow we will run faster, stretch out our arms farther . . . And one fine morning –
> So we beat on, boats against the current, borne back ceaselessly into the past.

Most of us dream the American Dream only semiconsciously, and the young Bob Dylan was no exception. Because the dream is necessary to America's survival as a nation, it is preached incessantly; because it is an impossible dream, what we hear is a simplified, näive version: God is on our side and will make us a 'suck-cess' if we will only 'please her, please him, buy gifts, don't steal, don't lift' and, in general, keep a clean nose.

This simplified gospel produces in most cases a good deal of mindless patriotism, church-going and war-mongering; in some cases, as in that of Bob Dylan and the generation which came of age in the sixties, it leads to a blanket rejection of the present and the immediate past, wherein the failed Dream is located. The present is trashed in favour of a future, which can more perfectly embody 'the virtues' – which are to be recovered from a romanticized, vaguely mythologized past: 'The time will come up when the winds will stop/And the breeze will cease to be breathin' . . .'

Bob Dylan And The American Dream is the subject of a more extensive essay of mine. What interests me *here* is Dylan's search for the past, for *the* past in which the vision manifests itself. Like so many of his generation, young Dylan rejected the immediate present and what I would call the *actual* past for an idealized, abstracted and largely depersonalized past (a past minus the grubbiness, a romanticized past), a mythological past, which he then projected into the future and finally talked himself into adopting as a useful – if also idealized, abstracted and mythological – present.

The rejection is well known and well documented: the whole new personal history Dylan invented for himself in songs like 'Long Time Gone'. Not without cause do the contributors' notes to *Broadside* issue 2 introduce Dylan as 'a young new songwriter and singer of New Mexico', a state in the American Southwest. 'The town I was born in holds no memories,' Dylan wrote in *11 Outlined Epitaphs*, not so much because it was not West but because it was too real, too actual. The present (read life in Hibbing, Minneapolis or New York) is:

> . . . just a dream, babe,
> A vacuum, a scheme, babe,
> That sucks you into feelin' like this.

> ['To Ramona']

Early Dylan lyrics are permeated with the theme of departure, leaving, clearing out and travelling on, escaping the inadequate present. I don't think it fantastic to consider a line like 'Look out your window and I'll be gone', or even a comic throwaway line like 'So long, New York. Howdy, East Orange' as a rejection of the immediate, personal present which has failed to measure up to the Dream. (Some other sixties songs spring immediately to mind in this context: Phil Ochs' 'The Scorpion Departs (And Never Returns)' and 'The World Began in Eden (But It Ended in Los Angeles)' and David Crosby's 'Wooden Ships' – songs of political self-exile.)

The subject at hand, however, is Dylan's search for a usable, if idealized past. We have not far to look for evidence: the first two lines of the first song of *Writings And Drawings by Bob Dylan*,[24] 'Talking New York' (1962):

101

Ramblin' outa the wild West,
Leavin' the towns I love the best . . .

The Hibbing, Minnesota described in *11 Outlined Epitaphs* and
'North Country Blues' is not exactly a part of the 'Wild West'.
The towns of 'the Wild West' are, in fact, fictions of Dylan's
mythic imagination, embodiments in his – and America's –
consciousness of a pure, if raw, American justice and democracy, a virtuous counterweight to a present full of 'people goin'
down to the ground' and folks who will 'rob you with a fountain
pen' and people who will 'kick you when you're up and knock
you when you're down'.

Significantly, Dylan localizes wholesomeness 'out West';
the corruption is East, in New York. Also significantly, the
wholesomeness is not only West, it is rural, as the decadence is
not only East but urban. 'Take all the smog in Cal-i-for-ne-ay',
and the dust of Oklahoma and the dirt of the Rocky Mountain
mines, Dylan claimed in 'Hard Times in New York Town': 'and
it's all much cleaner than the New York kind'. The glory of
America, he suggested in 'Let Me Die In My Footsteps', is to be
found in the rural West, where land meets sun, in Nevada, New
Mexico, Arizona, Idaho, the last of the true West.

As I have suggested, Americans fix their Golden Age in one of
three places: the colonies at the times of the Revolution, the
pioneers of the agrarian frontier, and the cowboy days (which
probably never were) of the Old West. Dylan embraces this
mythology and this past, not only in 'Talking New York' but in
songs like 'Rambling Gambling Willie'. Willie is, of course, from
'out West': the Mississippi River, up Cripple Creek, Colorado.
Like Pretty Boy Floyd before him and John Wesley Harding
after, he is honest, even generous, although an outlaw – a man
on square with God and neighbour. He supports his wives and
his kids, spreads his money far and wide, helps the sick and
poor. He is also more archetypal than actual. When the mythological West must give way to the *actual* West, as in a song like
'Ballad Of Donald White', we discover that folks in Kansas are
every bit as nasty and brutish as folks in New York Town. Even
in the Midwest we are taught 'the laws to abide' and that the
land we live in has God on its side. William Zantzinger may kill
Hattie Carroll in Baltimore, but Hollis Brown kills himself, his
wife and five children on a farm in South Dakota.

The most important lyrics in any analysis of Bob Dylan's search for a past are those which relate to his own youth in Hibbing: 'Ballad For A Friend', 'Bob Dylan's Dream', and 'Girl Of The North Country'. Unlike his poems on Hibbing and the North Country, which are realistic and therefore critical and dismissive, these songs are romantic, idealized and almost mythical. They suggest what we all know: that even in the most corrupt and corrupting societies, some measure of honesty and dignity can be found among members of small, personalized, 'humanized' communities. 'America is a lost nation today . . . but a saving remnant remains.'

Or 'remained'. These songs are all cast in the past: even young love and early friendship are best viewed over the shoulder. The 'Girl Of The North Country' *once was* a true love of Dylan's; right now she might or might not remember him at all. Still, he is kinder to her than to any other lover I can think of, sending a long-distance hello and admitting reverence, not so much for her as for her memory:

> . . . I've often prayed
> In the darkness of my night
> In the brightness of my day.

Idealized almost to the point of abstraction, she is love and warmth pitched against the wind and storm outside.

'Ballad For a Friend' is a less well known and slightly more complex song. Dylan's friend is gone, killed by a diesel truck on a Utah road. So the song is a celebration of personal relationships past – 'I had no better friend than he'. Dylan manages a larger dimension, however, by juxtaposing the truck against the railroad in the line: 'Now that train is a-graveyard bound'. One of the great sorrows of recent American history has been the passing of the railroad, so that the train has become part of that heroic, mythical past which is considered somehow morally superior to the present. 'The train – now *there was* a civilized way to travel,' you hear old-timers say. Dylan's friend is no more; the train is no more; both have passed into a mythology beside which the present pales.

'Bob Dylan's Dream' is the most complex of these three songs, the most fully developed. Dylan sets the story in a dream he had, interestingly enough on a train (again) goin' West (again). The direction is significant, for as we have seen, the West is associated mythically with the Dream, the East with the corruption of the Dream. Again, it is storming outside; again love – this time in the form of friendship – serves as a counter to the cold and the wind without. Bob Dylan's dream is lush and unabashedly romantic in the typical early sixties manner: a glorification of simplicity, poverty, unity against complexity, wealth and multiplicity. 'We longed for nothing and were quite satisfied,' Dylan tells us, implying what every good Protestant understands: the root of all evil is avarice.

'Simplify, simplify, simplify,' wrote Henry Thoreau, the spiritual mentor of this lyric and a prominent spokesman for the American Dream. Simplicity is the key here (and simplicity is possible only in the nearly allegorical mythologizing of the past which takes place in this song): in youthful simplicity come singularity of mind and vision, clarity of moral vision, camaraderie, self-sufficiency. In its inner simplicity, the company 'within' is healthier and happier than the world outside: a kind of 'Wild West' (here more a 'wild North Country', with the old wooden stove) contrasted to the New York City of 'Talking New York'.

This is all in the past, however. It's hard to say whether Dylan himself realized the convention he was borrowing, projecting the Golden Age into an idealized past. I suspect he did: the song was copyrighted in May 1963, scarcely enough time for Dylan to be looking back through 'many a year' passed and gone, many a gamble lost and won, many a friend gone and never seen again. Of course, Dylan was playing, during his early years in New York City, the role of the old ramblin' folkie just blowed in from Santa Fe with the dust of a million hard miles still upon him. This song is, in part, a piece of that role. But it is also one component in Bob Dylan's search for a mythological past on to which he could project a purity of life missing in the present. Significantly the song ends with a look to the future, a hope for redemption, for return:

> Ten thousand dollars at the drop of a hat,
> I'd give it all gladly if our lives could be like that.

104

The theme of the lost past does not entirely disappear from Dylan's work during the great years of 1964-7, although his attention was focused almost exclusively on the insane, poisoned present. In 'My Back Pages' he toys with a rebellion against the self-destructive complexities and hypocritical self-righteousness of the Protest Movement and a retreat into the simple past of 'Bob Dylan's Dream'. The present is (or has been) filled with confusion, phoney jealousy, pride, prejudice – all the sins which transform the American Dream into an American Nightmare:

> Ah, but I was so much older then,
> I'm younger than that now

Dylan sings. Salvation in the simplicity of youth.

Not until the period of *John Wesley Harding*, however, was Dylan to return fully to the mythology of the lost Golden Age. From *Blonde On Blonde* to *John Wesley Harding* is a great, great distance, and *Harding* is probably the pivotal album in Dylan's intellectual development. I have written at length on it elsewhere;[25] what needs to be pointed out here is that Dylan turned his attention from 'the diseased present' ('Rainy Day Women Nos 12 & 35', 'Memphis Blues Again' – all of the songs on the album) to a mythologized past in which he found a dream he could project upon the immediate future-become-present. *John Wesley Harding* ends with Dylan absorbed – musically and philosophically – into the mythology of the 'wild West'.

The album's first two cuts, 'John Wesley Harding' and 'As I Went Out One Morning', both operate within the mythology of 'Rambling Gambling Willie', the honest and generous hero of the American frontier. The difference between 1962 and 1968 is that Dylan now realizes he is playing mythologies like chess pieces, and this particular legend of lost innocence is a starting point for an album-long journey out of the Golden Past, through a confused and guilt-ridden present into . . . well, a mythological, idealized future which resembles (surprise!) the past of 'Bob Dylan's Dream'. In the lyrics of 'I Pity The Poor Immigrant', 'The Wicked Messenger' and especially 'Down Along The Cove' and 'I'll Be Your Baby Tonight', Dylan celebrates simplicity, honest relations, compassion, the moral vision and a small self-sufficiency. Like these two songs, subsequent work – the lyrics of *New Morning* for example – localizes this new state of grace in the West ('Day Of The Locusts' retains the old East/West dichotomy), so some of the old mythology remains.

The important difference between the early and late sixties, however, is that Dylan has moved out of the temporal past and into the geographically remote but nevertheless temporally present Now:

> Build me a cabin in Utah
> Marry me a wife, catch rainbow trout . . .
>
> ['Sign on the Window']

If there is any complaint at all, it is that complexification, acquisitiveness, pride – all the usual sins – cost Dylan a state of grace which could have been his long ago. In a small and often overlooked lyric, 'Wanted Man' (1969), a clue:

I've had all that I've wanted of a lot of things I had
And a lot more than I needed of some things that turned out bad.

Simplify, simplify, simplify.

Bob Dylan gained his reputation as spokesman for a generation which came to its maturity in the late sixties and has largely disappeared from any position of social and political prominence. It is possible that what drove the generation was the discrepancy between Is and Ought, between the grubby realities it found all around itself at the beginning of the decade and the ideals it had learned – in the abstract and tied to history – in school. Every member of that generation has had to come to terms with the betrayal of American idealism built into the American Dream. Most of the generation raged, with Dylan, during the mid-sixties. Part of the generation appears to have come to terms with itself and the country largely on terms outlined by Dylan in *John Wesley Harding* and prefigured in some of the earlier songs I have examined: a recovery of the small and idealized past (Western and rural) in a small and idealized present. This necessitated, of course, a departure from big politics and the revolution in town, out East. So it may well

106

be that in finding at least some qualities of the idealized past in at least some geography of the present, Dylan and the generation of which he was a part checked out of the scene deliberately. Dylan, at least, has returned more than once from his exile-into-salvation. The rest of the generation of the sixties seems, even at this writing, still content with personal grace.

Alias, Pat Garrett and Billy the Kid

Chris Whithouse

The comparatively recent death of Sam Peckinpah prompted this look at how much influence the man had, on Dylan's career and artistic development, during the short time they spent on location filming *Pat Garrett and Billy The Kid*. After all, there weren't many people who received regular dedications of songs on the Rolling Thunder Revue; nor is there any doubt that images of Mexico and the myth of the Wild West occurred with increased frequency in Dylan's work subsequent to that filming.

The year prior to the release of the soundtrack LP in July 1973 has been glossed over by biographers and interviewers, simply because Dylan himself kept a low profile in this period.

In June 1972, Dylan came to the end of his recording contract; he had not played a pre-announced concert since the Isle Of Wight Festival in August 1969 and he had not released an LP of new material for some twenty months. Although he had been rapturously received at the August '71 Concert For Bangladesh, he had announced that he was 'not about to go play concerts' some eighteen months earlier, and was still showing no inclination to tour. Indeed he had even stopped doing the occasional session-work which he had been undertaking for friends such as Allen Ginsberg. So what was happening?

Rolling Stone magazine reported a meeting with Warner Brothers Records in June 1972, at which Dylan 'appeared bored and didn't seem to want to, or seem able to, get an album together at the time'.[26] In the month following these talks, Dylan attended the Mariposa Folk Festival, Canada's equivalent of the annual Newport Folk Festival, and caught a Grateful Dead set in Jersey City, being seen chatting to Jerry Garcia afterwards. He also turned up at Mick Jagger's birthday party, complete with cowboy hat, got his photograph taken – at his own request – with Zsa Zsa Gabor, and grabbed a few words with Keith Richards.[27]

Dylan was clearly starting to circulate again, and, I believe, to look for new directions, well aware that he needed something to help him shake off his creative inactivity.

September saw him briefly on stage at the Bitter End in New York behind John Prine, before the session-work began again with his playing piano and singing back-up vocals (under the pseudonym Robert Milkwood Thomas) for Steve Goodman, whose LP *Somebody Else's Troubles* thanked Dylan but not Columbia Records on its sleeve. Then in October 1972, Dylan was in the studio with Doug Sahm, to contribute to the *Doug Sahm And Band* Atlantic Records album – Dylan having been friendly with Sahm since the mid-sixties and having expressed enthusiasm for the Sir Douglas Quintet on more than one occasion. Dylan also showed up at the 11th Annual Philadelphia Folk Festival with David Bromberg that same month.

Reports of how Dylan then came to accept the role of Alias are conflicting. Sam Peckinpah was still shooting film for *The Getaway* at this time, and Dylan didn't seem to have any firm plans about anything. When asked at the Doug Sahm session about future recording plans, he commented 'I'm not playing with anybody now'.[28] This comment was the first direct quote he had given *Rolling Stone* magazine in quite a while, suggesting that Dylan felt he had nothing to promote. Otherwise he might have felt like creating some favourable exposure for himself in a rock press which, if it had not already written Dylan off as a spent force, was certainly not treating him with the open reverence he had commanded throughout the sixties. (When it has suited his purposes, Dylan has been far from coy with the press – witness his extensive *Renaldo & Clara* interviews of 1978, or those to help promote *Biograph* seven years later, for example. In fact the supposedly press-shy and uncommunicative Bob

Dylan has given over 175 interviews to press, TV and radio in the course of his career – an average of one almost every seven weeks throughout the last twenty-five years!)

Yet after that October, things happened rapidly. While Nixon got re-elected, Dylan popped into the Wally Heider Studio in Los Angeles to play harmonica for Roger McGuinn – and then moved his family down to Durango, Mexico for the start of filming for Peckinpah. The Dylan entourage moved in on 23 November 1972.

If reports about Dylan's coming to accept the role of Alias are conflicting, probably the most reliable account – certainly the most thorough – is Michael Watts' for *Melody Maker*:

He got the part, in fact, through a combination of circumstances precipitated by Bert Block, Kristofferson's manager. Block, an old music pro who at one time managed Billie Holiday, was the guy who looked after the arrangements when he played the Isle Of Wight. He's the nearest thing Dylan has had to a business manager since he let his contract with Grossman expire. (Grossman and Block were partners for a while, indeed, and handled Janis Joplin together.)

Block mentioned to Dylan that Kristofferson was in a movie, and suggested it to him as well . . . Dylan had talks with Rudy Wurlitzer, the screenplay writer, and went to a private screening of *The Wild Bunch*. He was sceptical of the project at first. He only intended to see one reel. But then it stretched to three, four . . . Dylan came out of MGM's theatre with a celluloid monkey riding on his back.

He was fascinated with the idea of a movie part as much as he was daunted by his feeling of inadequacy towards doing it. Before there had only been documentaries. And Peckinpah was a frightening genius!

But he went down with Bert to Mexico to exorcise his doubts. The first night they dined at Peckinpah's house on a meal of roast goat. Then he was shown around the set. He was particularly captivated by the wardrobe of Western clothes, trying on the hats and costumes like a kid dressing for a fancy-dress party. He looked around for a while, and then, on the second day, quietly picked up a guitar and sang to Kris and [James] Coburn and Peckinpah this song he'd made up called 'Billy The Kid'. Peckinpah offered him a part there and then.[29]

In his book, *Peckinpah – A Portrait In Montage*, Garner Simmons quotes James Coburn, who played the part of Sheriff Pat Garrett, as saying: 'When Dylan came down to Mexico, Sam didn't know who the fuck Dylan was. But when he heard Dylan sing, Sam was the first to admit that he was taken with Dylan's singing. He heard Dylan's 'Ballad Of Billy The Kid' and immediately had it put on tape so that he could have it with him to play.'

It is possible to add here that Dylan had written the song 'real quick'[30] after he had been sent a script by Rudy Wurlitzer, who had himself told Dylan that he needed a song for the movie,[31] and also that Dylan had been called up by Kristofferson, who suggested that if Dylan came down to Durango, he would probably find himself getting paid for learning the techniques of cinema. Wurlitzer acknowledged this Dylan-as-pupil idea:

'Dylan is great. He's come down here to learn, he's turning in stuff and it's really been impressive. I think he's completely authentic . . . I don't know what he really wants to do but I would hope he would do his own film, because he's an artist and he can't help it. He's just finding out about films.'[32]

Rudy Wurlitzer was thirty-six years old at the time of the film's shooting. He had written three novels, one of which – *Nog* – achieved cult status on both sides of the Atlantic. He obviously had firm ideas about the film's story:

'Pat and Billy were two gunmen who essentially felt a kinship but had chosen two diametrically opposed roles in life, the former as a sheriff, the latter as an outlaw. Thus they were symbols of a changing America in the last century, the one a roving free spirit, symbolizing the pioneer nature of the Old West, the other selling out to the establishment for a steady job and security, representing, therefore, the solidifying respectability of the new America.'[33]

He commented further that he had not had Garrett and Billy coming together until the film's end, whereas Peckinpah had 'imposed' three scenes in the beginning to show them meeting. It also seems that Peckinpah's original opening for the movie showed the murder of Pat Garrett, and made the rest of the film appear as memory-images flooding into the mind of the dying Garrett (killed by the 'Santa Fe ring' which had hired him to kill Billy in the first place). However, the studio removed Peckinpah's opening and thus took away some of Garrett's nobility, as well as the irony of Garrett's claims of being out to survive.[34]

The inter-relationships between Peckinpah, Wurlitzer and 'the studio' (which seems to have meant Jim Aubrey, head of MGM) are complex. Aubrey began to pressure Peckinpah on the very first day of filming, and by January 1973 the film was already two weeks behind schedule and a million dollars over budget.[35] In large part this stemmed from technical problems – incredibly, almost a fortnight's filming had been spoiled by cameras being out of focus.[36] MGM sent down three executives from Culver City, and Peckinpah got more and more tense. He was constantly re-working the script – much to Wurlitzer's annoyance: he said later that he would walk onto the set to find scenes being directed which he had never written or discussed.[37] What with Wurlitzer's script being changed by Peckinpah and Peckinpah's film being edited by the studio, one wonders whose baby *Pat Garrett and Billy The Kid* finally is. Peckinpah certainly felt that edits and cuts forcibly changed the film's meaning: 'This was the story of a time – a legend – not about two gunfighters,' he was to complain.[38]

Yet Peckinpah's on-set domination of proceedings was enough to cause Kristofferson to speak with some trepidation about how best to approach the director with a new scene he and Wurlitzer had put together.[39] As for Peckinpah and Dylan – well, Wurlitzer was drawn to comment:

> That's the really interesting thing, what's going on between Peckin-pah and Dylan. Sam is really Western, like an outlaw, looking to the wide open spaces, and he didn't know about Dylan before. Dylan, you could say, was Eastern. He brings a different point of view, especially to a Western. The part is small but it is important in a funny sort of way. Do the two of them have any common ground to meet on? – *that's* the big question.[40]

It must have been a strange time for Dylan, two months in the heat and boredom of the Mexican desert, either cooped up in the trailer he shared with Kris Kristofferson on set, or in the rented house in neighbouring Yucatan with Sara, five children who – according to Maggie Netter, an on-the-spot MGM publicist – ran wild, and Rover the dog.[41] Add to this various people trying to gatecrash the set and it is perhaps not surprising to read reports that Dylan sometimes went for days without uttering a word.[42]

Michael Watts asked Dylan about the pressures:

> 'Tell me, how can you stand it down here?'
> 'It's not too bad because I'm making a film. If I wasn't . . .' The sentence was chopped off . . . The next time I saw Dylan was on the set later that day, and he was locked tight once more behind his stoniness.[43]

Dylan even seems to have hinted that he was tempted to give in. He asked Kristofferson how important it was to *him* that he (Dylan) finish the picture.[44] Presumably Kristofferson helped convince Dylan to stay on. Years later Kristofferson commented: 'He had a hell of a hard time down there, man. I admire him for sticking it out.'[45]

Some of Dylan's unhappiness was alluded to in the booklet that accompanies *Biograph*, where Dylan himself comments:

> Actually, I was just one of Peckinpah's pawns. There wasn't a part for me and Sam just liked me around . . . Rudy Wurlitzer . . . invented a part for me but there wasn't any dimension to it and I was very uncomfortable in this non-role. But then time started to slip away and there I was trapped deep in the heart of Mexico with some madman ordering people around like a little king. You had to play the dummy all day . . . It was crazy, all these generals making you jump into hot ants, setting up turkey shoots and whatever . . . I was too beat to take it personal . . . I was sleep-walking most of the time and had no real reason to be there. I'd gotten my family out of New York, that was the important thing, there was a lot of pressure back there. But even so, my wife got fed up almost immediately. She'd say to me, 'What the hell are we doing here?' It was not an easy question to answer.

Whatever was happening betwen Dylan and Peckinpah seems to have reached a peak when the principal characters flew down to Mexico City to the CBS Discos Studios that January. Peckinpah seemed jealous and perturbed that so many people were flying off to Mexico City to listen to Dylan record, and tried to arrange a rival attraction in Durango: a screening of his most recent picture, *The Getaway*. When this looked like being poorly attended, he called a 6.30 rehearsal for the Monday morning, knowing that anyone attending the recording-session would never make it back on time.

This element of rivalry between Peckinpah and Dylan was keenly felt by Wurlitzer, who when he got to the recording studio saw Dylan as exacting some form of revenge: deliberately performing a first take of 'Billy' that wasn't what Peckinpah was expecting. When he did a second take he also added a coda for good measure, as *Rolling Stone* reported:

> He bore down on the last line – 'Billy you're so far away from home' – and repeated it twice, and then addressed the control room: 'Keep that take and add this wild track to it: Corn. Beans. Succotash. Coffee. End of take.' . . . 'See, man, what he's doin',' said Wurlitzer, 'he's gettin' back at Sam. *Sure*. I don't know, man, if he's sayin' he's gonna quit the film or what.'[46]

Far more probable was that Dylan, as ever, was simply being spontaneous in the studio.

On the plane en route to Mexico City, the escapees had been feeling pretty good. Kristofferson was in a particularly talkative mood and was asked about Bob Dylan:

> 'Listen,' he said, 'this guy can do anything. In the script he has to throw a knife. It's real difficult. After ten minutes or so he could do it perfect . . . Listen, he does things that you never thought was in him. He can play Spanish-style, bossa nova, flamenco . . . One night he was playing flamenco and his old lady, Sara, had never known him to do it at all before.'[47]

Kristofferson told similar stories elsewhere:

> The first day we shot was also Bob's first day on camera. We had to be ridin' horses after these turkeys and he ropes 'em. Well, Bob hadn't ridden much and it was *hairy* ridin', down in gullies and off through a river. And then we had to rope these damn turkeys! I couldn't do it, but Bob did it all. I couldn't believe it. I've seen prints, and he's got a presence on him like Charlie Chaplin. He's like a wild card that none of 'em knew they had. I think they just

hired him for the name and all of a sudden you see him on screen and all eyes are on him. There's something about him that's magnetic. He doesn't even have to move. He's a natural . . . *fantastic on film.*[48]

But as stories of his jealousy or disgruntlement suggest, Peckinpah wasn't always awestruck by Dylan's many and charismatic talents during the shooting. Kristofferson (again) talked of other episodes (this time for Garner Simmons' book *Peckinpah – A Portrait in Montage*):

This one scene, Sam wanted him to come riding up to me, and, as usual, it wasn't in the script. So they put Bobby on a horse and told him what they wanted. Now it's hard for Bobby to hit his marks in a scene with his own feet 'cos he doesn't think like that. But he's supposed to come through these sheep to where I'm standin', and old Sam says, 'OK Bobby, you just come straight by the camera here.' Well, Bobby went into a gallop, man, scaring sheep, horses, cameramen and everybody. And I was laughin' so hard I was in tears. So was Sam. And old Sam says, 'No, Bobby, I really didn't mean that.' The strange thing is, I don't know yet whether Bobby did that on purpose or not.

The really big scene that Bobby kinda screwed up was the one where Garrett is supposed to be ridin' off into the sunrise at the end of the movie after killin' Billy. Only they were shootin' a sunset for sunrise and they had like five minutes of what they call 'golden time' when the sun is just right.

Well, the night before it had been the extras screwin' the shot up – lookin' at Sam, or somethin'. So we were doin' it the second time. Well, Bobby wasn't in the shot, and he and Harry Dean Stanton decided they were goin' on a health campaign and run five miles. Only the first part of the five miles was right through the shot.

I came out on the set, and it was like a tomb. I asked what happened and I hear 'The Dylan boys just ran through the shot.' And everybody is sittin' around not sayin' a word as Harry Dean Stanton comes walkin' in. It was about as quiet as a church, and old Harry Dean is sayin' 'Hi, Sam!' And everybody is sayin' to themselves, 'Oh shit,' and Sam growls, 'You just cost me $25,000.' And Harry Dean says, 'Sam, I knew it was wrong, and I was runnin' after him to tell him to stop.'

Now Sam throws a pretty mean knife. He can pretty near always make it stick. Well, he's got this knife in his hand, and he lets 'er fly, and it sticks in the wood next to old Harry Dean, who flies through the door like nothin' flat shoutin' behind him, 'I promise, Sam, it'll never happen again.' And when Dylan heard about it, he just said, 'Well, let's have a concert and pay him back.' It's like I said. I never know when he's doin' a number on Sam or not.

With Dylan and Kristofferson on the plane to Mexico City were Wurlitzer and Coburn, who wasn't so much looking forward to the recording-session as to a break from Peckinpah and MGM executives like Jim Aubrey (by this time known on the set as the Cobra). Rita Coolidge was there too, and even the film's producer, Gordon Carroll.

The recording session itself was intensive, and just about non-stop from 11 o'clock on the Saturday evening until 7 o'clock the following morning. Dylan had written only two vocal tracks – the title song 'Billy', and 'Holly', a lament for the character played by Richard Bright, whom Garrett guns down in the beans scene. There were a few instrumental tunes too. Dylan had already made a tape of these songs for Peckinpah, at the director's house in Durango, but even by the time of these recordings it was apparently not decided whether Dylan's music would be used in the film, or whether Kristofferson's own song 'Pat Garrett' would be included.

The session began with a take of a nine-verse version of 'Billy', apparently very different from the demo-tape version. But while Wurlitzer thought Dylan was being deliberately perverse, James Coburn said – in a rather Dylanesque phrase – that Dylan was just obviously 'so glad to be free'. There followed a second take of 'Billy' – again, nine verses: but two of these were new ones and a third was completely improvised. Animated by the experience of singing, and fortified with cups of vodka, Dylan whooped down a cut of 'Will The Circle Be Unbroken?', Kristofferson joining in halfway through, and his band (Mike Utley, organ; Sammy Creason, drums; Stephen Bruton, electric guitar; and Terry Paul, bass) backed Dylan.[49]

A galloping instrumental came next, though Dylan threw in a few 'Billy' lyrics for good measure; he announced the tune as 'Turkey #2'. A four-minute-long chunky jam between Dylan and Utley, with Dylan and Terry Paul la-la-la-ing manically was identified subsequently as 'Billy Surrenders' or 'Speedball'.

At this point Dylan came out with what seems, in context, an astonishing comment: 'Hey, we need Sam here, to say what to *do*.' A nervous Rudy Wurlitzer wasn't convinced. Looking over his shoulder, he said: 'Sam *is* here, man, I feel him.'

Another la-la-la, with Kris and Rita on back-up vocals, and Coburn saying one of his movie lines: 'Yeah, I'm alive though', was noted down as 'Turkey In The Straw'. It was, by this time, already three in the morning.

Then came 'Holly's Song' ('Goodbye Holly, Holly goodbye/ your wife's gonna miss you/your baby's gonna cry') and an ah-ah-ah instrumental called 'Peco's Blues', for which two Mexican trumpeters, who had been standing around waiting all evening, were required.

Coburn was wildly enthusiastic about the way the sessions were going. Then again, he had been smoking joints just about all the time since his arrival. Gordon Carroll, the producer, was concerned that he couldn't hear much of what had been on Peckinpah's demo tapes. In other words, he couldn't hear much of what the director of his movie was expecting to get brought back from Mexico City. A short and bitter exchange therefore followed between Carroll and Dylan, before the producer backed down.

At 4 a.m. the other actors left for the Sheraton Hotel, to get some sleep before Sunday's Superbowl football game on television. Dylan stayed on in the studio, called for another reel of tape and recorded 'Billy' again – with bass, drums and harmony and without harmonica. He didn't like it and sang it again, this time very slowly – eerie and mournful. Gordon Carroll was still listening, and Dylan turned to him enthusiastically:

'Right after this, Garrett rides into town, right?'
'Right,' the producer said. 'Right. That really is . . . unbelievable. Um, What do you think?'
'No,' said Dylan, 'I don't think. I hold it all in and then – act!' He laughed. 'I'm glad you were on the case because I forgot all about that original.'

Dylan came out of the studios talking about playing a concert in Durango:

116

'I'd like to. It's just a funky little hall. Real nice audience. They make a lot of noise. I'm kind of anxious to do it. I mean a *real* audience. I'm used to those audiences in the States, and they just come and gawp at you.'[50]

This never happened. More regrettable still is that in spite of its having been so striking an all-night session, of all its recordings only the second 'Billy' ends up on the 'soundtrack' LP and in the film (and even this has the harmonica cut out in the movie); on the album it is the track called 'Billy 4'(!). 'Billy Surrenders' was used in the film but did not make the LP. None of the rest was used at all. (Nor has it subsequently appeared in bootleg circulation; ditto – with the exception of one fragment – the demo-tape made earlier for Peckinpah.)

The other recordings which were used in the film and/or on the record were made later, in February 1973, back in Burbank, California, with Gordon Carroll producing. MGM PR executive Charles Lippincott was quoted as saying that Dylan cut three songs for a *new* album as well as the material for the film soundtrack.[51] He didn't expand on this, but we do know that by the time the soundtrack LP was released, in July '73, Dylan had certainly already written three songs intended for what was to become the *Planet Waves* album: namely, 'Forever Young', 'Never Say Goodbye' and 'Nobody 'Cept You'.

Since Dylan was still free of contractual obligations, the *Pat Garrett and Billy The Kid* album was auctioned off – Columbia Records outbidding MGM and Warner Brothers. Columbia's determination to win out perhaps suggested that they didn't like Dylan to be so free.

The record wasn't well-received. So long had elapsed since the release of *New Morning* (back in 1970) that people were looking to get something really substantial. But for Dylan, *Pat Garrett* was intended as nothing more or less than a film soundtrack album. Jon Landau in *Rolling Stone* reviewed it under the heading 'Dylan Redefines Himself – Merely Awful'.[52] Dylan was upset by this review and later said that Landau had '. . . got his head up his ass. He wrote that article from a very inexperienced and immature position because he had no reason to say that about it. He wasn't connecting it to the film.'[53] And then the slating that the film itself received at the time from the

117

New York Times apparently even resulted in Dylan's trying to persuade Columbia Records not to release the album.[54]

Before the subject of the film's music is left behind, it is interesting to note that Peckinpah had begun to feel uneasy about the work Dylan had done with Gordon Carroll, and had summoned one Jerry Fielding to supervise the work that had been done on the scoring of the picture, hoping that Fielding's 'professionalism' would give a gloss to Dylan's apparent näiveté. Fielding's comments (taken from the Garner Simmons book), emphasize how lucky we are to have what we have of Dylan's music for the movie at all:

> It was total frustration. Wasted effort. First of all, I was called in late on the picture after Sam began to doubt that Dylan's music alone could hold together a two-hour-plus motion picture.
>
> The producer, Gordon Carroll, was the one who subsidized [sic] Dylan as the major creative force musically on *Pat Garrett*. But just because you play a guitar and sing doesn't qualify you for scoring a picture. Everybody knew it, and everybody kept giving Dylan advice. The problem was he didn't know enough about the situation to tell good advice from bad. And then, of course, he looked at me, and all he could see was 'establishment'. So he wouldn't listen to me at all. And I resent that kind of superficial shit. I paid my dues in this business, and I've got the scars to prove it, but that's beside the point.
>
> I give Bobby Dylan credit for writing seven great pieces of music and a lot of nonsense which is strictly for teenboppers. I also give him credit for having a way with words that is often very effective but just as often meaningless. He plays a simple blues pattern and a number of repetitious chords that I honestly must say offend me as a musician. On that basis, considering the complexities of scoring a picture, Bobby Dylan has no more business attempting it than Sam Peckinpah has selling popcorn in the lobby of the theatre.
>
> But he was their boy, and I was supposed to make it happen. I set up two dubbing sessions. Dylan had this song he'd written for which he had a limitless number of verses that he would sing in random order. Actually, Kris Kristofferson had written a song as well which I thought had more potential in terms of scoring the picture, but I was overruled. So I had to tape Dylan's song, because he had nothing written down, and have it transcribed. It was my idea that by having Dylan sing a relevant verse as it fit the story at roughly nine separate points throughout the picture, it might be coherent. Dylan never understood what I wanted.

At the same time I asked that he write at least one other piece of music because you cannot possibly hope to deal with an entire picture on the basis of that one ballad. So, finally, he brought to the dubbing session another piece of music – 'Knock-knock-knocking on Heaven's Door'. Everybody loved it. It was shit. That was the end for me.

They all got into it. Bob Dylan – he talked to them all and he listened to them all and he believed them all and he tried to do what he thought they wanted in his limited way. And it was infantile. It was sophomoric. It was stuff you learn not to do the second year you score a piece of film. And for me to go back and try to do that shit and tell them why I can't be a part of that – why it's wrong that he's singing 'Knock-knock-knockin' on Heaven's Door' with a rock drummer in a scene were a guy is dying and the emotion speaks for itself. If I've got to explain that to a producer, then I've got to get out.

Finally, in the *Biograph* booklet, Dylan was to express his own dismay at the way his music ended up being employed in the movie: 'The music seemed to be scattered and used in every other place but the scenes which we did for it. Except for 'Heaven's Door', I can't say as though I recognized anything I'd done for being in the place that I'd done it for.'

Where were we? Oh yes: we'd left the tired troupe asleep in the Sheraton Hotel, Mexico City, dreaming of touch-downs and cheerleaders, referees with stars on their shirts and someone called Chisum working out the game-plan. The next day the Sheraton was briefly abandoned – no suitable TV set, apparently – for a specially-booked suite at the Fiesta Palace Hotel. The Miami Dolphins thumped the Washington Redskins, Coburn smoked on, and Bob Dylan went to bed.

In room 734, Dylan slept deeply. He was still asleep when the maid came to the door and said it was ten o'clock. Ten o'clock! No, it couldn't be! He'd missed that plane back to Durango and it was his big scene today, where he got to throw the knife he'd been practising with.

He slung all his stuff into a carpet bag and flung himself down to the lobby, his eyes still popping like a camera-shutter, just adjusting to being awake, to all these people down at reception, to the actual time it was! And then they tell him it's OK anyway, and it's really ten o'clock at night, and he needn't have worried after all. He shook his head in relief.[55]

119

Dylan made it for his knife-throwing scene at El Sauz the following afternoon. There were six takes, some of which were preceded by a scene in which Dylan was 'sitting on a chair surrounded by half-a-dozen ragged Mexican kids. He was strumming an acoustic, wearing a brown shirt, black pants and a grey top hat.'[56] A publicity still was taken from this scene, and has been much reproduced since, but the scene itself was excised from the much-butchered final version of the film.

The studio apparently made *huge* cuts – six men re-editing without Peckinpah's approval – after discovering the 'excessive' running-time. It might be that the part of Alias suffered quite badly from this studio editing. It would be interesting to know exactly what was discarded – and here I am disadvantaged by not having had access to a copy of Rudy Wurlitzer's screenplay[57] – but it is curious for example that both Kristofferson and Wurlitzer mentioned that Dylan played the part of Alias with a stutter. Wurlitzer observed even during shooting: '[the stutter] will have to be taken out. It becomes too much of a big thing if you only have a small part . . .'[58]

Kristofferson was getting frustrated because Dylan was doing so little in the film:

> The trouble is, man, Dylan aint had a chance to *talk*. His speaking lines have been a bunch of stutterin' that really pissed me off. He's called Alias, and in every fuckin' scene the sonofabitch is put in a different wardrobe and he looks entirely different and *that* could be why he's called Alias. And that damn stutter thing – that could be as big a defense as his change of clothing. Who knows? *I* thought it was supposed to be like the Fool in *Lear*. He sees it all, he knows the whole legend and can see where it's all going. But we never relate as characters. We're always chasing turkeys or some damn thing, and don't even *look* at each other . . .[59]

Although what speech we have left from Alias in the film is hesitant, it can't be described as stuttering. Either this was discarded before Peckinpah handed over his final cut to the studio or we lost the whole stutter in the subsequent edits.

An MGM handout for the film has a précis of the storyline which also reveals a couple of interesting discrepancies with the released movie version. Alias supposedly rides out of town after

Billy following the killing of the amiable Deputy J.W. Bell and of the unamiable Deputy Ollinger; but in the film we see him simply go back into the safety of the printers' office instead, and he is later seen in the barber's shop when Garrett has returned to Lincoln to learn of Billy's escape. Alias' next appearance has him in Billy's company at an unspecified location (probably Fort Sumner) which might lead one to wonder how Alias could have tracked Billy down when Garrett couldn't. There is also mention in the MGM handout of Billy accepting Alias' invitation to ride with him. This is not in the film, though the two men are certainly good friends by the time we are shown the turkey-chasing scene. ('I got me a turkey,' says Alias, perhaps anticipating the buffet requirements for the Mexico City recording session, at which Kristofferson's remarks were apparently made 'between bites of turkey and cheese'.)

There may be, in existing photographs, further clues as to footage intended for inclusion but discarded in the final edit. Several shots show Dylan/Alias wearing clothes he never wears in the film. *Talking Bob Zimmerman Blues* #5, August 1976, includes such photos, credited to Daniel Tehaney, who also took the shot used on the back of the hardcover of *Writings and Drawings*.[60] Unit photographer Bob Jenkins also has four nice location shots reproduced in Rinzler's *Illustrated Record*.[61] There is also the photograph which shows the excised singing-to-the-children scene, and note further that on the sleeve of the soundtrack album, Sara Dylan is credited under 'photography'. It would be gratifying to know what became of her shots: prior to the LP's release *Rolling Stone* ran a report that it would include a poster featuring some of them; this poster never emerged. (The same article also told us that the LP cover was to have featured a collage of paintings by Dylan, but that these had been accidentally destroyed in Mexico.)[62]

At any rate, in the final cut of the film we were left with 106 inutes of footage, in which there are only six scenes where Alias actually speaks. The part of Alias was always going to be relatively minor, even if Dylan's presence in the filming was major. Yet the first Alias appearance on screen implies, by recurrent cutting to him, that while he is only a spectator and takes no active part in the drama, he is to be significant nonetheless. This promise is never fulfilled. Alias' subsequent contribution is interesting but not 'significant'. The street-wise kid who can certainly 'throw the blade', rope himself a dinner and handle a rifle-butt when need be, undergoes what seems to me some sort of weird off-screen metamorphosis, to emerge as prepared to do Garrett's bidding with neither a word nor a look of protest. The label-reading scene is funny, and Dylan's performance here is surely a highlight of the film: but we are never given sufficient context in which to place Alias – a man who appears ready enough to crack a buddy over the head with that rifle-butt (again, most deftly) as soon as he's told to, and who has no comment at all on the shooting of Holly, nor even, finally, on that of Billy himself.

All in all Alias was a disappointment to most people, including Dylan himself. The acerbic, 'head-up-his-ass' Jon Landau called the film 'disjointed, confused and generally inept' and went on to describe Dylan as 'history's most nervous cowboy . . . always around to side with the winner.'[63]

On the other hand film critic Gordon Gow found much to admire, both in the movie and in Bob Dylan's Alias:

> To Alias, in fact, is assigned much of the film's neat recognition of fate. He broods silently, he worships and follows a hero but in time his left eye squints towards the camera, towards awareness of a hollow splendour. Dylan acts well, and he also furnishes the soundtrack with some moody tunes which fit the occasion ideally.[64]

Michael Gray is over-enthusiastic when he writes that 'it was partly Dylan's significant contribution, not only in writing the score but also by his own performance, and his re-writes of the script, that made *Pat Garrett and Billy The Kid* Sam Peckinpah's finest film'.[65] But his assessment echoes Gow's contention that, in spite of the cuts and edit-outs, Alias' role is still discernibly that of a commentator.[66]

The best assessment of the film I've come across is the summary by Terence Butler.[67] Butler tells us that the film presents a West where frontier vitality is down to dying embers. The authority taking control of the West is the cattle baron Chisum (who *was* played by Barry Sullavan, but was cut completely from the finished film). Characters have two options: they either conform to Chisum's invincible will, or they are destroyed. Against this repression, Peckinpah presents the fraternal loyalty of the old friendship between Pat Garrett and Billy The Kid. Garrett claims that he has become a sheriff in order to survive in changing times, but this ostensible pragmatism is self-deceit. Garrett's allegiance to (perhaps even subservience to) Chisum has taken away his outlaw identity. Hence his obsession with his own external appearance. We see his arrogant self-absorption in the scene in the barber's shop and we note too the great care he takes with his clothes throughout the film.

This article has already mentioned the studio's removal of the original opening – Garrett's death. Garrett was killed by the Santa Fe ring because he went against them. His revolt would have given him a belated claim to dignity, and thus lent to the film the dimension of tragedy which Peckinpah sought to include. As it is, all we see is the Garrett who sells out.

He tries to convince himself that he has not done so. He will not adapt his behaviour in deference to the businessmen who hire him, and he tells them plainly what to do with the money they offer as an incentive to bring Billy in: 'Stick it up your ass and burn it.' In company with Special Deputy Poe, Garrett is obnoxiously aggressive – probably because Poe represents what Garrett would not wish to see himself become, a Chisum sycophant. He defends Billy against Poe's disparaging remarks, and finally strikes him to the ground for wanting Billy's trigger-finger.

It is not just Poe who is on the receiving end of the aggression which Garrett cannot discharge against Chisum. More and more he pursues outlaws and drifters, bullying them, killing them – and getting old Sheriff Baker and his own old friend Black Harris gunned down in the process. He also uses women to bolster his self-image, as well as to provide another outlet for his violence. In the bordello he relies on force where Billy relies on charisma.

This Billy is increasingly romanticized by Peckinpah. He is a free man, as is emphasized in the scene when he hacks off his chains while singing the names of all the places he has passed through. While Garrett has to take every opportunity he can find to display his virility – shooting the chickens, shooting at the bottle in the river, beating Ruthie Lee, killing Holly and

123

Harris and sadistically humiliating Beaver, Alias and Lemuel –
Billy has an enchanting authority, which allows him to be loved
by his followers – by Paco, by Maria, by Bowdre – even as he
commands. He, like Garrett, appears at first to be committed to
survival, but as he becomes increasingly conscious of the legend
that has grown up around him, his attitude changes:

> Bob Dylan's deliberately colourless Alias, who has fled a job as a
> printer in Lincoln to join Billy's drifters, is a constant reminder to
> Billy of how a whole way of life derives its only real sense of
> identity from the *legend* [my emphasis] of Billy The Kid. When Billy
> asks Alias what he thinks about his going to Mexico, Alias replies
> that 'it depends on who you are'. Billy heads for Mexico all the
> same, but Alamosa Bill's dying words – 'Least I'll be remembered' –
> succeed in convincing Billy of the importance of the legend of Billy
> The Kid.[68]

And in fact only the spectacle of his gentle Mexican 'father',
Paco, being destroyed by the new Americans drives Billy back
north of the border.

Garrett's killing of Billy is his final betrayal of the frontier
past; Billy's death is itself a symbol of the passing of an era.
Actually Billy submits to Garrett, who punches the movie's
neatest crimson bullet-hole into Billy's neck. His second shot
hits a mirror, but the mirror does not break to allow Garrett
liberation from his second self – it merely cracks, so that Garrett
is left facing the distorted image of what he once was. As the
movie's missing opening would probably have made clear,
there is nothing left for Garrett now but to square off against the
men who sent him on this errand. The attack on Poe shows his
awareness of the right target for his aggression, but too late. The
coffin – for Billy, for Garrett or perhaps for the Old West itself –
is being prepared before the movie's final shot. The coffin-
maker, Will, refuses Garrett's drink and then says to him: 'You
finally figured it out, huh? Go on: get it over with.' The
coffin-maker is played by Sam Peckinpah.

When Bob Dylan had done his bit in Durango, he went back to
California to finish the soundtrack and then resumed making
the rounds (for a short time). He dropped into the Troubadour
to catch David Blue,[69] accompanied by Harry Dean Stanton,[70]

and then turned up there again to play harmonica for Roger McGuinn, who had played banjo on the *Pat Garrett and Billy The Kid* soundtrack sessions under the imaginative pseudonym of 'Jolly Roger'. Another soundtrack player, Booker T, was given a return favour by Dylan playing harmonica on his 'Crippled Crow'.

Dylan was certainly in a more positive frame of mind than he had been before he went off for his jolt of Mexico. 'He's gonna go out and *do* something,' commented Kristofferson on this revitalized Dylan.[71]

Dylan now settled in Malibu, and later that summer he began to rehearse with The Band for what was to be the 1974 'comeback' tour. Work on producing an album for Barry Goldberg in August 1973 was effectively the last of what had been a long sequence of insignificant sessions. By autumn Dylan was playing for himself again, recording the songs for *Planet Waves*, after sorting out his unsettled contractual situation.

There can be no doubt that Dylan's working with Sam Peckinpah was to have a profound effect on Dylan's later recordings – most notably on the *Desire* album. Although produced over two years after Dylan had worked in Durango, there is much Mexican imagery both in its lyrics and in the sound of the band, and in the tales of sudden, often violent deaths of travellers, drifters and outlaws, 'common folk' caught on the wrong side of love and the law. The overriding theme of the LP, moreover, is that of fraternity in the face of adversity or oppression. This, of course, was also a central interest of the movie. There was also – perhaps primarily – the inspiration of *filming* itself. Dylan had gone to Durango to learn. He came away with a light in his eye: 'I want now to *make* movies. I've never been this close to movies before. I'll make a hell of a movie after this.'[72]

On the Rolling Thunder Revue tours, when Dylan was singing the *Desire* songs for the first time, he dedicated several performances to Peckinpah, and as recently as 1985 (in the *Biograph* booklet) made the following statement about the late film-maker: 'He was an outlaw. A real hombre. Somebody from the old school. Men like they don't make anymore.'

Dylan himself formed the impression, at the time of the film's shooting and afterwards, that the character of Alias was a fictional one; and most people shared this assumption. But on the LP of a quite different project (yet with its own Bob Dylan connection, via Allen Ginsberg, as it happens) – the Giorno Poetry Systems LP *Disconnected* – there is a poem by West Coast poet Jack Spicer entitled 'Billy The Kid', which refers to someone called Alias being close to Billy, and this pre-dates the Peckinpah movie.

The possibility that Spicer created the Alias character, and that his poem inspired Peckinpah's scriptwriter, turns out not to be the solution to this small puzzle. Instead, a very different author – Pat Garrett himself – provides the answer.

Perhaps to cash in on the killing of Billy, the man who was his friend wrote a book: *The Authentic Life of Billy, The Kid, The noted desperado of the Southwest, whose deeds of daring and blood made his name a terror in New Mexico, Arizona and Northern Mexico*. This was declared to be 'by Pat F. Garrett, Sheriff of Lincoln Co., N.M., by whom he was finally hunted down and captured by killing him' and to be 'A faithful and interesting narrative'.[73]

In Chapter Two, Garrett describes Billy arriving at Camp Bowie, Arizona:

> ... with a companion, both mounted on one sore-backed pony, equipped with a packsaddle and rope bridle, without a quarter of a dollar between them ... Billy's partner doubtless had a name which was his legal property, but he was so given to changing it that it is impossible to fix on the right one. Billy always called him "Alias".

As for Pat F. Garrett himself, he was shot through the back of the head by an unknown assassin on 29 February 1908.

And a final historical note: US historian W.W. Hutchinson published an article after the release of Peckinpah's movie,[74] in which he takes the film to task for its historical inaccuracies. Two of his points are of interest. First, he establishes that while Billy The Kid derives from the name William Bonney, this was itself an *alias*, the outlaw's real name having been Henry McCarty. Second, Hutchinson adds that in appearance, far more than Kristofferson, it was Bob Dylan who looked 'like the real-life Billy . . .'

Dirge

John Bauldie

Another complex butterfly; another equivocal song. What on earth is Dylan singing about in this haunting, enigmatic piece? For all its obliqueness, the song's perspectives are well-defined, clearly in focus. But is it the looking back at love with jaundiced eye that John Herdman claims it to be? (*Voice Without Restraint*, Paul Harris Publishing, UK, 1982.)

It's certainly a song about a relationship that's past. I suppose it could be heard as a song to Sara – the obverse side of the coin to the same album's 'Wedding Song':

> I love you more than ever.
> I hate myself for loving you.

But 'Dirge'? A dirge is a song sung for the dead, for those passed. *Planet Waves* is very much about the past. The liner notes (omitted, presumably in error, from both the CBS reissue of the LP and from the Knopf/Cape collected works, *Lyrics 1962–1985*) are as open and personal as anything Dylan had written since *Some Other Kinds Of Songs* in 1964. A retrospective personal assessment, a thumbnail sketch of the past – boyhood, formative years, the fifties, New York, 'getting killed on motorcycles' and 'masks':

> We sensed each other beneath the mask

What else?

> Echoes of a star

127

Dylan hitting the road:

> joined the travelling circus, Love at first sight!

And then? Success. Fame. Fortune. A Star. Bob Dylan became a star, and almost got destroyed in a 'gone world going Wild!' But 'somebody got lucky', of course. 'I can't help it if I'm lucky'. 'Some good LUCK'. 'Lady Luck who shines on me'. Luck later became a 'saving grace' but (luckily) the pine box wasn't waiting for Dylan on the bend of Suicide Road, though the wheel exploded sure enough:

> peter pan of the throttle bums gets up to go someplace, it's growling . . . the engine slams into first gear – and it sounds like john lee hooker coming & oh Lordy louder like a train . . . & you Know he knows something is happening & it ain't the ordinary kind of sound that you can see so clearly & carrrrrashhhh & a technicolor passion of berserk & napoleonic & suicide . . . Babylon's sweetheart & the redblooded boy oozing all over & shock, the defunct rock-abilly . . . & into the most northernmost forest he can find . . .'
>
> [*Tarantula*]

So, off to Woodstock to get it all evened up. Straightened out. Look at the ceiling. Look back for once. How did it happen?

> the sideshow took over . . . I lit out for parts unknown

Dylan got confused in 1966. He was sucked into being Tiny Montgomery, the Mighty Quinn. They both had their Bob Dylan masks on. The performer's mask. Renaldo's painted face. It was the star persona who was left at the side of the road, next to the bent Triumph. Bob Dylan got lucky.

In 'Dirge' Bob Dylan looks back to his time as a rock superstar – to 1966. The imagery presents the performer in theatre:

> the stage was set, the lights went out . . .

Dylan sings of 'loving' the role which demanded the 'painted face' while in retrospect he can see that this love was symptomatic of 'weakness'. Dylan is singing to a persona in 'Dirge'. Time has brought both recovery and wisdom. He can see the 'foolish game' and 'the need that was expressed', and he's 'glad the curtain fell' because it was a 'hollow place', Lower Broadway, with its theatres and shabby bright lights – a place where martyrs lament their own demises and where those who yearn for the chance to become martyrs, 'angels', continue to 'play with sin', presumably having started out on burgundy and just come in from the coast. Dylan was looking positively ghost-like in 1966.

The process which brought the Minstrel Boy (remember his name?: it was Lucky) to the top of the hill and made him everybody's Wanted Man began worthily enough with those 'songs of freedom', in which the young prince sought to expose the 'naked truth' of man's folly but found himself 'a slave in orbit' (marvellous phrase, prising its aptness out of the tired analogy used habitually in the word 'star'). The orbit is the endless road of concerts, interviews, appearances, photographs ('Don't forget to flash!'), heading along for that million dollar bash. Cue the squeals of delighted anticipation: 'Ooh baby, ooh-ee' – a million dollars! But chasing a pot of golden rainbow is chasing an illusion and it can strip life of its sense. One can find oneself running on a hilltop following a pack of wild geese.

Fame takes the star from his home and from his past and from his past lovers:

> I wish I was there beside her but
> I'm not there, I'm gone.

'All of them ladies' cannot take away the loneliness. They unwittingly push him ever closer to the edge. He'll probably finish up with a million friends:

> Everybody from right now
> To over there and back

but he'll be 'hitting it too hard', or punching himself in the face. There must be some way out of the confusion:

> . . . hello, goodbye
> Then push 'n' then crash

129

No wonder, then, that he's 'glad the curtain fell'.

It fell on a slave who had been 'beaten till he's tame'. Where's the Lenny of yesteryear? The angry young ironist? And what was it all for?:

> All for a moment's glory . . .

So. Escape from the slavery: but at a cost – and the price is high. 'Loneliness', 'solitude', the traumas of alienation from self. Finally though, things are evened up and the expenditure is justified:

> At least I'm out of debt.

Now Bob Dylan Superstar didn't make himself, of course. It was 'every boy and girl' or 'every girl and boy' who pushed Tiny or Mighty up the charts. But he who has escaped the shackles of stardom has no thanks for the boys and girls:

> Can't recall a useful thing
> You ever did for me
> 'Cept pat me on the back one time
> When I was on my knees.

'You' is Henry and Mrs Henry – it's you (me) – the Henry in the street. 'Don't ya tell Henry' that Dylan's just ordinary, average, common too, no different from anyone: 'You see, you're just like me'. But that won't satisfy. Henry doesn't want to know that. Henry wants a star to pat on the back, or wants a lock of hair; and Henry has shears which can slit through the singer's thin-spun life.

Acclaim is ultimately destructive. It's the kids who killed Ziggy Stardust. Remember the ego-bubble? The 'leper messiah' in 1966? Remember what Ziggy shouted as he was going under, being leant on?: 'Oh Henry, leave me alone!/Oh Henry, get off the phone!' Remember Dylan:

> I believe I'm strangling on this telephone wire . . .

The penultimate stanza of 'Dirge' is an unparalleled expression in Bob Dylan's work of the relationship between performer and public:

> We stared into each other's eyes
> Till one of us would break

The lines might present Dylan coming face to face with himself too (I and I): looking into the mirror and seeing the past not-so-darkly. The situation brought the artist to his knees, but there was Lady Luck, in the nick of time. No more mistakes now, no more self-delusion: 'I hate myself for loving you,' Dylan tells Renaldo, 'But I should get over that.' The self-hatred, that is. The self-love he has, thankfully, already gone well beyond. That's why the song's a dirge.

1976 and Other Times: Ronnie Hawkins, Rock 'n' Roller

Interview by Michael Gray, St John's, Newfoundland, Autumn 1985

You played in Britain in the 1950s, didn't you?

I played there in '59. I was on a show . . . 'Boy Meets Girls', with Marty Wilde . . . And the Vernon Girls . . . Oh! we had some fun! There was Adam Faith, Billy Fury.

Eddie Cochran was on that show once.

Yes, we had the same manager then – and Gene Vincent . . . 'Be-Bop-A-Lula' had died down in the States, but he was over there in England making money when he couldn't even get arrested in the States.

Well one of the good things about Britain is that the Eddie Cochrans are really still revered there when they've long been forgotten in the States. Buddy Holly –

131

I played with Buddy a dozen times, and I never did understand Buddy too much either. Bright guy, and new stuff. You know how Dylan writes: he says you shouldn't criticize what you don't understand, right? Rapid Robert, that's what I call him.

How did you first meet Dylan?

I met Robert through Albert Grossman and through the band. I didn't know too much about Bobby. I just knew he was one of those folk-singers that was supposed to be a hero. I'd never seen him and I'd never paid too much attention to any of his songs. Then Robbie Robertson and them came down and said boy, he writes a *lot* of good stuff. So I started listening a little bit, you know? And so in Toronto, when they decided to go with Bob, the band was playing up there and Bob came up to, I think it was the Friars Tavern – and they rehearsed some songs. That was when they were gettin' ready to go on the road. They had a lot of problems, with people booing and throwing things. Then, when Bob took a little vacation for a while after that motorcycle wreck, that's when Albert gave Robbie and them a chance to go in there and do their own thing. That's how the *Big Pink* album came about. But I dig a lot of Bob's songs an' all. I call him the Poet Lassoo . . . y'know: laureate, lariat?

So were you not on the road when the band started to work with him? Had you already stopped using them yourself?

Oh, yeah. I was playing, but I had already put another band together – because they had a chance to better themselves, and anytime somebody has a chance to better themselves, you just wish 'em well and hope they can make it. You've done all you can do. And I wouldn't travel in those days much. I was up there in the Coq D'Or Tavern in Toronto, because my kids were kids then. I wouldn't travel till they got grown up.

When Dylan took the Hawks on the road, Levon Helm wasn't with them –

He left. He walked off in the middle of a set, they say. Then they took my other drummer, Sandy Konikoff . . . they used him because Levon had disappeared on 'em. Levon took off because they were having problems. They were being booed and it was embarrassing, y'know. So then they brought in Sandy Konikoff for a while. Then they took ... Mickey Jones. But Mickey, I knew him when he was just a *kid* – I mean a young kid, down in Texas, from when I played the Texas circuit ... Yeah, Mickey Jones was in a band I booked into my club at Fayetteville – we say *Fedville* – it's the University of Arkansas. The leader of the band killed himself in his motel room playing Russian roulette.[75] Then [Mickey] played with Trini Lopez. Can you remember who Trini Lopez was? The hubcap stealer from Texas! Ha! Then later on [Mickey] played with Bob Dylan and then he played with Kenny Rogers. But I saw Mickey just a few months back, out in California ... They're putting a movie together called *The Black Hawk Story*. It's a story out of my life, about when I had the black musicians, about 1957. They took me out there to tell a few stories to some of the scriptwriters, and Mickey was out there on that. Mickey Jones is doing movies now. He gets bit parts in a lot of movies. I've seen him in all kinds of television movies and stuff. Yeah. And he weighs three hundred pounds now.

OK, now tell me a story I can't print.

Oh, I caint do that! Everybody's got their problems in this business, and you can't tell what they do in their after-hours, when they're on their own time. There's a million stories 'bout that stuff – sayin' and doin' things that you're not supposed to do: but it's not good for journalists to print that kinda stuff because they're supposed to print the good stuff, not the private lives, y'know? Bob's only human like the rest of us, so he does things – everybody does things that they don't want the world to know about, sometimes, I mean, and Bob's no different.

But that was so striking about Renaldo & Clara. *He'd always kept his wife and all that stuff very private, and then suddenly there it is all up on the screen.*

Yes, I'm surprised he did that. I couldn't understand that. Bob is so intelligent, y'know – and he's mysterious. He's hard to figure out. I can figure out people pretty quick, because I've been in the business so long, and I can judge an audience and all that. But Bob is like a – what's the word? – a *schizophreniac*. I'm not sure he's like that, but he has different personalities for diffe-rent things.

133

On Renaldo & Clara, *I'd like to know about the actual filming and how people got ready for it, how much rehearsing there was, or not –*

Ha! There was *no* rehearsing, y'know. Bob was directing and producing and doing everything. I did three or four little skits, and he'd just call me up, three or four o'clock in the morning, and say, 'Come on, let's do somethin'.' I did one with Mick – what was his name? um, Mick . . .

Mick Ronson.

Yeah. He was a git-tar player.

Yes, where he was playing the guy on the door who wouldn't let you through –

Yeah! That's right! That's the truth! . . . And then we did one with some girl that Bob had discovered from Israel. All ad-libbed. *All* of it.

And did you see it afterwards, the film?

No. But when I was down in California doing something or other, why, Bob invited us down and they had the showing of it. I went down with Kris Kristofferson and we watched about *eight hours* of film. And he had everybody in it: all the freaks, the greeks, the cripples, everything. It was kinda like the story of his life. He had his wife and he had his girlfriend, Joan Baez, and they were both there. He lived with one of 'em and then he lived with the other one, and then he lived with both of them, and they were both there! I said, 'Bob, howja ever did this, boy? It's amazing!' I told Bob, I said, 'I don't know how you ever got this job done.' But he managed to handle it somehow!

The girl you were doing the seduction scene with, in Renaldo & Clara –

Yeah, the girl from Israel. Who *was* she? I don't even know who she was.

You're asking me? I'm asking you!

No. I never seen her before in my life. And that was all ad-lib, y'know. Bob just says, 'Listen, the thing is this – see what happens.'

How much did he tell you about what he wanted, and how much did you have to guess?

I didn't know anything about it: nothing. You know what Bob is, he's mysterious. He's always been mysterious.

So he'd just spring it on you?

Yeah. He woke me up. He said. 'Come here, here's what we're doing. We're doing this, we're doing that, strictly all ad-lib.' Fakin' it, or whatever the word is.

He just told you what the basic situation was, and that's all?

Uh-huh.

Can you remember what he said at all?

He just said, 'OK, here's the situation: you're talkin' to this lovely lady. You're tryin' to get her to go home with you, and her father wants her home.' We just started talking. That was it. I don't have a clue who that girl was, what she's done, or nothing. I heard later, from Allen Ginsberg, that she was just a friend of Bob's, an actress from Israel. That's all I heard.

And then there's the scene where you're being Bob Dylan, and you arrive at the hotel, and there's the TV interviewer –

Yes . . . and she thought I was Bob Dylan. She actually *thought* I was Bob Dylan. She knew nothing about Bob; she was just doin' her TV thing. So when I came in with the hat and a lot of people around me, she thought, 'Wow, must be Bob!'

She was genuinely an interviewer for local TV?

Yep. And I think that's where Bob got the idea for me being Bob Dylan, because I'm answering questions, and when I saw that she didn't know any better, I started answering Bob's questions for him – just for fun, y'know. And he was laughing. He was standing alongside and he said, 'Go ahead, go ahead!' So I'm goin' ahead . . . It was somethin'! So she's askin' me all these questions about all the songs I'd written: 'Blowin' In The Wind' and all that, and we were just puttin' her on . . .

Did you tell her, afterwards?

No. I never did tell her any different. I'm sure she found out quite quick, but I didn't tell her.

And you never saw the finished film?

No. Never did.

It's four hours long, even the finished version.

Where did it play? . . . It must be the art theatres or something. But it's going to have to be a classic, because no matter how bad the film stuff was, he had so many people on there that nobody else could have gotten on the film. I mean, he had everybody. I think that film was mostly just about the sixties. I think you'd have to know that era. He had eskimos in there, and some of the old punch-drunk boxers; he had *lots* of different people in that booger. Bad photography, bad everything, *but* he's got the people. People that nobody else could get; and a lot of cats who most of the world won't even know who they are; and people who just happened to be around, like the rich girl that died – Edie Sedgwick. She was there. She wanted me to run off with her! She was crazy! But as a matter of fact she was still beautiful. But burnt. Burnt. People that – a lot of them are dead now. Gosh, there's a lot of 'em gone. Had too much fun. That beautiful rich girl was so beautiful she was on the cover of every fashion magazine in the world. She OD'd. And she had everything . . . She was a lovely lady, I'll tell you that. Burnin' both ends of the candle, though: livin' too fast.[76]

People think you do that yourself.

I kinda pace it. Have to heal up now and then.

How many concerts were you around for during all that Renaldo & Clara *filming?*

I was just there to do what he wanted me to do while they were in Canada. Just the Canadian thing. Just a little while. I just did one show. I wasn't even going to do the show, because [of] the promoter . . . Bill Graham . . . he's got another cat: his assistant – I call him the Guru [pronounced Garoooohh]. He also did *The Last Waltz*. But Bob wanted me to go on and do some stuff. Here come the Garooh and said 'Bob's got too long a show, you better not go on.' So I said fine, I didn't go on – the first show. Then

136

Bob came back and said, 'What are you, chickenshit? You didn't go on!' and I says 'No, because your cat said not to go on.' So the second show we went on. I called it a breakdown of communication.

And did you get to talk to Sara Dylan much?

No. I saw her, though. She was a beautiful lady. She was a dandy. They were having a few problems. Like I said, he lived with Joan Baez and then he lived with Sara and then he lived with both of 'em together.

When Dylan was doing the filming, did you get the impression that he knew exactly what he wanted and what he was doing?

Well, my opinion of Bob Dylan is, he's Bob Dylan. His film is like his music. You don't understand it but it seems like it's right after you listen to it. It aint kosher, no big-time production, and you don't understand it, but it seems OK.

How much of the Winterland event, The Last Waltz, *were you around for?*

I was out there for a month, before it was recorded. See, The Band were trying to finish a new album – the last album with Capitol. I stayed out there, at the Shangri-La. The Shangri-La was the studio that The Band and Dylan owned, y'know. And it was *reverse* shangri-la. That's the place I said you come in at nineteen and you leave at 300 – in about six months. So anyway, they were trying to get that together: and all these heroes of the world came in. And I had never seen a lot of them, y'know. I'd played in the bars of Ontario: I didn't know that much about what was going on, except that Rolling Thunder Revue I did and that *Renaldo & Clara* with Bob. This was my chance – I got to see all the heroes, and their lifestyles. Boy, it was fast! Ha! Fast pace! It was one hell of a party.

The Last Waltz?

They were lucky to get through that, you know, because there were so many *great* artists. And then all the heroes of the world that weren't even on the show were there. And so it was a rough schedule. Robbie and The Band were trying to rehearse some of the important stars, plus they had the last album for Capitol to

137

do: all going on that last month. Robbie's fingers were bleeding, man, he was doing all this stuff. They had Van Morrison who would come in. Y'know Van is a little temperamental; Bob is a little temperamental. These were Big Time Temperamental Artists. So I'm just sat back there – I didn't even rehearse, I just went on cold.

But I was there watching the whole thing. I had never seen anything like this in my whole life! Because these were all the superheroes of the world at that time – *all* at the Shangri-La. Even those who weren't on it were there. They were pulling up in the limousines, y'know, coked out of their heads, smacked out of their heads, bumpin' into walls. And I was sayin' 'Boy, is this the Big Time?'

The Rolling Stones were there. Eric Clapton was there. I think he was doing an album on his own right then. Ron Wood was there playin' some guitar with Eric Clapton. They were nice cats – Old Man Ron – and Eric Clapton was really nice. I got half-drunk and talked them into doing a thing with Kinky Friedman and The Texas Jewboys. I wrote this song called 'Kinky' and he recorded it. I don't know whether it ever came out. I never heard no more about it . . . Ron Wood, Eric Clapton played a little bit on it, and Levon. That was at Shangri-La.

Was Robbie trying to get Dylan to rehearse? And Van Morrison to rehearse?

I don't know about that. Robbie was working himself half to death, I know that. Van Morrison rehearsed a couple of things. Joni Mitchell came in. Joni's so different. It was rough – I'd have hated to have that schedule. It was amazing how *The Last Waltz* came off, with the time they had to rehearse with each act. It was fast-paced. Rushed and hard.

And Neil Young was there too –

Yeah. Neil's beautiful: what a nice cat he is. Oh yeah, you gotta like Neil; he's so laid back, he just takes life with ease. They kicked him out of the Coq D'Or a few times, when I used to play. He used to try to come in. They kicked him out: because he was a hippy before the time . . .

Did The Last Waltz *have an impact as far as your career was concerned?*

138

Well, yes. Any time you do anything that gets good publicity you probably get a job or two. I don't know – but it certainly did *me* good. I was really honoured to be on it.

You looked very pleased when you came out on stage.

Oh, I had a great time.

Do you still talk to Robbie at all?

Yes. We talk to Robbie every now and then. He's always got something going for him, but it never comes about! Of course these days Robbie and Martin Scorsese and Robert De Niro, they do a lot of things together: they do a lot of projects. Everybody out there is always on a project, and most of them don't never come through. But I hope they do. I'm still waiting.

And did you enjoy doing Heaven's Gate? *That had the same cinematographer as* The Last Waltz, *didn't it?*

Yes, a Hungarian. He's won every award there is to win. Oh yes, I loved it. I learnt such a lot: about movies, about life, everything. That was so different from my scene. And some of the cats there . . . That John Hurt, he passed out in my room almost every night. Me and him had a hell of a time. See, I had the music in my room, so everybody was there every night, all night long after working, y'know? Half of 'em passed out there. I had to get that John Hurt up in the morning . . .

Going back to The Hawks/The Crackers/The Band: as far as you're concerned, did Robbie and The Band make a sudden leap musically?

Yes. Especially the second album. 'The Night They Drove Old Dixie Down' and all that. I was so surprised that Robbie wrote that stuff, because they were a rhythm 'n' blues act. They played rhythm 'n' blues *great*. And they didn't *like* country music. We even had a few arguments about that in the old days. I wanted to play that to people and they wouldn't play it. And then when their albums came out, man, I was shocked, because they were definitely country roots. So different. I thought it was great, though. They've certainly left their mark on musical history, because it was a different thing altogether – a brand new style of music. It wasn't straight country and it wasn't rock. It was a whole new thing. I remember John Lennon told me he'd sent them telegrams about it. Boy, an awful lot of *heavy* people liked The Band's music.

An awful lot of ordinary people liked it too!

Yes.

And back when they were with you, did Robbie and Richard Manuel ever write songs?

No! Nothing! I couldn't even get Robbie to sing, or nothing! But they were really good. This was rhythm'n'blues before Motown: the real heavy stuff. Richard Manuel could really sing that stuff too at that time. I hired him strictly as a vocalist. Richard wasn't a very good piano-player at that time: his piano-playing was very average, or even less than average. I hired Garth Hudson to come in as a teacher to teach us more music, right? And he taught Beak – The Gobbler, we called him, that's Richard Manuel – all the proper chords and all this stuff. Garth was always strange. He's still strange. I saw him in California, and he took me around, showed me a bunch of stuff. He represents Laurie Organs, or something, and he puts on exhibitions or whatever. I used him on an album that I did out there at the time. He has different projects that he's working on all the time. I never did understand Garth Hudson. Still don't . . .

At that time in the sixties I was the only one that could make Bob Dylan smile, y'know. 'Cause he was having a few problems in the sixties – because they was having too much fun. They was grabbin' hold of the old snuff-box a little too much . . . Bob called me the High Garooh Of Rock 'n' Roll! You know, I have never seen Bob Dylan play when he did his single thing. But Ramblin' Jack Elliott used to tell me that in the early days in Greenwich Village when Bob was in there, he couldn't tune his guitar and he sang out of tune but something about him was good. Ramblin' Jack! Boy, he's a character. He's a classic! Likes trucks. He likes to drive trucks . . .

Who else do you remember from Renaldo & Clara?

Well, there was that fiddle-player, Scarlet Whatwashername – Rivera? She ran off with Darlin' Doug. He used to play rhythm guitar for me. A good-lookin' kid. Had a body: slim hips and a golden head of hair on him there, better than any woman you ever seen in your life. I can't remember his last name. We called him Darlin' Doug. He didn't like that so he changed his name legally to Marshall. So then we started calling him Marvellous Marshall. Anyway, I pulled a little joke on him with Allen Ginsberg when the Rolling Thunder thing was up in Canada . . . Anyway, Darlin' Doug was a blonde kid, and Scarlet Rivera, she fell in love with him and, er, they did a lot of weird things!

Then there was that girl who was in *Nashville* – what was *her* name? [Ronee Blakley.] She plays good piano and she's been around some. We were at her apartment in California, having a party, and she had all the heroes, all the celebrities there. And Bob was there . . . And Bob Neuwirth. You know Bob Neuwirth, doncha? He wrote 'Mercedes Benz' for Janis. He's crazy. They tell me that he's a reborn Christian preacher. Well, I've got to see *that*. He's the wildest bugger I've ever seen. He was the one that almost set Gordon Lightfoot's house on fire. Ha! Ha! ha! Bob Neuwirth!

Anyway . . . at Ronnee Blakley's party I got in a little trouble, because somebody was there knockin' Bob, Bob Dylan, y'know. He and Levon got a little high, and they were singing, and cutting up, and this and that, and Bob was kinda nodding out. I tell ya who it was – what was Barbra Streisand's first husband's name? The big goof? Elliott Gould. He and the bodyguard for Willie Nelson. They were there, and they were drunk, and they were mouthing off at Bob and Levon. And I was a little drunk myself. I was gonna whip their ass right there at the damn party . . . They were knockin' things, sayin', 'Look in there – Bob's drunk and he's doin' this and aint it awful? I said, 'Yes, it is awful: he can draw more people drunk than all of you boys could if you were straight as a damn string.'

So you rushed to defend Bob's honour?

Yeah! I was a little bit high, y'know. And this cat was supposed to be so rough and tough – had whipped three or four hundred people in Texas, and broke people's backs and stuff – Willie Nelson's bodyguard that is – well, I was gettin' ready to hit him in the head with a poker! They had a fireplace and I grabbed the poker and I was ready to whip him and that Elliott Ghoul real easy. I could have done it real easy; but they apologized and left.

So when was this party: was it during Rolling Thunder?

No, it was way after that. It was after they'd filmed everthing. In fact, I think I was out there maybe seeing the Rolling Thunder footage at the same time. I can't remember time. But Bob was there and he was having a party, y'know – doing his own thing. He'd had a few drinks and this 'n' that and he pulled out the git-tar and started singin' and nodding off a bit, and these two big goofs, Elliott Ghoul and that big muscle-bound fucker, they started mouthing off ... I don't think Bob knew that was happening at the party because he was in the other room with all the heroes, and everybody was a bit drunk. And of course when you're as big as Bob you caint hardly do anything in front of anybody because, you know, everybody expects you to ... they expect him to be like Jesus Christ: to walk on the water all the time. And of course that's impossible.

And had you ever met Allen Ginsberg before Rolling Thunder?

Brilliant man, you know. And you know he's a bit gay ... Oh yes: I was going to tell you the story about Darlin' Doug. Darlin' Doug was beautiful, but he wasn't gay. But he wanted to be a hero. He couldn't figure out why he wasn't on top of the world, he was so good-lookin' and this and that. And so I played a little joke on him. I was over talking to Allen, and Allen said, 'Who's that good-lookin' kid over there?' I said, 'Oh, that's my rhythm-guitar player,' I said, 'But he's a little mixed-up.' I said, 'He thinks he wants to be gay.' Of course Allen – the sweat broke out on him! Then I went over there and told Darlin' Doug, I said, 'Now listen, see that guy over there? His name is Allen Ginsberg. He's the one that made Bob Dylan. He's worth *billions*. If he likes you, he'll buy a record company for you!' So Darlin' Doug goes over, and they sit down with each other, and meanwhile I'm hid in a corner watching the play! Oh man, it was a classic! Should have filmed that one.

A Profile of Howard Alk

Clinton Heylin

Howard Alk is one of the key people who have aided Bob Dylan directly with his creative output. As well as producing the *Hard Rain* 'TV film' made in 1976, Alk was co-editor, with Dylan, of both *Eat The Document* in the sixties and of *Renaldo & Clara* in the seventies. These films can't be properly appraised without scrutiny of the editing skills Alk brought to them – perhaps especially in the case of *Renaldo & Clara*, in which much of the import of the film communicates itself through the edits themselves, rather than through the narrative action between them.

Larry Sloman offered a sketch of Alk's imposing appearance:

> . . . A bear of a man, huge, with a tremendous beard that covers virtually every inch of his round, warm face, and an old shopping-bag-man fedora precariously balanced on his head.[77]

As with many other friends of Dylan, it would appear that Howard Alk began his long association with him through mutual acquaintance with Albert Grossman. Grossman appears nearly as frequently in Alk's story as does Dylan, and their relationship remained a cordial one long after Dylan had shrugged off Grossman's management of his affairs.

In the late fifties, Alk's main interests were in music – mostly folk, blues and jazz – theatre and film. In 1958 he combined two of these passions by making a crude documentary film called *The Cry Of Jazz*. He also co-founded an improvisational theatre company, Chicago's original Second City Troupe, with which he was subsequently to move, as an actor, to New York.

Alk's association with Albert Grossman dates from Chicago, where Grossman ran a folk-music club called The Gate Of Horn, about which ex-folk-trainee and ex-Byrd Roger McGuinn much later wrote a song. (Grossman was later to move into management in New York, whilst Alk was to return to Chicago – to open a folk club.)

In the Dylan biography by Scaduto there is only one reference to Alk:

In late April [1963] Dylan went to Chicago where he appeared at The Bear . . . he did not get paid for the two nights [sic] at the club, which had just opened . . . Howard Alk, the owner, said he couldn't afford to pay Dylan, but Al Grossman booked him in anyway because he wanted Dylan to get exposure.[78]

I suspect that Scaduto isn't quite accurate in crediting Dylan and Grossman with playing The Bear simply for exposure; more likely Grossman booked Dylan in as a favour to Alk to help his newly-opened club. After all, Dylan had already played his first major New York concert by then – at the Town Hall on 12 April. And perhaps Dylan was just as pleased as Grossman to do the favour: Dylan too knew Alk by this time, having already met him in New York in the early sixties.[79]

While in Chicago, Grossman got Dylan booked to appear on the great Studs Terkel's radio show, Wax Museum, recorded on 1 May. That *was* exposure.

From late April 1963 until the making of the film *Don't Look Back* in mid-1965, there is no documented link between Alk and Dylan, although it seems that they became firm friends in the meantime.

Howard and his wife Jones Alk helped with the making of *Don't Look Back*, but it was very much director D.A. Penne- baker's film. Pennebaker told *Movie Magazine*[80] in 1981 that the Alks were used in 1965 for reasons of economy – that they were 'a couple of Dylan's friends'. Alk's role was clearly just that of helper, as Pennebaker specified in another interview elsewhere:

'Howard Alk . . . was kind of helping out; he had a camera. I think I had a camera for Howard . . . It was a fallback camera, but he didn't shoot very much on that.'[81]

Pennebaker's perhaps somewhat dismissive statements ab- out Alk may be touched by the inability of the two men to see eye-to-eye on theories of film-making. Pennebaker felt that Alk's editing of the following year's *Eat The Document* was far from admirable, and explains this concretely in his interview elsewhere in this book (see page 63).

'I think he [Dylan] was very influenced by Howard's film ideas, which didn't interest me much, frankly, at the time, and they still don't.'[82]

If Alk's role in the making of *Don't Look Back* was far from substantial (and obviously while he might have held a camera, he wasn't involved at all in the film's editing), the reverse was true with *Eat The Document*. Here, Alk's film ideas had an impact. As Pennebaker implies, Dylan was understandably uncertain, working in a new medium, and in consequence relied particularly on the editing skills of Alk.

Although Alk also played more part in the filming itself in 1966 than he had the previous year – sharing the work with Pennebaker and even filming without his direction for two or three days while Pennebaker was absent from the tour in Cannes – his most important role in the making of *Eat The Document* was as editor.

Dylan and Alk were in the process of editing when Dylan's motorcycle accident occurred. Dylan was obviously feeling the effects of many kinds of pressure, and this new and tedious process of film editing was very time-consuming.

It was also tremendously frustrating. The more they looked at the 1966 footage, the more they seem to have felt that they could do very little with it. Dylan has repeatedly said something to this effect in interview:

In 1968:

> What we had to work with was not what you would conceive if you were going shooting a film . . . we were very limited because the film was not shot by us, but by the eye, and we had come upon this decision to do this only after everything else had failed.[83]

In 1973:

> We didn't have enough good footage. There was forty hours of it, but the camera was jumping around all the time. That was the only stuff we could salvage.[84]

And in 1975:

> That film was a project which we did to rescue a bunch of garbage footage that was shot on one of our tours.[85]

Not only was the editing proving very difficult but there were problems with the deadline that ABC Television were imposing for production of the film that they had paid for in advance and had already advertised.

Though the motorcycle accident allowed this deadline to be passed, completion of the editing work on the 1966 tour footage still seems to have taken an inordinate amount of time. Having worked on it off and on throughout 1967, Dylan and Alk were still putting the finishing touches to the film at the beginning of 1968.

By this time, of course, the plan to make it an hour-long film for ABC-TV had long since been abandoned. *Eat The Document* remained unseen for a lot longer.

What arose from it, however, was an idea for a film to be actively directed by Dylan, with Alk advising. The product of this resolve was realized years later in the making of *Renaldo & Clara*.

That this epic film was an eventual result of the months of labour on *Eat The Document* is evident from many parallels of style, structure and symbolism in the two films. Dylan actually echoed his own words in linking the two films in interviews in 1968 and 1975. About *Eat The Document* he said in 1968:

Now if we had the opportunity to re-shoot . . . we could really make a wonderful film.[86]

In 1975, referring to the '66 film experience, he said:

The whole thing fell through, but Howard and I, we got together and decided if we ever get the chance again to shoot good footage before we get to the editing room, some things that we can connect, we can make a fantastic movie on the screens.[87]

Alk as editor has always had a very distinctive style. One Alk trademark is his use of music to illustrate a point raised in conversation, and to highlight that point's significance or lack of it that way.

In *Festival* for instance, Alk brilliantly contrasts Dylan's new form of 'folk-rock' music with the traditional image of 'folk' music – people sitting around a whiskey still playing a wash-board – by splicing conversations with old-timers against shots of Dylan's afternoon rehearsals for the Newport '65 set, finally

146

cutting from one elderly woman directly to the opening song of that set:

> 'I don't know that what we call "folk" now two or three hundred years ago was called "pop". You see, we change . . .'
> '. . . Aint gonna work on Maggie's Farm no more!'[88]

It's a neat way of providing a context for Dylan's tirade against, among other oppressive aspects of American society, the (often folk-disseminated) concept of the Puritan work ethic – 'man and God and law'.

Another example of this Alk trademark, this succinct providing of context through adroit editing, shows up in his film *Janis*. Ms Joplin is asked: 'Do you have any explanation why you're so popular?' She breaks down in tears, and the film cuts to her performing, shaking out her soul and with the band playing full-tilt boogie. With a loud rasp she wails 'Woahh, yeahhh!' – and thus the question is answered.

There is a similarly clear-sighted, determined stance, combining music and talk, taken in *Eat The Document* itself, in a delightful sequence which splices excerpts from 'Ballad Of A Thin Man' with a parade of Mr Jones-style conversational fragments to counterpoint the lyrics:

> '*Just what you will say when you get home . . .*'
> '. . . I'm not sincere at all. I'm not any more sincere than you are . . .'
> '*You say "Oh my God, am I here all alone"?*'
> '. . . crawling through the bloody gutter just making a bloody pile out of it . . .'
> '*You've been with the professors and they've all liked your looks . . .*'
> '. . . Oh, I don't know if I'll accept that . . .'[89]

In the years between finishing *Eat The Document* and starting work on *Renaldo & Clara*, Alk was by no means idle. He continued to edit musical films, but also – in two films made with a Michael Gray (no relation) – he moved into radical politics.

The musical films which Alk worked on were *Festival*, *You Are What You Eat* and *Janis*.

147

You Are What You Eat was released in 1968, and again suggests connections between Alk, Dylan and Grossman. Alk worked on this film too as editor, with Barry Feinstein shooting and directing. Feinstein was at one point working with Bob Dylan on a book, for which he would provide the photographs and Dylan the text. Nothing came of this project, but it had been Feinstein who took the front-cover photograph for Dylan's *The Times They Are A-Changin'* LP, and it can be assumed that Feinstein had met Alk in Dylan's company in 1964–5.

You Are What You Eat was one of those groovy West Coast happenings: a hippiesque movie. This commentary from the soundtrack LP's sleeve-notes sums it up (while suggesting, at the same time, the presence of Howard Alk's handiwork):

> If what you see on film is one reality, what you hear on the soundtrack is another. If the two simultaneous realities contradict each other, they also free us from the slavery of our cultural clichés of experience. What emerges is a new reality . . . there is no literal plot.

The film featured, among others, Peter Yarrow of Peter Paul and Mary (like Janis Joplin, another Albert Grossman act), who co-produced the film with Feinstein; John Simon, who was a close friend of Grossman's and was working closely with The Band at this time, producing their magnificent first two albums (and playing on the second); Paul Butterfield; The Electric Flag; Barry McGuire and Tiny Tim. The film also offered the song 'My Name is Jack', written by John Simon, which Manfred Mann covered with moderate success.

The original intent with Alk's widely-seen documentary film *Janis* had been to feature footage of both Janis Joplin and The Band, to be taken from the 'Festival Express 1970' tour. Again, both acts were managed by Grossman, who was first approached with the project by producer Frank Cowley. In the end, the film not only stuck to Janis Joplin but stuck mainly to her music, rather than her lifestyle. In putting this film together, Alk's role was 'really more than that of an editor; more like that of a post-mortem director, or perhaps "orchestrator"'.[90]

It was in this same period that Howard Alk made two political films, about the Black Panthers and other contemporary American radical organizations: films in which a general theme was the degradation and oppression of the American black.

The first of these was called *American Revolution II*. It centred around the notorious Democratic Convention in Chicago in 1968, and included interviews with various radical groups. In an interview about the film in *Take One* magazine, Alk makes clear his support for the basic aims of the Black Panthers:

> One of the things we're trying to do is let you see that these men are revolutionists – political revolutionists. But they're not terrorists; they're not irresponsible madmen ... The actuality is that these men believe this society is bad pie, and they don't want a slice of it.[91]

In the course of a later interview in the same magazine, writer Gerald Peary is concerned to emphasize that

> to talk of Howard Alk in any but political terms is to misrepresent him. His conversation is filled with ... expressions of his total support for the programs of the Black Panther Party.[92]

Gray and Alk made another film directly after *American Revolution II*, which dealt with the murder of the leader of the Chicago Black Panthers by government agents: *The Murder of Fred Hampton* (certainly an uncompromising enough title).

This was sequential to *American Revolution II*.[93] Not surprisingly, Gray and Alk had difficulty raising the capital to finance this project. The identity of the person who eventually put up the money *is* perhaps a surprise: 'Al Grossman ... gave us money. He said of Fred Hampton – "That man's got to be heard".'[94]

Consistent with Howard Alk's political views, then, and relevant when we come to consider how much he contributed to *Renaldo & Clara* – in terms of ideas rather than technical expertise – is the reply he gave interviewer Peary at the end of the sixties to the question 'What kind of film would you *like* to make?':

> There are a lot of white people out there who have been stepped on and victimized, and who don't have the vision of how else it could

be. It seems to me that it is this lack of vision which is one of the main things preventing people from moving. So I think here is the valid function of film-makers. The film I would most like to make at this moment is one that is not my vision imposed on people at the other end of the camera, but coming from them.

I would like to go around the country presenting people with a proposition: 'OK, we're making a movie. It's cool. You can do what you want because this is only a movie. But assume for the purpose of this little movie that you had the power to run the community, what would you do? Let's play a little game called Running It.'[95]

While this tends to suggest a film far more overtly political than a work like *Renaldo & Clara*, we can recognize in Howard Alk's comments here thoughts and ideas which must surely have influenced the way certain scenes in *Renaldo & Clara* were set up.

Indeed, there is one major, sustained sequence – the brilliantly rendered series of street-interviews about Hurricane Carter – which combines the two main characteristics we have identified as belonging to Alk's work as a film-maker: it shows both his political solidarity with black America (and his commitment to using the camera to let the disenfranchized speak for themselves) and his trademark of cutting from conversation to music and back again to emphasize points and set contexts.

In retrospect the 'Ballad Of A Thin Man' sequence in *Eat The Document* appears like a practice run for this memorably effective 'Hurricane' sequence in *Renaldo & Clara*.

It might be interesting here to speculate on Bob Dylan's alleged meeting with the Black Panthers in 1970. The unsatisfactory encounter supposedly took place between Dylan and Huey Newton and David Hilliard. It must be assumed that Dylan and Alk had discussed the subject of the Panthers, and one can imagine that it was at Alk's prompting, or at least with his encouragement, that Dylan eventually agreed to a meeting. Years later Alk commented: 'Bob Dylan is by nature not a political person.'[96]

In the same article in which Anthony Scaduto raised the question of the alleged Dylan/Panthers meeting, he quotes Dylan as making this interesting comment about his activities at the end of 1971: 'I'm helping other people out, making records with them, helping one friend edit a film.'[97] It used to be thought that this was a further Dylan–Alk project, and that either it came to nothing or at least has remained unreleased; we now know, however, that Dylan was not at work with Alk at this time but was instead helping George Harrison on the editing of the *Concert For Bangla Desh* footage.

Howard Alk's return to working with Dylan, on what would become *Renaldo & Clara*, seems to have been activated by his receiving, characteristically, an unexpected cryptic message. In autumn 1975, Alk was woken one night at home in Montreal by the phone ringing. He picked it up to hear a voice say simply: 'Bob wants to know if you're ready.'[98]

Howard Alk joined the Rolling Thunder Revue at the Seacrest Motel in Falmouth, Massachusetts and shot footage throughout the tour. Was it to be the project Dylan had thought of as long ago as 1968: 'to make a story which consisted of stars and starlets who were taking the roles of other people'?[99] Sam Shepard, also summoned by an unexpected phone-call, and hired to help write a script for the film, seems to have become immobilized by its uncertainties. Mel Howard, a cameraman and a friend of Alk, wasn't at all sure it was working, and confided to Larry Sloman, who insinuated himself onto the tour to write about it (and to enjoy it), that he was 'bummed out about the film'.[100]

However, Dylan insisted that he and Alk 'knew where the film was going' all the while, even if there were times when they 'weren't sure exactly how it would get there'.[101] When asked, in 1978, if the end result was the film he had foreseen, Alk said: 'It's clear that this is the film that wanted to be made: the film that Bob had in mind.'[102]

This of course suggests that Howard Alk was stressing that in the end it was far more Bob Dylan's film than his. Larry Sloman, who after the tour seems to have stayed in contact both with Dylan (for whom he helped make the 'Jokerman' video of 1983) and with Alk, said when asked directly how much Alk had contributed to the film that certainly Alk had contributed technical expertise but that his creative input had been minimal. This might be overstating the case, but evidently it is primarily Dylan's vision, and wholly Dylan's symbolism, on which the film trades.

The actual editing of the film, calling upon all the technical expertise Alk was able to offer, involved dealing with extensive concert footage plus something like eighty hours of non-concert footage. Work on this seems to have started at the beginning of 1976. In all likelihood what happened at this point was that the footage was screened, notes made and cuttings taken – a process which Alk says took six months. The second Rolling Thunder tour obviously meant a hiatus in the work on the film, and this was extended by the editing of the TV Special *Hard Rain*. (Alk was also probably involved in editing the shelved so-called Clearwater TV Special from the same period.)

Possibly partly because of the breakdown in Dylan's marriage, work doesn't seem to have re-started on *Renaldo & Clara* until 1977, when an intensive six-month spell in the editing room by Alk and Dylan brought the film to completion.

According to Larry Sloman, his book about the tour – *On The Road With Bob Dylan* – also intervened between the two long stints of work on the film, by making Dylan re-evaluate some of the footage already edited:

> Howard told me [years later]: 'You know that fucking book? We worked for five months [sic] on *Renaldo & Clara*, and after we read that Bob turned to me and said, "This is the kind of movie we should have made." ' He said they scrapped everything they had done and went back and recut . . .[103]

Towards the end of the editing, Dylan started to give interviews to promote the release of the film (which suggests that ahead of completion he felt confident that he knew what he and Alk would be ending up with). Despite these concerted attempts to 'explain' some of the concepts and symbolism in the film, the majority of the press slaughtered it when they saw it, calling it obscure, narcissistic and impossible to follow.

Prior to its release, and this reception, Alk and Dylan were considering making at least one more film. According to Alk, 'You can believe that Bob is fully committed to film-making. That we are discussing the next *two* films.'[104] And according to Barbara Kerr, in her interview with Dylan prior to *Renaldo & Clara*'s release: 'There has already been some discussions between Dylan and Alk about scripting the next film.'[105]

It is likely that the critical – and commercial – failure of *Renaldo & Clara* in the USA scuttled any such plans. However, this did not altogether terminate Howard Alk's filmic association with Dylan. He seems to have filmed at least two concerts during the 1981 tour, and to have been present all the way through it. (Confirming this, all the photographs in the *Shot Of Love* songbook are by Alk, including shots of posters pasted up in London advertising the Earls Court dates; and Alk can be seen behind Dylan in the Vienna street-interview filmed and shown by Austrian TV.) He was seen filming the last concert of the (European) tour, at Avignon; he was also apparently shooting some footage on the subsequent American leg of the tour; and Dylan sang 'Happy Birthday To You' for Alk at the 25 October concert at Bethlehem, Pennsylvania.

Howard Alk committed suicide in 1982. His influence on Dylan's filmic vision through the years should be acknowledged; so should the expertise he gave to help Bob Dylan put across his ideas in a medium he could not call his own.

Jacques Levy and the *Desire* Collaboration

John Bauldie

Jacques Levy is the man with the beard on the back of the *Desire* sleeve, in the picture with Dylan at the microphone. He was born in 1936 in New York City. Educated at Michigan State University, Levy trained as a clinical psychologist and after obtaining his PhD, worked at the Meninger Foundation Clinic in Topeka, Kansas. There, he directed amateur dramatics at a local community theatre as a hobby, but found theatre so stimulating that by 1965 he'd decided to give up his career in psychology and return to New York to try his luck as a director.

Off-off-Broadway – alternative theatre – was just taking off at the time, and Levy got involved with a group called The Open Theatre. He directed at the New Dramatists Committee, the Judson Poets Theater and the La Mama Experimental Theater.

By 1967 he'd moved a little more up-market, directing a couple of off-Broadway successes: *America Hurrah* by Jean Claude Halie and Bruce Jay Friedman's *Scuba Duba*. It was the London production of *America Hurrah* which brought Levy to the attention of Kenneth Tynan, the English critic who, towards the end of his life, conceived *Oh! Calcutta*.

Tynan's ideas for 'an evening of Victorian esoteric pornography' were adapted by Levy, who shifted the *Oh! Calcutta* project to the USA and commissioned various writers to contribute. Among those who did were Samuel Beckett, John Lennon and Sam Shepard (who, many years on from Levy's collaboration with Dylan on *Desire*, and from involvement in the Rolling Thunder Revue and *Renaldo & Clara*, was to find *himself* in songwriting collaboration with Dylan, resulting in 'Brownsville Girl' on 1986's *Knocked Out Loaded* LP).[106]

Levy shaped the material – sketches and songs – into a stage show that opened in June 1969 on Broadway and won notoriety for its nudity: an aspect that wasn't planned, but which grew out of sense and movement exercises practised by the cast (it says here).

A little earlier, Levy had begun working on a country-rock musical version of Henrik Ibsen's play *Peer Gynt*. The show was to be called *Gene Tryp*. Levy's musical collaborator was to be Roger McGuinn of The Byrds. The two wrote all the songs together and McGuinn had Bob Dylan in mind to play the lead role. Tim Buckley and Jon Voight were other possible choices. The show was conceived as a lavish spectacle – moving towards a (then hefty) million dollar budget. However, the withdrawal of backers David Merrick and Don Kirshner meant a budget cut to $300,000. Columbia Records' offer of $150,000 for rights to the score didn't help enough to meet the show's financial needs, however, and interest in the project began to wane.[107]

The co-written *Gene Tryp* songs did appear, however, on Byrds albums. 'Chestnut Mare', 'Lover Of The Bayou', 'All The Things' and 'Just A Season' were all on (*Untitled*); 'I Wanna Grow Up To Be A Politician' and 'Kathleen's Song' were on *Byrdmaniax*. Subsequently Levy and McGuinn remained friends and collaborators, many of their songs appearing on McGuinn's solo LPs *Roger McGuinn*, *Peace On You*, *Cardiff Rose* and *Thunderbyrd*.

It was through Roger McGuinn that Jacques Levy first became involved with Bob Dylan. The opening track on McGuinn's first solo album, *Roger McGuinn*, is 'I'm so Restless', co-written by McGuinn and Levy. It has a verse about Bob Dylan, and Dylan liked it enough to contribute the harmonica break in the middle of the song (with McGuinn himself doing the one at the beginning).

Levy had met Dylan by chance in the spring of 1974:

> I was just walking out of the house right here on Bleecker Street and he [Dylan] was coming this way. I said 'Hey, hi!' and he didn't know who I was, but he was familiar with my work with Roger. We started talking and spent the evening together.[108]

Dylan had just finished his 'comeback' tour with The Band, and was writing the songs for *Blood On The Tracks*. He was also studying painting at classes run by an old man Dylan identifies only as 'Norman' ('I'd rather not say his name. He's really special and I don't want to create any heat for him').[109] Both Dylan and Levy were tied up so much with their own projects that it was a year later before they met again:

> I bumped into him again on Bleecker Street, and again we came up here [Levy's loft in La Guardia Place]. He had no specific plans at that time to do anything, and he said something like, 'I really like the stuff you do with Roger, how about if you and I do something together?' Which was slightly strange, right? Because he knew *I* did lyrics and I knew *he* did lyrics. But I said, 'Sure, let's give it a shot.'

Dylan's version of this meeting corresponds just about exactly:

> I was just in town, you know, and saw Jacques on the street. We ran into each other and we had seen each other off and on throughout the years, so we wound up just over at his place sitting around, and I had a few songs. I certainly wasn't thinking of making a record album, but I had bits and pieces of some songs I was working on and I played them for him on the piano, and asked him if they meant anything to him, and he took it someplace else and then I took it someplace else, then he went further, then I went further and it wound up that we had this song.

155

The song was 'Isis'. Here's Levy again:

> We were just sitting, just talking . . . then he went to the piano, sat down and started to play 'Isis', but it was a very different style of 'Isis' than you hear now. It was almost a dirge, unlike anything I'd ever heard before, slow, obviously setting you up for a long story . . . Dylan had already put together the first verse: 'A guy married Isis and left' . . . He had the general feeling of the song but he hadn't got further . . . so now what? . . . So the two of us started working on that together. I started writing words, then he would say: 'Well, no, how about this, what about that?' – a totally co-operative venture. It was just extraordinary, the two of us started to get hot together. And we began to work on this thing and we just kept going with it, and we'd stop and we didn't know where the story was going to go next . . . we were just having a great time laughing and coming up with one verse after another . . . and we kept on going until five in the morning and we finished the song. And both of us thought it was great. We were just knocked out by it . . . It's impossible to remember now who did what, it's like we'd push each other in the sense that he'd have an idea then I'd have an idea until we'd finally got to a point where we both recognized what the right idea was and what the right words were and whether it came from him or me it doesn't make a difference.

The 'Isis' that was finished by the dawn wasn't quite the final version:

> We re-did some stuff but the basic story was there. I would write this stuff down and then type it up and we would go over the stuff. And we went down to the Other End and Bob read the lyrics to a bunch of people sitting around the bar – just read them, and everybody responded to the thing, because everybody gets hooked in that story, apparently. The two of us didn't know that at the time. I mean, we were getting hooked . . . I don't know how that story came about and Bob doesn't either. It came through the two of us, just a kind of unconscious connection we were making . . . it doesn't have anything to do with the Egyptian goddess; the only thing is that at some point we threw in the Pyramids instead of the Grand Teton Mountains, which is probably really what it's about. Going up into the hills in Wyoming or something.

After the first completed version of 'Isis' the energy flowed:

We got together again the next day and we wrote another song and we both got a sense that it was getting serious . . . we wrote another couple of songs . . . then Bob would pick up a guitar and rush around to the Other End and get up on stage and sing it – but it wasn't the right atmosphere to write too seriously . . . What was happening was that we were going out and hanging out late at night and we were getting together the next afternoon and there were lots and lots of distractions . . . Then a week went by when the two of us couldn't get together and finally I said: 'Why don't we get out of New York and go somewhere where we can really work?' He had a place on Long Island, so we went out there . . . East Hampton, and stayed out there totally cut off from everybody . . . We had already written a couple of songs and there was a feeling of confidence that we both had that we could really do it.

In three weeks at East Hampton the two wrote a reputed fourteen songs. Dylan had already finished 'One More Cup Of Coffee' while he was hanging out with some gypsies in the south of France and in Corsica a couple of months earlier. And he also wrote 'Sara' alone:

Bob had been fooling with 'Sara' for a long time. He'd got the choruses down but the verses were actually written out at this place on Long Island where we stayed . . . There was a place out there that he and Sara had stayed at . . . out there are the dunes and the beach and all that stuff mentioned in the song. He would try things out on me, but it was a very personal song for him to write.

Nobody visited during the three-week stay:

We went out a couple of nights. One night we went to a bar and Bob sang a couple of the songs and we hung out with some people that night just to get away from things. The pressure was tremendous and intense on both of us, and we'd stop in the middle of a song and go shoot a game of eight-ball.

'Romance In Durango' started out because Dylan had a Mexican-type tune but no words:

. . . the first thing that came was an image I had from a postcard that was once sent to me by Jack Gelber, the playwright. He sent me a postcard with a picture of a Mexican hacienda or something – some

Mexican shack, not a hacienda – a shack with a bunch of chili peppers on the roof in the sun. So the first line was 'Hot chili peppers in the sun' and I remember saying, 'No, *blistering* sun,' so we got the first line. And then there was this escape.

Perhaps the duo's most renowned collaboration was on the protest song 'Hurricane'. Richard Solomon, an independent screenwriter, put together a defence committee for Rubin 'Hurricane' Carter in 1975, and contacted celebrities who might be useful for the cause. He sent Dylan a copy of Carter's book *The Sixteenth Round*, which Dylan must have taken with him when he went to France in late spring. On his return to New York, Dylan went out to Trenton State Prison with Solomon to meet Carter, and as they spoke – probably as Carter spoke! – Dylan jotted down notes. The subsequent song didn't come easy. Levy commented:

> When the Hurricane thing started, Bob wasn't sure that he could write a song at that point. He was just filled with all these feelings about Hurricane. He couldn't make the first step. I think the first step was putting the song in a total story-telling mode. I don't remember whose idea it was to do that. But really the beginning of the song is like stage-directions, like what you would read in a script:
>
> 'Pistol shots ring out in the bar-room night.
> Enter Patty Valentine in the outer hall.
> She sees a bartender in a pool of blood.
> Cries out, 'My God, they've killed them all.'
> Here comes the story of the Hurricane . . .'
>
> Boom. Titles. You know, Bob loves movies and he can write these movies that take place in eight to ten minutes, yet seem as full or fuller than regular movies.

The song that Dylan and Levy completed had one major factual error. They put Alfred Bradley in the bar at the scene of the crime, when it should have been Albert Bello. On Friday 24 October 1975, the stanza was corrected after Dylan, staying at the Gramercy Park Hotel, had been contacted by George Lois, another Defence Committee organizer (a Madison Avenue adman, who, years later, was to be the producer of Dylan's 'Jokerman' video). 'Hurricane' was re-recorded that night.

Among the other songs co-written by Dylan and Jacques Levy were 'Mozambique', 'Oh Sister', 'Black Diamond Bay', 'Rita May', 'Catfish' and 'Money Blues'. It is also likely that 'Wiretappin' ' was co-written. Then there was 'Joey'.

'Joey' was written back in the city. One night Levy and Dylan went to dine with Marty Orbach, a New York author who was working on a book about Joey Gallo. Levy comments:

> She [Marty] and her husband [Jerry] knew Joey well and I knew Joey through them. I spent a lot of time with Joey in that last year he was alive [1970] and Bob became very interested in it all. We were telling stories about Joey and when we left their house we came back here and started work on the song.

Dylan has also talked about the composition of 'Joey':

> I was with Jacques. I was leaving town and Jacques says he was going up to some place to have supper and I was invited to come up if I felt like it and I was hungry. So I went with him and it was up to Marty and Jerry Orbach's place, and as soon as I walked in the door Marty was talking about Joey. She was a good friend of Joey's. They were real tight. I just listened for a few hours. At that time I wasn't involved in anything that he was involved in, but he left a certain impression on me. I never considered him a gangster. I always thought of him as some kind of hero in some kind of way. An underdog fighting against the elements. He retained a certain amount of his freedom and he went out the way he had to. But she laid all these facts out and it was like listening to a story about Billy The Kid. So we went ahead and wrote that up in one night.

Levy added later that Dylan 'got knocked a lot for that song. People don't get knocked for writing songs about Jesse James, but he got knocked for that one. Most of the people who knocked it took this moralistic point of view. They'd just seen *The Godfather* three times and they said "How can you dare write a song about someone like that?" '

With this whole bunch of new songs (plus the acclaimed *Blood On The Tracks* collection), and with old friends gravitating to the Village, Dylan picked up on an idea that had long been with him. After tossing ideas around in talk with Levy, David Blue, Roger McGuinn, Bobby Neuwirth and Ramblin' Jack

Elliott – among others – the basic scheme for what became the Rolling Thunder Revue came about. Scarlet Rivera's friend Sheena comments to Larry Sloman that Dylan had been excited by the *Desire* recordings:

> He immediately started talking about a tour. He said 'Oh, man, I would really like to take this band out on the road with everybody.' That was what was in his mind. For the road. One more cup of coffee. For the road. For the road. Everything was getting ready to hit the road.

Levy was hauled in as director for the show:

> Bob said: 'Can you figure out a way of doing it – a presentation? What would it be like?' So I sat down and I did something not unlike the kind of work I had to do in *Oh! Calcutta!*: to figure out what goes first and what follows what – the batting order. I knew we were talking about a big show – four hours or more. So I wrote up a thing like that and I left open spots so there could be guests and shifts. It wasn't really a rigid thing at all [but] the key point [was] how exactly we'd get to the point where Bob came on, and when to play his new material. We rehearsed the show in New York for almost two weeks. Again we had this enormous pile of material, and it had to be arranged and worked out and staged. And the idea was that it should not *look* staged. We didn't want it to be a flash show, because that didn't fit anybody's style. The thing was to make it appear like it was a spontaneous evening – totally impractical, like a travelling vaudeville show or a travelling circus – the jugglers and the clowns. There was almost a hootenanny feeling . . . [but] . . . there was no tuning up between songs, there were no pauses. Big chunks of the show were the same every night.

It was also Jacques Levy who worked on the way the show was lit:

> There's a big difference between seeing Bob stand up there in a kind of grey expanse, seeing nothing in the background, and seeing him picked out with a pin spot that half shades his face and gets shadows all over his guitar, and you see nothing else but that, except maybe a red glow in the background. Immediately you see the two different images. We weren't using spotlight. All the lights were on the stage. So even in these big places, the show still had

160

At the Savoy Hotel, London, April 1965.

Filming *Hearts of Fire*, October 1986.

ghost of electricity: on stage in Paris, 24 May 1966: his 25th
hday.

With guest Van Morrison at Slane, Ireland, last date on European tour, 8 July 1984.

:h Muhammad Ali, backstage at Madison Square Garden,
v York City, 8 December 1975.

Onstage at Idraetsparken, Copenhagen, 10 June 1984.

h Regina Havis at the Fox-Warfield Theater, San
ıcisco, 21 November 1980.

v York City, 1983.

At a Singers Club party, the Pindar Of Wakefield pub, Grays Inn Road, London, 22 December 1962. The man behind Dylan is legendary folklorist A. L. Lloyd.

this wonderful look to it. The house would be dark, and there, down there, would be this little jewel box all lit up.

And Levy had one more function on the Rolling Thunder Revue, according to Roger McGuinn – that of 'camp counsellor':

Because he was a practising psychologist, he knows how to work with people. I *know* he knows how to work with me, because it's worked. And it's worked in Dylan's case too.

The success of Dylan's work with Jacques Levy is evident in a set of some of Dylan's finest songs and in two of his best tours. I wouldn't swap 1975 for any other year in Bob Dylan's history.

Interviews and a Poem: Allen Ginsberg, Poet

Introduction

The main features of the more than 20-year relationship between Bob Dylan and Allen Ginsberg are touched upon in what follows.

After meeting Dylan in 1963, Ginsberg has reappeared in the Dylan story, as he says himself, every couple of years. He's there throughout the truly formative years: in *Don't Look Back* in a hotel room, and at the very beginning, lurking in the London alley where Dylan card-mimes 'Subterranean Homesick Blues'. He asks a question at the December '65 San Francisco press conference and around the same time is pictured famously with Dylan, Robbie Robertson and poet Michael McClure in a San Francisco street. That Christmas Dylan gives him a Uher tape recorder and encourages him to 'learn an instrument'. He revisits a far more reclusive Mr D after the 1966 motorcycle crash, bringing boxes of poetry up to Woodstock, New York

161

State, for him. In 1968 Dylan is able to return to its author an old typescript of *Gates Of Wrath*: the first time he'd had a complete copy since the manuscript had been 'carried to London by lady friend early fifties' and had 'disappeared'.

In 1971 Dylan is (unbeknownst to the older poet) in the audience for a Ginsberg poetry-reading at New York University in Greenwich Village – prompted by which they record together: a TV show and a studio session.[110] At both, Ginsberg includes his 'September On Jessore Road': written, he says later, 'to make Bob Dylan cry.' Ginsberg writes sleeve-notes for Dylan's *Desire* album, hangs out on the Rolling Thunder tours, and plays a prominent part as the Father in *Renaldo & Clara*, a film which he helps Dylan and Howard Alk to edit. Far less consequentially, Dylan and Ginsberg together attend sessions for Leonard Cohen's album *Death Of A Ladies' Man* in late 1976 (produced by Phil Spector), emerging together in the deep background on the track 'Don't Go Home With Your Hard On'.

In the eighties their recurrent association continues. In February 1982 they record together again, this time at Dylan's Rundown Studios in Santa Monica;[111] then Dylan writes – most uncharacteristically – a lit. crit. testimonial for Ginsberg's *Collected Poems 1947–1980*, published in 1985; and, most recently, the respect in which Dylan holds the pioneering beat poet has him calling on Ginsberg in 1985 to ask his opinion of the newly-finished lyrics for the *Empire Burlesque* LP (about which Ginsberg is obviously too kind). Altogether a tight connection of hearts.

Part One (1977)

An interview by Alan Ziegler about Dylan, Ginsberg and the 1976 Rolling Thunder Revue, extracted from Poets On Stage: The Some Symposium on Poetry Readings, *Some/Release Press, USA, 1978.*

Did Dylan let you do any singing on the tour?

Actually, he's done me a favour; he was dubious about my singing but he kept pushing me to recite poetry, till finally in Fort Collins [Colorado, 23 May '76] I did: and in Salt Lake City [25 May: these were the very last two dates of the tour].

Why did he have to talk you into it?

I sort of had this fatuous idea of myself as a singer. They have enough singers and musicians and rock and roll stars there. He was interested in the poetry part. I was shy about that, partly scared. I couldn't figure what you could say to 27,000 people: what could engage the minds of that many people in the hysteria of a giant rock and roll thing.

One day in Fort Collins as Dylan came off in the intermission, casually, over the shoulder, he said: 'Why don't you go out there and read a poem?' So I went out there and read a very brief poem called 'On Neal Cassady's Ashes', because that's Denver area (half the audience did know who Cassady was) – seven lines. One exact clear, sharp, solid, brilliant image, in the middle of this rock and roll hysteria, saying: 'All ashes, all ashes again'.

How did the audience react?

Well, cheers. I couldn't tell whether cheers of recognition, derision, or just to have somebody talking. I wasn't announced. I just went on and bellowed words out over a microphone, and when I got off Roger McGuinn shouted my name and then the band went into their thing.

I think it would be entirely appropriate to read poetry in that setting.

It turned out to be. Dylan's imagination was just right. I hadn't realized. Then I read again in Salt Lake, a poem which was just right for a Mormon, mystic town. ('Holy Ghost On The Nod Over The Body Of Bliss') But it had to be fast, sharp. And there was no announcement (before or after), who I was or anything. I just went out and knocked that language out. So the review in the paper said that a gentleman in a tuxedo got up and recited a poem in the intermission. I had gotten a five-buck shantung silk tuxedo from Salt Lake Salvation Army and wore it on stage.

Many years ago Bob Dylan read a poem to Woody Guthrie in the middle of a concert, and the audience responded enthusiastically.

Everybody wants to hear Dylan talk anyway.

The spoken voice in the context of a music setting can be very startling.

Well, I must say I was a little scared because I figure after all the rhythm and harmony and powerful enunciation of vowels and consonants on Dylan's part, how could talked poetry engage people's consciousness and rivet attention? At best, poetry is soft-spoken actual speech, like someone talking to himself very quietly, but saying things so clear that it is literally comprehensible and the sound is clear and the mind is clear. In rock and roll, the mind is not necessarily clear. So the poetry can have the clear mind talking directly and not raising the voice. It would be interesting in the middle of Rolling Thunder to get to *that*.

Another thing is the oratorical 'Howl' or 'Sunflower', like that 'Holy Ghost' poem I did in Salt Lake – in an oratorical rock and rolling voice. But to do Reznikoff or Williams style work that doesn't have rhyme – Whitman is still oratorical – it's an open field for experiment. But Dylan seems to want experiment.

It's such a great opportunity to get the work out there . . .

Dylan, I think, saw the space there before I did, and tried to encourage me to do it, which is an amazing piece of generosity on his part: intelligence, or just natural mind. Dylan has common sense, freedom – ease, ease. So he's talking about continuing working on that.

Is he going to keep on touring?

Well, we talked about it . . . He said he's a gypsy and he wants to go on touring for the rest of his life, absolute wandering; and I said, 'Well, I have to go home and take care of my father,' and he said, 'Listen, when you're an old man we'll take care of you on your death-bed.' He said, 'We're gonna be gypsies, go around the world and tour forever, never never never never come home again.' It was late at night, and we were all drinking.

Are you going to hold him to it?

No, I'm sure he was just babbling poetry.

Part Two (1978)

From a transcript by John Hinchey of a discussion between Ginsberg and students at Swarthmore College, Pennsylvania, 4 November, 1978. On the film Renaldo & Clara:

It's built in a very interesting way. You would have to study it like *Finnegan's Wake*, or Cezanne, to discern the texture, to discern the composition of the tapestry. It's like a tapestry.

What he did was, he shot about 110 hours of film, or more, and he looked at it all. Then he put it all on index cards, according to some preconceptions he had when he was directing and shooting. Namely, themes: God, rock and roll, art, poetry, marriage, women, sex, Bob Dylan, poets, death – maybe eighteen or twenty thematic preoccupations. Then he also put on index cards all the different characters, all the scenes. He also marked on index cards the dominant colour – blue or red . . . and certain other images that go through the movie, like the rose and the hat, and Indians – American Indians – so that he finally had an index of all of that.

And then he went through it all again and began composing it, thematically, weaving in and out of those specific compositional references.

So it's compositional, and the idea was not to have a plot, but to have a composition of those themes.

So you notice the movie begins with a rose and a hat: feminine and masculine. The rose is sort of like 'a travelling vagina' – those are his words. The hat is masculine – crowns. The rose . . . travels from hand to hand. The truck drivers eating are the meat universe.[112] Remember the truck driver with the big rose right in front of his nose?

. . . reviewers got upset because – it was like being upset at Van Gogh . . . it's a painter's film, and was composed like that.

Part Three (1983)

This interview was conducted for The Telegraph *by Michael Krogsgaard on 20 January 1983 in Copenhagen, Denmark. Ginsberg begins by talking about the (then forthcoming) release of his album* First Blues *(John Hammond Records, W2X 37673):*

Two Blake songs, 'The Tyger' and 'My Pretty Rose Tree', will be on the album . . .

You also did 'A Dream' by Blake, didn't you?

Well, I have a whole unissued album by Blake that I did in 1972, and a couple of Blake songs that I did with Dylan in '72 also ['The Tyger' and 'Nurse's Song'; actually '71], that have never been put out.

The problem is, the stuff we did together wasn't really good enough for an album. Just a couple of good tracks – three good tracks, I think. I think the best thing we did was 'Jimmy Berman' . . . I tried 'Jessore Road' with him but my harmonium is not in standard pitch and when he tried to tune his guitar Dylan didn't get it tuned right, so the whole thing's a little off key.

It's interesting because he played both guitar and piano on it. The piano was really terrific – like a lightning bolt. But it wasn't good enough. Nobody wanted to put it out. I didn't even try.

But [John] Hammond liked those songs, three of them. Then I did a set of songs with Hammond in '75 which Columbia wouldn't put out because it was too dirty, they said. Hammond now has his own label, so we'll get it – I think it's out already, or will be out in the States this month.

You also did a television programme in '71 called Allen Ginsberg *and Friends.*

Yeah. Happy Traum and Dylan and David Amram came. Plus there was a drummer from Swami Muktenander who was awful, and had all sorts of Indian bells and spiritual/ materialistic sounds, and the soundtrack drowned out the guitars and the words even – so that wasn't usable either. It was an hour programme, with Philip Wayland, who was a poet. I sang 'Jessore Road' all the way through, which is a long thing for television, and some mantras and I think that was all the songs we did.

When did you actually do your first recording?

1968. An album of Blake, with Don Cherry, Elvin Jones and several musicians suggested by Charlie Mingus, who was a neighbour then. So he suggested I use Herman Wright on bowed bass and Julius Watkins on French horn. Did you ever see that? A couple of people here have it. And in Amsterdam. I've seen copies around in Europe after fourteen years.[113]

Was it a natural thing for you to do after you'd been a writer, to do records too?

Well, no. It was Dylan's suggestion. The Blake was my own idea, but then he heard me and Peter[114] improvising in a poetry reading and so he called up and said could I do that whenever I wanted? I said sure, because I used to do it with Kerouac under Brooklyn Bridge. So he came over with Amram and we jammed for a night.

I'd known him [Dylan] already about seven years. I met him in '63 and we'd spent time together over the years and I'd seen him a little bit earlier than that. He went to see a performance of *Kaddish*, which is a play of mine – and he likes *Kaddish* a lot, which is why he put it in *Renaldo & Clara*.

So he suggested we go to a studio and try to just improvise, with no preparation, nothing on paper – which was Kerouac's method; and it was also my Tibetan Meditation teacher's method and suggestion. So I thought it was interesting and thrilling to do it with Dylan. I thought I'd be a big rock star. I had visions of grandeur and getting rich. But nothing like that worked out. It was a terrible disappointment. Then finally Dylan said, oh don't worry about it. Just sing the songs to your friends. So that's what I did. It was good advice.

Besides the back-up vocal you did on Leonard Cohen's 'Don't Go Home With Your Hard On' –

I never heard that: never heard the record.

Oh, it's pretty disco!

It was a good song, I thought. It sounded good when we were doing the back-up.

Why were you involved in that?

Oh, er, it was in Los Angeles. I was staying with Dylan at that point for a couple of days. He was editing *Renaldo & Clara*. I was on my way passing through to Hawaii. So we went out one night with Ronee Blakley to Cantor's Delicatessen, which is on Fairfax. And we didn't have anything to do and he said that Cohen was recording with Phil Spector – and he had introduced me to Spector in '65.

So we went over there, and Spector was taking a lot of cocaine and was in a kind of hysterical frenzy: totally Hitlerian and dictatorial and sort of crazed. He started pushing us all around, saying get in there! get on the microphone! The whole thing was total chaos.

Cohen was in despair and Spector went in and started twiddling the dials and mixed it all, and it sounded perfect. It was amazing. It was total chaos. I don't see how he could have remembered what was on the twenty-five or three thousand tracks or whatever. Twenty-four tracks.

He just ordered Dylan around – it was really amazing. Dylan kept telling Spector, 'You ought to work with me cos I got words.' It's a funny way of putting it. He's got words. He's got words. It's just local Los Angeles talk; I had never heard it before. I haven't seen him since last year. Don't know what he's up to now.

He did a pretty good tour last year: well, in '81, that is. In America too.

What was the band?

It was basically the band from the Saved *album . . .*

I think we recorded in the same studio in Santa Monica [in 1982], but I think he's selling it – that's what I heard. Because he spent a quarter of a million dollars, he said, and he said it was a lemon . . .

But when you first recorded with him – that wasn't until late 1971?

Yeah. Just that one period of a week or so. Then '82. Every ten years!

Part Four (1985)

This more recent interview with Allen Ginsberg about Bob Dylan

168

was also conducted for The Telegraph *– by Wes Stace, in Cambridge, England, on 27 April 1985. It was during the National Union of Mineworkers' strike, and Ginsberg was giving a fund-raising poetry-reading for the benefit of striking miners who had been imprisoned. The interview began with Ginsberg just finishing talking to a third party:*

Third Party: You said in a recent interview that you'd retained the anger but grown more compassionate . . .

Ginsberg: I didn't say that. I never was angry. That's somebody else's interpretation. I don't think anger is useful. Wrath, maybe, but not anger . . .

Stace: Do you remember in the mid-sixties when Dylan was doing press conferences, some of which you were at, and he was saying just that?

Yeah, yeah.

Do you think that what people maybe took for drunken or drugged humour was more true than they wanted to believe?

He was intelligent about his responses. He always gave zen-like, metaphorical answers to stereotyped questions. He always gave very poetic responses.

Why did you ask the question in San Francisco about the possibility of Dylan's one day being hanged as a thief?

Because he had a line about a thief in some poem. I was just being playful, and the other reporters were being so serious. I thought it would be nice to say something comic. His answer, 'You weren't supposed to ask that question', was play. And then I thought that in twenty years people would read about that exchange and see how funny it was.

They're very funny interviews now.

They were then. I was sitting at the back in the press corps and I knew that he was a great poet and he knew that I was a great poet, and everybody was asking him relatively uninformed and unspirited questions, so I thought I'd ask him something funny, something nonsensical in his own style . . .

169

He had a style of response that Gregory Corso used to use – of crazy wisdom or serious nonsense. Nonsense on the surface but if you actually picked up on what he was saying, it was a very straightforward way of talking about something real. Like him saying 'my music is mathematical' – that's what he means.

He didn't like to be pinpointed on specific things, did he? Like who was Mr Jones, or where was Desolation Row?

I don't think there was a pinpoint. His interest was in improvized verses which he would sometimes blurt out into a microphone without knowing what the next word was going to be, without calculation, but out of spontaneous playfulness in rhyme. And sometimes he would listen to what he had said and write it down and straighten it out a little. He didn't necessarily mean something in the sense that he set out to mean something, but it would mean something in terms of indicating the cast or direction of his mind or mood, or specific references and thought-forms that were passing through his mind at that time, or the interests that he had at the moment, or things he was reading or what he'd read in the newspaper ... so it was a composite of what was going on in his mind.

When you first met Dylan, in 1963, was he already reading more meditative authors by then?

Like who?

Herman Hesse, people like that.

Probably by then, yeah. I do know that he did read a lot of Kerouac's *Mexico City Blues*, Grove Press, 1958. He read that in '58–9 and it had a big influence on him, he said.

Do you think your works –

I'm telling you something specific. Somebody gave it him and it influenced his poems – or 'blew his mind', as he said – it being the first book of poetry which talked the American language to *him*, and so influenced his writings, or turned him on to poetry, as he said at Kerouac's grave. A specific book, a specific text at a specific time. 1958–59. *Mexico City Blues*. Grove Press.

Who would you say Dylan's favourite authors were?

170

Emily Dickinson. You know Circuit Films? That comes from 'Success In Circuit Lies', which is an Emily Dickinson poem. It's about making the truth slant.[115] He had that poem pinned up on the wall while he was editing the film [*Renaldo & Clara*]. That's why it's called Circuit Films.

He likes Isaac Bashevis Singer. He studied painting. He had some old Jewish Russian teacher in a Carnegie Hall studio.

What books have you recommended to him?

When he was ill in the sixties – when he had his crash – I brought him a box full of books of all kinds. All the modern poets I knew. Some ancient poets like Sir Thomas Wyatt, Campion. Dickinson, Rimbaud, Lorca, Apollinaire, Blake, Whitman and so forth.

He mentioned Apollinaire in a recent TV interview; but sometimes he's very opaque about his influences, as though he doesn't want to let on –

Yeah, well, nobody sits down and asks him about his reading list and what years he read what. If he was asked directly he might answer. Have you ever seen an interview in which somebody asked him precisely what he'd read and in what year?

Well, people have tried to pin him down.

They've tried to pin him down instead of ask him.

That scene in Renaldo & Clara *when you visit Kerouac's grave: was that moving for you?*

I was moved: by his interesting talent and knowledge.

What was it like to travel on the Rolling Thunder tour?

There's a whole movie about that!

Was it truly representative of the tour?

Yeah. The *whole* movie: the four-hour version.

Is Larry Sloman's book good, about that tour?

Yeah, pretty good. Sloman's accounting of the conversations is pretty accurate.

One of my favourite photographs is from then: that one of Dylan showing you some chords.

He actually did teach me the three-chord structure for the blues, but not on that occasion. That was – we were just making fun because there was a friend of mine, Ellie Dorfman, who took a couple of good pictures. There's a kind of funny humour and awareness that he has that let him get into that particular situation. Lowell, Massachusetts, I think.

Have you known Dylan regularly since 1963?

No – I've known him on and off ever since. We were friends and we were acquaintances and there were times when we were together and he was very kind to me, and very affectionate professionally and quizzical, curious and inquisitive personally – and sometimes mysterious – but I only see him when he has some business with me, or some spiritual amusement, or music or language to play; so it's usually every couple of years, that's all. A very modest friendship.

I saw Dylan a couple of weeks ago, and we hadn't met in some time . . . He came over with a cassette of his new album [*Empire Burlesque*]. About midnight. He came over with an old friend of his and his girlfriend about one in the morning. They stayed till about three and played the album through. He was interested in what I thought, what kind of language I thought would be interesting for the title.

He said he had a title but people didn't like it . . . *Empire Burlesque* – and I thought that was as good as anything. The only word I could think of was razzmatazz: *Country Razzmatazz* or something. But I thought *Empire Burlesque* was fine.

You thought that suited the material?

Yeah. Empire equals nation, and Burlesque equals variety, and what goes on. The most interesting song, I thought, apart from one or two of his own solos, was 'Clean-Cut Kid'. 'You've been to all the best schools, played all the rules, and I'm afraid they're going to kill you, murder you.' Interesting.

What has been your favourite period of his creativity?

I follow him as he goes through. Almost every record has some

172

colossal classic. He was put down for *Pat Garrett and Billy The Kid*, yet 'Knockin' On Heaven's Door' is an extraordinary thing. He was put down for *Planet Waves*, but 'Forever Young' is a beautiful song. (I've heard that sung round camp-fires, not recognizing it was Dylan, and they'd go, 'Oh my God, that beautiful old favourite is Dylan?!') He was put down for 'Idiot Wind' but 'Idiot Wind' was a great song. *Desire* I like a great deal – the cantillation on 'One More Cup Of Coffee'. 'In The Garden' on one of the later albums [*Saved*] I think is a great song. The 'Lenny Bruce' song is a great song – every album has some.

What do you like about 'Lenny Bruce'?

Oh, just the rawness of the voice, and the directness, and the statement, and the kind of pathos. He's really talking about himself also, and all us artists.

His unexpected sympathy for Lenny Bruce at a time when he was supposed to be a Born Again moralist Christian, and he was coming out for the injured and the insulted and the wounded and the supposedly damned.

What did you think about his conversion?

He always seemed to be seeking some ultimate eternal truth. It might have been expected that he'd have a visionary experience, which he did, and it might *not* have been expected that he would have solidified it into the symbolism of Born Again Christianity. Well, why not?

It might have been expected that he'd evolve out of it as something closer to his natural Judaism, which he has: long ago. He hasn't been a Born Again Christian for a long time now. People still think he is and five years ago he changed.

In the conversation we had a couple of weeks ago there was a great deal of judgmental Jehovaic or Nobodaddy – 'nobody daddy up in heaven', a figure of judgmental hyper-rationality. There's this judgmental Jehovaic theism in his recent work, and he said: 'Allen, do you have a quarrel with God?' And I said: 'I've never met the man.' And he said: 'Then you have a quarrel with God.' And I said: 'Well, I didn't start anything!'

So he still has a fixed notion of divinity, and I think that's a mistake, as a non-theistic buddhist: that any solidification of the ideal God like the ancient Jews warned against – naming the name of God – is a mistake. It's a psychological error on a simple point.

Did Dylan seem happy with things, his new material?

No. Not happy, not unhappy, just working on it. He's always working. Neither happy nor unhappy. He wasn't going around with a simpering smile. He was serious and he wanted to know honestly what my reaction was to his language. He was willing to repeat a lot of it out aloud. He's always a hard-working guy and he always produces something . . .

And he's always a little ahead of me in his social thinking, and a little behind me in his metaphysical thinking. I think. I'm guessing. It's a presumptuous thing to say. Who knows? I wanted a line or two about my writing [as a blurb for *Allen Ginsberg Collected Poems 1947–1980*], and I went back to some old interviews and phoned in to his publishers for permission to use them – some crazy thing he said about my being an inspiration.[116] And then when I called back to his office he'd written me a little paragraph, which is outside on all the posters. He wrote that about two months ago for me. It was amazing. He put himself out unexpectedly. He said he was reading the book and enjoying it. So that's as much as I know at the moment.

Part Five: 'Blue Gossip'

One of a number of Ginsberg poems about Bob Dylan (see also Some Bob Dylan Lists *in this book), 'Blue Gossip' was written 23 October 1972; it is not in his* Collected Poems *(see above) but was published in* First Blues: Rags, Ballads and Harmonium Songs 1971–74, *Full Court Press, NY, 1975: a slim pink volume which has the dedication 'To Minstrel Guruji Bob Dylan' and includes a photograph of Dylan and Ginsberg together at Kerouac's grave:*

BLUE GOSSIP

I guess he got sick of having to get up and get
scared of being shot down
Also probably he got sick of

174

                              being a methadrine clown;
Also he wanted to go back explore
                          MacDougal Street New York town

I guess he got sick of a Cosmic
                          consciousness too abstract
I guess he wanted to go back
                          t'his own babies' baby shit fact
Change his own children's diapers not get lost
                          in a transcendental Rock & Roll act.

I guess he thought maybe he had
                          enough gold for the world
Saw red white & blue big enough now
                          needn't be further unfurled
I guess he felt prophet show good example,
                          bring himself down in the world.

I guess he took Zen Chinese vows
                          and became an anonymous lout
I guess he figured he better step down off stage
                          before he got kicked out
I guess he felt lonesome and blue
                          and he wanted out.

I guess he did what anyone
                          sens'ble would do
Otherwise like Mick Jagger go out on stage
                          wearing curtains of blue
And fly around the world with great big
                          diamonds and pearls made of glue.

I guess he felt he'd used up
                          'nuff of the 'lectric supply
I guess he knew that the Angel
                          of Death was nigh –
I guess he sighed his
                          next mortal sigh.

I guess he guessed he could
                          find out his own mortal face
I guess he desired to examine
                          his own family place
I guess he decided to act with
                          more modest silent grace

I guess he decided to learn
           from ancient tongue
So he studied Hebrew
           as before he blabbed from his lung
I guess he required to learn new
           tender kind songs to be sung.

I guess he thought he was not guru
           for Everyone's eyes
He must have seen Vajra Hells
           in old visions he'd devised
He must've seen infernal assassins
           stealing his garbage supplies.

I guess he decided to die
           while still alive
In that way, ancient death-in-life,
           saints always thrive
Above all remember his children
           he already pickd a good wife.

I guess he decided to Be
           as well as sing the blues
I guess he decided like Prospero
           to throw his white magic wand into the Ocean blue –
Burn up all his magic books,
           go back to Manhattan, think something new.

I guess he decided like Prospero
           World was a dream
Every third thought is grave
           or so Samsara would seem –
Took Hebrew Boddhisatva's vow
           and saw golden light death agleam.

I guess he decided he
           did not need to be More Big
I guess he decided he was not the
           great Cosmic Thingamajig
I guess he decided to end that sweet song
           as such is his Suchness I dig.

Three Other Poets on Bob Dylan

Philip Larkin

I'm afraid I poached Bob Dylan's *Highway 61 Revisited* out of curiosity and found myself well rewarded. Dylan's cawing, derisive voice is probably well suited to his material – I say probably, because much of it was unintelligible to me – and his guitar adapts itself to rock ('Highway 61') and ballad ('Queen Jane') admirably. There is a marathon 'Desolation Row', which has an enchanting tune and mysterious, possibly half-baked words.

[*Jazz Review*, 10 November 1965.]

John Berryman

'I can never forgive that young upstart for stealing my friend Dylan's name,' he roared about Bob Dylan.

'Yes, but don't you agree he's a poet?'

'Yes, if only he'd learn to sing!'

[John Hoffenden, *The Life of John Berryman*, 1982]

Robert Lowell

Bob Dylan is alloy; he is true folk and fake folk, and has the Caruso voice. He has lines, but I doubt if he has written whole poems. He leans on the crutch of his guitar.

[*The Review*, Summer 1971]

1970s: Bob Dylan's Favourite Electric Guitars

Most Dylan watchers were surprised when, in the middle of the 1976 Fort Collins Colorado concert, as seen in the *Hard Rain*

TV-film, Dylan strapped on an outrageous white guitar and played a slide riff for 'Shelter From The Storm'. For Dylan to play slide guitar in concert was unheard of – and where on earth did he get that guitar anyway?

It was sold to him in the spring of 1976 ˇ Don Vargas, of Woodland Hills, California. The guitar is a National, made in the early fifties. Vargas sold Dylan *three* Nationals, the other two being a lap-slide and a jazz model.

The white one is a Glenwood 98 model, and it seems likely that it was its looks which attracted Dylan. Norman Harris, a specialist dealer in rare guitars in Reseda, California, from whom Dylan has bought many of his favourite instruments, once commented in *Guitar Player* magazine: 'Dylan has a lot of strange things – though he's not really into guitars – just because of what they look like.'

This comment recalls the scene halfway through *Don't Look Back* which has Dylan peering into a music-shop window in Newcastle, on his 1965 British tour, and being delighted by some exotic instruments. He says to the film-maker, D.A. Pennebaker: 'Look at this guitar, man, this one right here! Do you believe *that* guitar? They don't have those guitars in the States, man. They're incredible!'

Dylan carried the white National Glenwood 98 with him throughout his 1978 world tour, but though it was sometimes brought on stage, it seems never to have been played in concert since that 1976 Rolling Thunder tour.

He can be seen playing it on the back-sleeve photograph of the *Hard Rain* LP. More prominently, he is pictured posing proudly with the guitar backstage at Madison Square Garden, 29 September 1978. This photograph, by Morgan Renard, graced a cover of *Rolling Stone* magazine that November.

More recently, another Renard shot was included in the booklet issued with the *Biograph* box-set. The white guitar is just visible in the shadows.

Norman Harris sold Dylan two of his other favourite guitars: a 1959 cherry-sunburst Stratocaster which Dylan must have used as often on stage as any other electric guitar, and notably a mint condition Fender Telecaster – yellow, with a black pick-guard – which Dylan bought for the 1974 tour.

Dylan has been photographed with this one many times; it is

to be seen in Dylan's studio in a photograph in the American magazine *Spin*, November 1985. (This shot is one of several terrific pictures accompanying an excellent interview-feature.)

This guitar was sold to Norman Harris in the first place by one Joe Broome who, before he became a car dealer in San Fernando, had been a professional guitarist. He had been given the guitar by Leo Fender himself. Broome used it on a tour with – bizarrely – The Three Stooges. When the tour was over, he put the guitar away in its case and never got it out again until he sold it to Bob Dylan's dealer.

Finally, the jazz model National Dylan bought from Don Vargas can also be seen in a photograph in the same issue of *Spin* magazine.

Bob Gets a Little Cross

Last time I was here in San Diego – I think about a year ago, I don't know – I was coming, coming from some place, and I was feeling real sick when I came through here and I was playing the show – no, I don't think it was this place: I think it was another place. Anyway, I came just about a year ago, I think. After – just about towards the end of the show someone out in the, someone out in the crowd – they knew I wasn't feeling too well, I think they could see that – and they threw a silver cross on the stage.

Now, usually I don't pick things up in front of the stage. Once in a while I do, sometimes I don't, but, ahh, I looked down at that cross, I said, 'I gotta pick that up.' So I picked up the cross and I put it in my pocket. A little silver cross, I'd say maybe so high.

And I put it – I brought it backstage and I brought it with me to the next town, which was out in Arizona. I think it was, uh, Phoenix. Anyway, I got back there: I was feeling even worse than I'd felt when I was in San Diego. I said, 'Well I need something tonight.' I didn't know what it was. I was used to all kinds of things. I said, 'I need something tonight that I didn't have before.'

And I looked in my pocket and I had this cross. So if that person is here tonight, I just wanna thank you for that cross.

[On stage at Golden Hall, San Diego,
California, 27 November 1979.]

179

Slow Train

John Hinchey

The song 'Slow Train' opens with Dylan feeling 'lowdown and disgusted' because his companions seem not to share his own spiritual independence. Their spirits appear still mastered by 'earthly principles' they haven't yet learnt to 'abandon'. But Dylan feels so lowdown, not because his companions are lost – he doesn't even say that, asking 'Are they lost or are they found?' – but because he 'can't help but wonder' what's happening to them.

He gradually recovers his spirits as he discovers, at first unwittingly and then with full consciousness, that his companions' seeming unregeneracy is not their problem so much as it is his, a function chiefly of his ignorance of them except from the outside, through the necessary veil of 'earthly principles' through which even the regenerate must lead their lives.

In short, he gets down from his pulpit and enters the common fray of sex and politics, 'economy' and 'astronomy' in which, if anywhere, he will have to find his companions.

Thus the third verse (of seven) seems to mock us: 'Look around you, it's just bound to make you embarrassed' for all the earthly addictions that have made us hostage to foreign oil and foreign politics – the implication being that our loss of political and economic independence is but a symptomatic consequence of our prior loss of spiritual independence.

This seems to me a splendid insight, but there is also something puritanically cold-blooded in the way political and economic realities are implicitly reduced to object-lessons for spiritual truths – as if, having abandoned earthly principles for spiritual ones, we then have some choice other than to repossess the earth in terms of spiritual principles.

However, by the sixth verse, all this has changed, and his citation of grain elevators in which surplus food rots while millions starve is resonant with the full gospel awareness that it is the generosity with which we care for each other's earthly hungers that alone nourishes our own and our companions' spirits. Whereas earlier he had appealed to our paranoia by

180

playing not so much upon our worldly fears of foreign domination as upon our spiritual fears of entrapment in the whole insoluble mess to which the flesh is heir, here he appeals to the latent 'brotherly love' within us. And if he continues to mock us, he incorporates the mockery as an element within a challenge he throws out to us:

> Talk about a life of brotherly love, show me someone
> Who knows how to live it

And finally this challenge is thrown out by the force of his own search for companions – 'Show me . . .' is the only line of direct address in the song – the burden of which he has now openly taken upon himself.

This self-transformation is very deliberately acted out. That third verse is followed by a verse-long instrumental break, after which Dylan returns with renewed energy to the impasse in his relations with his companions.

His first step, paradoxically, is to get downright nasty: 'Man's ego's inflated, his laws are outdated'. This is an angry mockery, not the cold-blooded mockery of the previous verse, and it proves regenerative in that it opens his voice to the burdensome pressure of his own impatience:

> They don't apply no more, you can't rely no more
> To be standin' around waitin'

'Standin' around waitin' ' is just what he's been doing himself prior to this, but now he makes his first real move, by citing earthly precedent for his desire for a community of spiritual companions:

> In the home of the brave
> Jefferson's turning over in his grave

which, in turn, opens his imagination for the first time to an awareness of the spiritual futility from which his companions suffer: 'Fools glorifying themselves, trying to manipulate Satan'.

The opening sense of conflict between heaven and earth is giving way gradually to a sense of a war within the spirit, between heaven and hell, for possession and mastery of the earth – and this revision frees Dylan's imagination, in the next verse, to undertake an assault, for the first time, on behalf of his companions against all those who would cheat them of their spiritual birthright by reducing human companionship itself to mere connivings of our self-interest:

> Big-time negotiators, false healers and woman-haters
> Masters of the bluff and masters of the proposition

to whom he adds, with a self-implicating force that can't be unintentional, those who connive with Satan in the Lord's name:

> But the enemy I see wears a cloak of decency
> All non-believers and men-stealers talking in the name of religion

The flesh will eventually lose its war against the spirit, since we are always coming to the end of our earthly ropes, but the spiritual warfare between those who merely take away our lives and those who give them back to us, between those who ask us to waste our lives and those who ask us truly to spend them, is a contest whose outcome remains for us to determine.

By the song's end, then, Dylan has fully earned his dismissal of 'earthly principles'. He may not care about them, but he does take them seriously, because they are his sole access to what he does care about. In the second verse he had cited his own rescue from spiritual ignorance by a lover who gave him a good talking to, but he cited this as if to say, 'I got the message, why can't you?' The answer, of course, is simply that that's no way to talk to a companion; no one who has to listen to that kind of talk is going to show much of himself to whoever's asking. All this seems to be both acknowledged and corrected in the song's powerful final verse, in which Dylan's spiritual independence is shown not to shield him from, but to open him to, earthly pains – pains compounded by his earthly powerlessness here, and by his implicit self-recognition in that 'bad-talking boy':

> My baby went to Illinois, with some bad-talking boy she could destroy
> A real suicide case, but there was nothing I could do to stop it
> I don't care about economy, I don't care about astronomy
> But it sure does bother me to see my loved ones turnin' into puppets
> And there's a slow, slow train comin', up around the bend.

When it first appeared, that choric slow train had seemed to augur on the one hand Dylan's own present salvation and, on the other, his companions' oncoming doom. But here it finally discloses its full and true significance as the emblem of that dual lot of tedious earthly troubles and ecstatic spiritual ease in which we all presently share.

Bob Dylan's Leadbelly Parable

This is a 12-string guitar. First time I heard a 12-string guitar was played by Leadbelly – I don't know if you've heard of him? Anyway, he was a prisoner in, I guess it was Texas State Prison; and I forgot what his real name was but people just used to call him Leadbelly.

He was recorded by a man named Alan Lomax – don't know if you've heard of him? Anyway, he got Leadbelly out and brught him to New York.

He made lots of records there. At first he was just doing prison songs, and stuff like that . . . He'd been out of prison for some time when he decided to do children's songs.

And people said, 'Oh my! Did Leadbelly change?!'

Some people liked the old songs, some people liked the new ones. Some people liked both songs.

But he didn't change. He was *the same man.*'

[On-stage at the Fox-Warfield Theater,
San Francisco, 12 November 1980]

"I don't know what Bob Dylan sees in it!"

What He Can Do For You

Christopher Ricks

A true thing was said about art by the arty old fraud Jean Cocteau, that if artists have a dream, it is not of being famous but of being believed. Bob Dylan's Christian songs ask, reasonably enough, to be believed. This isn't to say that the personal faith of the artist, a matter of biography, is the point; an artist is often someone who is especially good at, generous about, imagining beliefs that he doesn't himself hold. A lot of Dylan-listeners, though, persist in treating the Christian songs as if they were a personal affront, rather than something to confront flexibly; as if such songs only have either the passively low-level interest of a biographical report or the actively repellent interest of an allegiance 'we' don't share, thank you. Yet to trust that these songs, like others of Dylan's, ask to be believed is quite different from concluding that if you don't believe them, then there's nothing really in them for you. To take this party line is drastically and impoverishingly to curtail what we have art and imagination for at all. Art becomes then only a matter of preaching to the converted, a monster rally for the faithful, instead of being no less something else, something more magnanimous. One of the chief functions of art, as William Empson used to say, is exactly to give us sympathetic access to systems of belief that are not our own. How else could it enlarge our sympathies?

I am not myself a Christian believer; the delight I have in, and the understanding I get from, Dylan's Christian songs arise from what an unusual pleasure it is to be able (without stubbornness or rancour) honestly and unservilely to acknowledge that my own system of beliefs doesn't have a monopoly of intuition, sensitivity, scruple and concern. Most of us Dylan-lovers are liberals (granted, there is a smattering of radicals, some on the radical right); and the big trap for liberals is always that our liberalism makes us very *il*liberal about other people's letting us all down by not being liberals. You can believe whatever you like *so long as it's liberal*: this isn't any less dogmatic than most Christianity, and is rather more sleazily menacing.

185

The gratitude that I feel for the best of Dylan's Christian songs (they don't all succeed, but so what? Nor do all his political songs) is related to the fact that so many of them – as with so many of his other great songs, those of friendship, 'Song To Woody', or of love, 'If Not For You' – are themselves supreme acts of gratitude. Dylan is a notably imaginative sayer of thank you.

My own gratitude comes to this: that it is good to meet a heartfelt expression of faith which would constitute – if you were ever to find yourself converted – so true an example as to become a reason. If I were ever to become a Christian, it would not be because of any poem by Gerard Manley Hopkins but because of many a poem by George Herbert. Or because of a Dylan song like 'What Can I Do For You?':

You have given everything to me
What can I do for you?
You have given me eyes to see
What can I do for you?
Pulled me out of bondage, and you made me renewed inside
Filled up the hunger that had always been denied,
Opened up a door no man can shut, and you opened it up so wide,
And you've chosen me to be among the few
What can I do for you?

You have laid down your life for me
What can I do for you?
You have explained every mystery
What can I do for you?
Soon as a man is born, you know the sparks begin to fly
He gets wise in his own eyes, and he's made to believe a lie
Who would deliver him from the death he's bound to die
Well, you've done it all and there's no more anyone can pretend to do
What can I do for you?

You have given all there is to give
What can I give to you?
You have given me life to live
How can I live for you?
I know all about poison, I know all about fiery darts
I don't care how rough the road is, show me where it starts
Whatever pleases you, tell it to my heart

186

Well, I don't deserve it but I sure did make it through
What can I do for you?

Of course Dylan's imaginative decisions in singing this are an inseparable (*not* indistinguishable) part of the song's penetrative power; I think of the way in which, throughout the first two verses, the title-question – 'What can I do for you?' – is sung by him with an impetuosity, an eagerness, which runs ahead of the music and of the chorusing voices. It's a touching effect, this very human haste, this anxious hopeful striving, but – or rather *and* – it is at the same time something less than a perfectly disciplined acquiescence in God's will, something less than *fitting*. It is only in the last verse, in the very last line, that Dylan's voice reins itself in more to the music's timing and to a chastened patience, a truer fit – yet (and this is what saves the song from spiritual complacency) even there the fit isn't quite perfect, isn't a conclusive sanctity such as would sound sanctimonious. Humility, as T.S. Eliot wrote, is endless.

Or again there is the tender unfieriness with which Dylan sings that he knows all about 'fiery darts' (it takes you back to its political counterpart, the tender unaggression with which he once voiced 'How many times must the cannon-balls fly?', his pacific voice giving the cannon-balls the gentleness of cotton-wool). Except that Dylan doesn't simply sing 'fiery darts' but something of a pun, combining 'doubts' (sufficiently suggested for that to be what was printed in the original songbook) with what is nevertheless asked for by both the rhyme (*darts*/starts/ heart, positioned where the previous verses have given the sure-footed inside/denied/wide, and fly/lie/die) and by the Biblical allusion: 'The shield of faith, wherewith ye shall be able to quench all the fiery darts of the wicked' (*Ephesians*, vi. 16). Dylan's phrasing and voicing amount to a great act of quenching; the fiery darts of the wicked are quenched, first by the coolness of his voice's utterance and next by the tempering of the words, so that there is this tentative doubt as to whether we heard *darts* at all or *doubts*.

But it is the song's progress which contains and releases these local movements. What the singer, like any devout lover, wants is reciprocity – and yet reciprocity with God is unthinkable. 'What can I do for you?' is one of Dylan's great and characteris-

tic questions (like 'How does it feel?' or 'Are you ready?')
because it permits of – more, insists on – two antithetical
answers. From one point of view, the answer to the question
'What can I do for you?' when addressed to God is 'absolutely
nothing'. From another, the answer is 'everything'. 'A condition
of complete simplicity/(Costing not less than everything)' (Eliot
again). From the very beginning of the song, we are implicated
in Dylan's yearning for the perfect matching reciprocity of an
answer, for a true fit; and continually the song has the honesty
to deny us this. Patience, hard thing . . . So the first line, 'You
have given everything to me', is not followed by – not matched
with – the complacency of an echo (which would be 'What can I
give to you?'), but by the unremitting question which is central
and yet at a tangent: 'What can I do for you?' It is this imperfect
alignment which animates the relation of statement ('You have
. . . You have . . .') to the succeeding question, 'What can I do for
you?', throughout the first two verses. Then, with the end of the
second and the start of the third and last verse, Dylan modulates
his pattern (as he so beautifully does, just when he had settled
into comfy parallels and reversals, in 'Do Right To Me Baby');
for in these successive instances, he comes very near (so near
and yet so far) to finding the reciprocity which he hungers for –
and yet still not quite. The second verse ends with:

Well, you've done it all and there's no more anyone can pretend to do
What can I do for you?

— with its parallelism in the return ('you've done . . . What can I
do . . .') – and the third verse varies the terms of this while
repeating its shape:

> You have given all there is to give
> What can I give to you?

But this still isn't the exact fit, the perfect returning of a question
to its statement, which is what it's aspired to; for the move is
not from 'you've done it all *for me*' to 'What can I do for you?',
and again the move is not from 'You have given *me* all there is to
give' to 'What can I give to you?' At which point Dylan reaches
for – no, it's better than that, it's that he reaches – the realization

of how the question itself must be turned so that it will, in its very questioning, return a true answer:

> You have given me life to live
> How can I live for you?

Not *what* can I *do* for you, but *how* can I *live* for you. The deepest question turns out not to be a *what* question but a *how* one; and it is with that recognition that Dylan can then legitimately return to asking the good old (not the best new) question, with his rueful matching of 'Whatever' against 'What':

> Whatever pleases you, tell it to my heart
> Well, I don't deserve it but I sure did make it through
> What can I do for you?

Deaths Around Bob Dylan's Life: Last Thoughts on David Blue

Michael Gray and John Bauldie

A number of people who have played significant parts in Bob Dylan's life and work have died in the comparatively short span of time since Dylan turned forty: enough such deaths to show that here is another aspect of reality that the artist, as well as the man, must deal with and measure the cut of, as he enters middle age.

As an individual, Bob Dylan finds himself still a survivor in an especially volatile milieu inside our volatile civilization. ('By this time, I'd have thought that I would be sleeping/In a pine-box for all eternity . . .') As an artist, Bob Dylan may find that this apparently accelerating process – the deaths of those around you becoming a part of your life – presents itself compellingly as a theme for exploration in his work, as other explorations within the kingdom of middle age (weariness, and

189

the onset of new confusions, for instance) have done recently.

This theme may not emerge at all as the early deaths of friends and heroes of Dylan's youth did, in individual lamentation-songs. They, after all, come not only from another era but from a very different vantage-point: partly because youth can more easily afford a romantic fascination with death – can play with feeling close to it – and partly because back then, those who died were the odd ones out by dying.

Dylan's first album is so soaked in this romancing, so enthralled with giddy delight in its use of the ancient blues-man's voice, that it is obvious its creator was very young. Its obsession with death is suffused with youth's sense of immortality.

But while that first flood from Dylan the performer showed him to be, in his eccentric way, the archetypal immortal youth, he soon arrived – at an early age and with a remarkable sustained clarity – at a wise working relationship with death. ('Obviously,' he said in 1966, 'death is not very universally accepted.' It is one of the ways in which he has been maturely unAmerican.)

In the 1965 British-tour film *Don't Look Back*, the Bob Dylan who wasn't a fraction as derailed by his fame and fortune and hipness as most of us would have been, put in the same position, and who wasn't yet twenty-five years old at the time, offered this unblinking belief to the *Time* magazine reporter:

> I'm saying that you're going to die, and you're gonna go off the earth, you're gonna be dead. Man, it could be, you know, twenty years, it could be tomorrow: any time. So am I . . . All right: now you do your job in the face of that – and how seriously you take yourself, you decide for yourself.

Since Dylan turned forty in May 1981, death has taken Howard Alk, David Blue, Paul Butterfield, Albert Grossman, John Hammond Richard Manuel, Richard Marquand, Sam Peckinpah and Tom Wilson. And these are only the public names.

Of them, the last six mentioned can all be said to have achieved wide recognition in their chosen areas of work, while Howard Alk's less celebrated talents are discussed in some detail elsewhere in this book.

This leaves actor and singer-songwriter David Blue (né Cohen). In tribute to his always-underrated talent, here, in slightly expanded form, is the obituary notice first published in *The Telegraph* in February 1983.

MG

David Blue, 1941–82

I first heard David Blue singing on a tape which Bill Allison sent me. It was the first Elektra album, and it's remarkable because of its sounds: a cross of *Highway 61 Revisited* and the Butterfield Blues Band at Newport in 1965. For the years between my hearing that tape and now, I've been tracking and tracing the other David Blue albums.

It was in early December 1982 that I finally found a copy of the *Singer-Songwriter Project* album – Dave Cohen (he changed his last name too . . .) plus Richard Farina, Patrick Sky and Bruce Murdoch. I may just have bought it on the day that 41-year-old David Blue collapsed and died on his get-in-shape jog around Washington Square.

I bet David Blue was melancholy for most of his life. If I can judge fairly from his cameo/chorus appearances in *Renaldo & Clara*, he was also the kind of person whom you might not suspect was feeling as bad as he really was. But the pain showed in his eyes in the photographs, and it does in the film. Bob Dylan's film.

David Blue loved Bob Dylan. He loved him as a writer and as a singer and as a human being. He loved him as an old friend . . . He tried to write it down in a song called 'Cupid's Arrow', written after the Rolling Thunder tour:

> It was obvious God loves you
> It's obvious so do I
> The simple things we've shared together
> Helped both of us survive . . .

(I learnt later of David Blue's performance at the Phil Ochs Memorial Concert at the Felt Forum, New York City, in May

1976. He sang 'Cupid's Arrow' and introduced it by saying: 'I wrote this for Phil Ochs.' A sincere gesture for the occasion, I'm certain, but also, I'm certain, not true. It was far from obvious that God loved Phil Ochs. But this is no place for an argument.)

David Blue was the same age as Bob Dylan. He may not have been a genius but he did have a very special gift. As an actor, he will be remembered for an exceptional, powerful performance in *An American Friend*. He was also a singer and songwriter of considerable and, it seems now, ever-to-be-unrecognized talent.

JB

Bruce who?

WERE it not for the fact that high court judges so regularly demonstrate their ignorance of modern tastes and trends, it would be tempting to assume they are indulging in a little judicial leg pulling to keep us all amused.

After all the hysteria about Bruce Springsteen it seems hardly credible that an English judge should have to ask counsel during a copyright action: "Who is Bruce Springsteen?"

The question ranks closely behind that of a Scottish High Court judge who was told during a divorce hearing that the woman's

BRUCE SPRINGSTEEN

husband used to disappear.

On one occasion he went to London to see Bob Dylan."

"And this Mr Dylan," enquired his lordship, "is he a friend of the family?"

A Meeting with A. J. Weberman, Summer of '82

John Bauldie

I think I'll call it America, I said as we touched down.

It took two phone calls to persuade A.J. Weberman that he'd like to see me. I used to write to A.J. sixteen years ago. I sent him money; he sent me tapes the like of which the world had never heard – concerts from 1963! Studio cuts that hadn't been released! Not just that: A.J. had this key to a secret code . . . Now it's common knowledge but it wasn't then. Not too many of us knew A.J. then.

Shelly did though. Shelly used to be in A.J.'s class. He was on the field-trip down MacDougal Street when Dylan confronted Weberman and his students; he was at The Bob Dylan 30th Birthday Street Party (organized by the Dylan Liberation Front and staged outside Dylan's Greenwich Village house on Sunday 23 May 1971); he was in the Dylan Archive when A.J. was neck-deep in his researches, pounding out the Book which would finally tell the truth – the concordance-based work on symbolism in Dylan's writing.

I stayed with Shelly in New York. (Saw more Ribakoves in his drawer than I've seen in any one place.) So I told A.J. on the phone that the two of us would like to see him.

I wanted to see his Dylan Archive too. The Dylan Archive! It used to be written on A.J.'s notepaper: *Dylan Archive – A.J. Weberman, Dylanologist*.

'Don't come here!' the A.J.-like voice at the other end of the telephone wire yelled. 'I'll meet you on the corner of Mercer and Houston at 11.30. I'll be with the dogs.' He hung up.

The following morning we were there early. A fine rain fell for a few minutes.

'Think he'll show?' I asked doubtfully. Shelly didn't see A.J. as a punctual appointment-keeper, and street-corner rendez-vous in strange and potentially hostile territory isn't really my scene, man.

As the second hand on my Seiko watch hit the top of the dial at 11.30, there he was! A.J. Weberman, Dylanologist, champion of causes, liberator of garbage. But wait. Was that really A.J.? He'd cut his hair, cut off all of his hair – real short. He walked two Dobermans – Helga and Mordecai – on iron chains.

'John. Shelly.' A.J.'s handshake was firm and cool. It was a hot day. He took us into the local dog-walking pound: through two chained gates, behind railings, a concrete oasis at the bottom edge of Greenwich Village, bordering on the Bowery. He let the dogs run free. We sat down on a bench. I tried to talk to him for about twenty minutes. He wasn't too responsive.

Shelly had written to him months back, and sent some cash for a copy of the ill-fated Weberman book-manuscript. 'Hey, Shelly, I couldn't find the book. I'll give you your money back.' The money wasn't important. Shelly had wanted the book.

Weberman stood up and walked into the shade. Shelly and I sat sweating in the sunshine.

Weberman talked to some neighbours, kicked one of his dogs and came back: 'We'll go see if we can find the book.'

Shelly hadn't heard. 'Come on Shelly, we're going back to A.J.'s!'

We walked down Elizabeth Street.

A.J. suddenly turned. 'This is where Dylan jumped me!' A strange light glowed in his eyes. ' "Laughter down on Elizabeth Street"! Can't you see these buildings, how they close in? This is "the valley of stone".' There was certainly a stream of pure heat. ' "It felt out of place, my foot in his face"! Just here, man, near this trashcan. "The book that nobody can write". That's my book!'

We got to Bleecker. The Yippies were just getting onto their bus. We stopped at A.J.'s door.

'Still got the same place?' Shelly asked.

'I got the whole building,' said A.J.

The whole building? He pushed a big key into the steel door and swung it open. It clanged, locked behind us. It was as if we were in an airlock. Another solid steel door faced us. Up to the right a TV camera peered at us. To our left were tear-gas canisters, ready to be triggered by remote control.

The second door opened. We went up some stairs. 'This is the dog's floor.' We went up some more stairs. The office. No Archive.

194

'Do you still listen to Dylan?' I asked, as A.J. changed into camouflage shorts to match his shirt.

'I listen to the records, man, I don't have much to do with anything else.'

'What about the symbolism, A.J.?'

'Still there, man, still exactly the same.'

'Do you still write, A.J.? The last thing I read was your review of *Renaldo & Clara*.'

'That was the last thing I did.'

'You should write it down,' I said, 'some of us still want to hear it.'

'I guess so,' he said. 'Nobody knows more than I do about Dylan's poetry.' He turned to the cupboard and pulled out a loaded shotgun.

'See this? Nobody will get me in here.' He glanced at the TV monitors which focused on the steel doors and the tear-gas bombs.

'Let's get the boxes.' We went briefly upstairs. 'This was A.J.'s flat,' said Shelly. No Dylan pictures. No records. No tapes. No Archive.

'Do you still do the garbology, A.J.?'

'Naw, not much.'

The garbology murals were still there – perhaps the garbage too. Down in the stairwell were three hefty cardboard boxes. 'Bring those up here,' A.J. directed. The boxes were brought and opened.

Dylan. Piles of articles, cuttings glued to sheets, sellotaped to sheets; yellow, musty, stuck together. Piles and piles. Photographs. Dylan 1965, Columbus, Ohio; November 1966, Seattle; New Year's Eve with The Band. Galley roughs for the original *Freewheelin'* sleeve, discarded covers for *Tarantula*. A *Tarantula* badge! Dylan in magazines: colour photo in 1966 *McCalls*; *Movie World, Intellectual Digest*. A treasure-chest and a terrible mess. And in the second box, more and more. And in the third box, Weberman's book.

More than 400 pages, and this is just volume one: up to *Blonde On Blonde*.

'Here, Shelly, you can have the book.' Shelly didn't know what to say.

A.J. looked at both of us: looked very carefully.

'You want this stuff?' he asked, casually pointing to the boxes.

'You're kidding,' I said.

'Take it,' he said, 'I'm all through with it.'

Shelly went to get the car. While he was gone, A.J. began to talk about Dylan again, but he seemed very confused and I felt sorry for him – for something that had been lost.

'What do you do with your time?' I asked him, although I already knew.

'I manage.'

'What about money?'

'I have more money than I ever had. I get more in a day than I got in a lifetime. I don't need money.'

Then Shelly appeared on the grey monitor screen.

We loaded the boxes into the VW, and left A.J. Weberman, the world's first and greatest Dylanologist, staring at a steel door on a flickering TV screen in an empty building at the bottom of Bleecker Street. New York New York.

And yes, Weberman did scare me; but then again I'm easily scared, and anyway those are my best days, when I shake with fear.

Postscript on Weberman's Work

The garbology book, *My Life In Garbology* by A.J. Weberman, was published by the Stonehill Publishing Co., 1140 Avenue of the Americas, New York, NY 10036, USA, in 1980, and cost $8.95. It has twenty-five chapters, the first and longest of which is 'Bob Dylan's Million-Dollar Trash', in which A.J. gives the background on, and the findings of, his expeditions into Bob Dylan's garbage-can from September 1970 onwards.

A.J. analyzes the garbage and prints photos of some of the tastier items – Dylan's incomplete letter to Johnny Cash, his driving licence (signed 'Robert Dylan' and apparently for a 1954 MG) and some other stuff of Dylan's wife Sara's. The rest of the book is devoted to other people's trash and to a rundown on the science of garbology.

Incidentally, A.J. has his name on at least one other published book: *Coup d'état In America: The CIA And The Assassination Of John F. Kennedy* (The Third Press, NY, 1975), co-authored with Michael Canfield.

196

A Note on Bob Dylan and Bob Marley

supplied by Tony Jowett

Stephen Davis' *Bob Marley: The Biography* (published by Arthur Barker, London, 1983) is worth reading in its own right, but also has an intriguing mention of a Wailers' version of 'Like a Rolling Stone', with words altered by Marley:

> Although few of Bob Dylan's early records reached Jamaica, Bob Marley was very attentive when one of Dylan's mid-sixties AM radio hits came beaming in from Miami. One of the most amazing Wailers' cover versions was the group's take (credited to Bunny and Coxsome) of Bob Dylan's 'Like a Rolling Stone'. After a spooky blues piano intro, the Soul Brothers slip into a sinister groove that's a mixture of 1965 American folk-rock and early Jamaican rock-steady. Although the chorus is the same as Dylan's, the verse and melody are different: 'Nobody told you he was on the street/But that's what happens when you lie and cheat/You have no nights and you have no morning/'Cos time lights come just string without warning/How does it feel/To be on your own/With no direction home/Like a complete unknown/Like a rolling stone?' It's a sentiment that Bob Marley knew all too well.

Various other references establish that Dylan had an important influence on Marley – and Marley, in a succinct quote in his own inimitable patois, acknowledged his admiration for Dylan. Introducing this, the book refers to a Wailers concert at Santa Monica in the summer of 1976, which Dylan attended:

> The show at the Roxy was a particularly brilliant and gem-like performance, in part because Bob Dylan was in the audience and Dylan was a favourite of Bob's. 'Him's really say it clear,' Marley had said of Dylan earlier in the year.

The Oppression of Knowledge: No-one Can Sing the Blues Like Blind Willie McTell

John Bauldie

Among the ghosts who haunt Bob Dylan's street, there are several whose names have occasionally been moaned from the shadows: Robert Johnson, Arthur Rimbaud, Hank Williams, Woody Guthrie, William Blake – ghost poets and rainbow angels. Sometimes the voice of the long-dead may be heard in the spaces between the lines of songs. Dylan's past is peopled with ghostly presences and from time to time he has written songs to bewail deaths.

His earliest lamentations were of the deaths of unnamed friends – 'He Was A Friend Of Mine' and 'Ballad For A Friend'. Many other songs lament the demises of named, often public, figures – 'Ballad Of Donald White', 'The Death Of Emmett Till', 'Who Killed Davey Moore?', 'The Lonesome Death Of Hattie Carroll', 'Only A Pawn In Their Game', 'George Jackson' and 'Lenny Bruce'.

Most recently, there is 'Blind Willie McTell', recorded at the sessions for the *Infidels* album.

Here, we are dealing also with everybody's death. Man has invented his doom (as Dylan insists on another *Infidels* song, 'License To Kill'): not *determined* or *decided* but *invented*. It is a technological doom. The world is already condemned, marked out by the arrow of truth for damnation and demolition:

> I seen the arrow on the doorpost
> Saying 'This land is condemned'
> All the way from New Orleans
> To Jerusalem.

All the way from the new world to the old world, from the land of the last Adam to the land of the first Adam, from the place of Bob Dylan's musico-spiritual roots to the place of his ethno-spiritual roots.

Planet waves. We are living in the end times, and our floors are most certainly not fireproof. The land took a lot of building: a lot of blood and sweat and tears and toil, a lot of labour, a lot of pain and suffering and slavery, exploitation and martyrdom out on Highway 61. Now it's sundown on the Union. This land, your land, my land, the great God-given land – the whole world (your world, my world) is

condemned.

Man has invented his doom, but that in itself is not the problem here. The problem is, how is such a doom to be lamented? How is the imminent passing of the world to be bewailed? How is the world to be elegized?

A real problem. The world cannot be allowed to pass unwept. Some melodious tear must be shed – but it's no use pleading, bleating, blah-ing 'Don't fall apart on me tonight/I just don't think that I could handle it', or sitting there shivering in fearful apprehension, looking up at that green hill far away and asking, 'Who's gonna take away/His license to kill?'

The self-contradictory songs on *Infidels* reveal, in spite of themselves, someone who sounds like Bob Dylan in a state of frustration, saying over and over: 'I can't . . . I can't/I wish I'd have been . . ./I'm stuck . . . I can't move/I can't stumble or stay put/I just don't think that I can handle it.' But *Infidels* does not offer what it could have offered – a quite remarkable, because quite perfect, classic monody: 'Blind Willie McTell'.

In this great unreleased song, Dylan conjures the ghost of a long-dead blues singer who might have offered appropriate lamentation were he not dead, and gone. Meantime, Bob Dylan offers his own lamentation, bewailing not just the damnation of the world, and not just his own inability to offer an appropriate response to its imminent passing, but bewailing also the fact that there seems to be no-one who can appropriately mourn that passing.

The vision of desolation and expected destruction which opens the song is oppressive. Singing the blues is one ages-old way of addressing and attempting to relieve such oppression. Sing while you slave. It must have started by the waters of Babylon. The world's doom is already invented, the land already condemned. There's really nothing anyone can say that

199

can change that, but that is not to say that what is about to come to pass ought not to be lamented. Indeed, responsibility for such lamentation ought to be assumed. The problem which brought this song into being is the singer's feeling of being unable to shoulder the responsibility that he's always liked to think he inherited from those ghosts who haunt the darker side of his street – Robert Johnson, Leadbelly, Blind Lemon Jefferson, Blind Willie McTell. How can Bob Dylan offer appropriate homage, how can he address and relieve the oppression? He cannot.

There is no-one who can, and Bob Dylan *knows* that:

> No-one can sing the blues like
> Blind Willie McTell

and he continues to tell us throughout the song that he knows that; and it's that knowledge that is being bewailed – not just the fact that no-one can sing the blues like Blind Willie McTell, but that Bob Dylan knows that no-one can.

It is both the lack of a singer and the knowledge of the lack that are worthy of lamentation. Each verse in the song concludes its picture of desolation or degradation with this same statement, though the second verse recognizes another voice: one lonesome enough, mournful enough, to harmonize with an image of the world's demolition:

> I've heard that hoot-owl singing
> As they were taking down the tents.

The trees are barren: not about to bud again, not about to renew; the tents are being pulled down, the show is over, and the hoot-owl is doing its best – despite its lack of a worldly audience – to lament, to mourn, to address or relieve.

> But nobody can sing the blues like
> Blind Willie McTell.

Them charcoal gypsy maidens have dressed themselves in borrowed robes, having appropriated the bird's feathers, and

200

have strutted their stuff; but this response to circumstance, no matter how well effected, is totally inappropriate. (In another unreleased song, 'Yonder Comes Sin', sin itself comes strutting along dressed up in feathers.)

Because there is a great deal of strutting and fretting upon the stage, inside the tents – temporary shelters which are about to be taken down – all eyes and ears are directed *away* from the only performer (the hoot-owl) who is not wrapped up in vanity:

> The stars above the barren trees
> Was his only audience

and who is making his own instinctive attempt to sing the blues, but who, even as he hoots, does not have the emotive power of Blind Willie McTell, whose own blues singing was the product of human experience – with its bitterness and sweetness, its frustration, grief and love, its unkept promises and its broken hearts – of which the hoot-owl can know nothing.

It is to the bitterness of experience that Dylan's thoughts turn in the third verse. He replays time past, moving backwards through American history. Shots of the South ablaze. Subliminal freeze-frames of the freeing of the slaves amid the flames give way, in this continuing retrospection, to the cracking of the whip in the days before the blaze, and then back further to ghostly ships sailing in with human cargo, and finally, initially, to the moaning of wandering tribes all the way from New Orleans to Jerusalem.

The South in its power and in its pride is personified by the 'fine young handsome man' (who is not a squire but who dresses – in his coat and tie, in his cloak of decency – as if he were), drinking bootleg whiskey. He's a pretender: he represents the ghost, as was, of America's future. The land of the free was founded upon the bone-filled graves of slaves. Now it is condemned to face its inevitable, man-invented, doom. Despite the tolling, from generation to generation, of the undertaker's bell, man is still what he was, is what he is. All that there is in the world is all that there ever was in the far-beyond lands of the forefather slaves:

> Power and greed and corruptible seed.

201

The seed will bear the corruption to the future, should there be much of a future, whatever future there is. Power and greed, vanity, selfishness: it is as it was and as it will be.

In former times, the oppression of such knowledge might have been addressed and relieved by the blues singer. Now there is no-one to play the tune. The singer of *this* song, as he gazes at the condemned land from inside 'that old St James Hotel' as others have gazed before him – hotels are like tents: temporary residences, occupied in passing – the singer of *this* song cannot find the words, or the voice, to adequately express what he sees as he gazes.

The irony is that in attempting to express that inadequacy, in lamenting the oppression of his knowledge, Bob Dylan sings the blues indeed: and such a soul-rending blues as any of the old bluesmen – Blind Willie McTell, Robert Johnson – might have sold their souls to be able to sing.

Postscript

From *Rolling Stone* magazine, 21 June 1984:

Kurt Loder: I heard an out-take from the Infidels *sessions called 'Blind Willie McTell'. Is that ever going to come out? It's a great song.*

Bob Dylan: I didn't think I recorded it right.

Highway 84 Revisited

John Lindley

Bob Dylan tours, like Bob Dylan albums, take time to settle in the mind. If 'journalistic reviewing' is to be avoided then any series of concerts needs to be considered, revisited via memory and tape, and somehow slotted into the general perspective of Dylan's career.

'The best since 1978,' a friend of mine observed after that 7 June 1984 concert in Brussels: but of what 1978 was he speaking? Dylan at Budokan? Dylan at Earls Court or Blackbushe? Dylan in Miami that December? When we speak of Rolling Thunder as one of his finest hours, are we thinking of 'Isis' from 1975 or of 'Idiot Wind' from 1976? Which is more indicative of the 1974 tour with The Band – the riveting 'Ballad of Hollis Brown' at the start, or the mutilated 'Just Like A Woman' at the close?

With Dylan, possibly more than with any other performer, the kind of show you see and hear when you hand in your ticket will depend very much on the particular time you catch that tour.

The comparative brevity of the 1984 tour should have made things simpler, and to an extent it did. The programme, barring certain minor changes, steadied itself relatively early, and what diversions there were came chiefly in the occasional inclusion of unexpected things, like 'To Ramona', or in the superstar sessions which illuminated the later encores. But inevitably there are problems in trying to come to a coherent overall assessment.

'The best since 1978'. Reports that filtered through of the early gigs on the '84 tour spoke of performances that were rough and untogether – little more than on-stage rehearsals: and video and tape recordings lend credence to this. Simply to dismiss these shows as inferior to the later ones, however, would be altogether too tidy. It's true that in that opening week Dylan was fronting a line-up that seemed both unfamiliar with the material and uncertain how to approach it, but the experimental nature of these first few shows brought some fascinating glimpses of Dylan's creativity in performance.

At Hamburg we were treated to a 'Just Like A Woman' pitched high, with a long harp intro and Dylan on electric guitar – and, conversely, an 'I And I' and an 'All Along The Watchtower' with him on acoustic guitar. At Verona, first night, we got a shakily caressing 'Shelter From The Storm' and an 'It's Alright Ma (I'm Only Bleeding)' with an unusually light touch. Same place, second night, there was an acoustic and gentle 'Blowin' In The Wind' with Carlos Santana playing eloquently delicate Spanish guitar with a fluency he had been seeking, and failing to find, in the opening concert. There was also a 'Masters Of War' that strutted with a venom that had dissipated to a cold, slick anger by the time Dylan played it for the twenty-seventh time, at Slane.

The result, when the tour hit England, was one of losses and gains. An appealing ramshackle quality, as well as a degree of freshness, had disappeared from the set, but in its place there was a swaggering authority.

Inevitably there were song casualties along the way: Willie Nelson's 'Why Do I Have To Choose?'; the (poorly) reworked 'When You Gonna Wake Up?'; and, sadly, a magnificent 'Man Of Peace'. In came 'Knockin' On Heaven's Door', 'Simple Twist Of Fate', 'Tangled Up In Blue' and the previously (and subsequently) unheard 'Enough Is Enough'.

Apart from that last song, Dylan was, by the close of the tour, playing only four or (as at Wembley) five songs written since 1974. Four songs from his last six, as it then was, studio albums! In fact, Dylan placed such strong emphasis on his earlier material that an uninformed observer at the Nantes show, for instance, could have been forgiven for thinking that the latest album was *Highway 61 Revisited*.

And a current album, or lack of it, seemed to be the problem. The recording of *Infidels* had been more or less completed over twelve months before Dylan first took to the stage at the end of May '84 – and for an artist who outpaces his own songs and attitudes at the speed that he does, twelve months can be a very long time. The energy reserved for songs like 'I And I' on this tour proved once again that Dylan is at his best when performing songs that he is still both musically and emotionally in step with. The inclusion of only three songs from *Infidels*, however, would suggest that interest or belief (or both) in this material was already waning.

None of this, though, sheds much light on Dylan's uncharacteristic bias towards his sixties catalogue to the exclusion of so much excellence achieved since.

It is the most famous of those sixties songs – 'The Times They Are A-Changin' '', 'Blowin' In The Wind', 'Mr Tambourine Man', 'It Aint Me Babe' and more – that shackle Dylan now. Other singer-songwriters may have had more chart hits, but it is doubtful whether any has written more classic songs than has Bob Dylan. How does he handle such a situation? 'Don't look back' was the catch-phrase once, and though only the years

1966, 1979 and 1980 can be cited as steadfast examples of this policy, Dylan has mostly shown a sense of proportion when uniting his present with his past.

The irony is that while the chameleon nature of Dylan as an artist is one of the attributes his fans most cherish, the public display by his audience often transmits a very different message. At Earls Court and Birmingham in 1981, powerful readings of 'When You Gonna Wake Up?' and 'Slow Train' were greeted with a tepid reaction bordering on indifference, while lack-lustre versions of 'Maggie's Farm' and 'Like a Rolling Stone' brought the house down. It is of course no more than an example of people responding to *what* is being played rather than to *how* it is being played, but what must be the effect on Dylan's psyche?

That some songs on 1984's tour were there because they were *expected* to be there seems unquestionable. 'Ballad Of A Thin Man' and 'Maggie's Farm' should have been dropped long ago: on recent form they have been drained of all atmosphere and theatre (in the case of the former) and all variety and humour (the latter), coming across as no more than hollow and mechanical crowd-pleasers. In contrast, the (once again) rewritten 'Simple Twist Of Fate' and 'Tangled Up In Blue', and occasionally an untired 'Girl Of The North Country', revealed instead Dylan in full command of older songs for which he has obvious affection and in which he has continued belief. The ease with which those convictions were transmitted to us showed up the redundancy of some of the other material the more pointedly.

This dilemma was still more apparent in the sections of the concerts where Dylan was alone on stage. The song choices here were often so predictable that Dylan seemed as guilty as many of his audience of relating his 'solo performer' image to the songs only of his early career. This has not always been so. Remember 'Nobody 'Cept You' in 1974 and 'Abandoned Love' at the Other End in 1975?

'He has got to decide whether he wants us to go into his past or whether he wants us to go into his future,' said Christopher Ricks on television two days after the Newcastle concert. Should Dylan realize his recently-expressed desire to include some solo performances on future studio albums then perhaps the emphasis on the dichotomy between early-acoustic and later-electric will shift.[117]

205

Did the demands of the audience, or at least Dylan's interpretation of them, dictate his selections for the 1984 tour, or was it felt that the songs of *Bringing It All Back Home* and *Highway 61 Revisited* were more suited to the stripped-down sound of the tour band?

This would be an explanation, but hardly a justification. To let the band dictate to him would be to put horse and cart together the wrong way round, and nearly as disappointing as letting the audience do the dictating. It's possible instead (and, I would like to feel, more probable) that after three years of touring on chiefly new material, followed by a two-year lay-off, Dylan simply saw the time as ripe for a reminder: a clearing of the decks before embarkation on a new journey.

'The best since 1978.' Well, in 1978 it was Billy Cross on lead guitar, occasionally stepping out, as on that heavy-metal 'Masters Of War' on the American leg, but more often content to let the spotlight also turn towards saxophone, violin, congas and more. No such possibilities this time around. The small backing unit assembled for the 1984 tour – a band that was to progress from its shambolic beginnings but rarely reach anything better than general competence – had far fewer resources to draw upon.

In *this* band the attention was squarely on Mick Taylor. Dylan has never in the past had much time for extended instrumental breaks; here though he found himself with a guitarist of such pedigree and reputation that he seems to have felt the occasion demanded them. As a consequence, obligatory guitar solos invaded every song, often more than once, and made one yearn for a player with the sense of economy (and bite) of a Robbie Robertson.

Some of the time Taylor handled his responsibilities adequately, very occasionally supplying inspired work, as on the final verse of 'Masters Of War' at Newcastle, when his guitar punctuated the vocal with a tight musical parody of Dylan's phrasing. More typical, though, was 'Every Grain Of Sand', which repeatedly featured totally inappropriate guitar-work. Far too often he seemed dull-mindedly lost with the material, and incurious about it. And – visibly failing the infallible test of whether a musician enjoys coping with, or even comprehends, Dylan's eccentric, magical, live-the-moment creativity – Taylor appeared baffled as to what to do whenever Dylan took up his harmonica.[118] Ironically it was left to Carlos Santana, whose own set produced the most deadeningly boring music it's ever been my misfortune to stand through, to bring a degree of flair and sensitivity to the songs on which Dylan played harp.

Even without singing or playing at all, Dylan is a knock-out on stage. Whatever you call it – charisma and magnetism both seem inadequate words: too commonplace and suggesting something too unspecific – whatever it is, Dylan has it in abundance. It's that nervous energy, that cool, that visible intelligence and panache which is present in virtually every move and gesture he makes. Watch *The Last Waltz*, *Renaldo & Clara*, *Concert For Bangladesh*, *Pat Garrett and Billy The Kid* and it is evident in them all, Dylan had it on this tour, had it back in 1965 in *Don't Look Back* and, though we haven't the film to prove it, you can bet he had it on those freezing nights at the Gaslight as the sixties rolled in.

Above all, the 1984 shows were a reaffirmation of this *performing* genius. Despite the band being undistinguished and uneven, Dylan's own undiminished assertiveness – which gave us the driving black humour of 'Tombstone Blues', the superb vocalizing on the reworked 'Simple Twist of Fate', and the astonishing 'Tangled Up In Blue' – made it all worthwhile. And although vocally he never quite reached the dizzy heights of his David Letterman Show appearance earlier the same year, the solo sets, for all their predictability, were sometimes literally breathtaking reminders of his immense talents.

But what proportion of an '84 audience could readily have picked up on all this? – for if the soundness of Dylan's choice of both songs and musicians was dubious, then the very nature of the tour itself was even more questionable. The unsuitability of the venues chosen, and the problems of seeing, or more to the point not seeing, Dylan in such stadia, were striking. Unlike most first-time punters, long-time connoisseurs like me knew enough to insist on putting ourselves within those rewarding first twenty yards at the concerts we attended: but since this access physically *cannot* be the experience of any but a tiny minority of those there, *most* people *must necessarily* come away having in a sense been hardly there at all. Especially among those coming to see this strange, puzzling, legendary old figure for the first time, it must have been all too easy, standing way back amid the detritus, to miss the genius altogether.

I can't help but wonder what ultimately damaging effect these kinds of shows must have on both the state of Dylan's art and his status as an artist. It very much worries me that Dylan himself should court this detrimental shoddiness by appearing on the same bill as the likes of Santana and Lindisfarne in fodder-for-the-masses package tours. Remember Michael Gray's remark (published in *The Telegraph* issue 16, summer 1984) about a recent 'lack of self-regard on Dylan's part, as if he were beginning to piss away his stature as an artist'? And 'I think he has a problem with concerts now because a concert is a rally,' said Christopher Ricks on *Saturday Review*, 'the occasion is one that actually likes all that thumping community and fervour.' Quite.

Dispensing with peripheral of support bands and playing smaller halls might have gone some way to offering us, and him, a Bob Dylan unassailed by community singing or inane cries of 'Rock 'n' roll!!' and the company of an audience there for the music as opposed to The Event. There were a couple of utterly marvellous '84 concerts – Barcelona and Paris, I'm told; Newcastle was pretty damn good too – but sooner or later, as Bob Dylan must know, his unique performer's art demands that he undertake an altogether different kind of *concert* tour.

Brief Encounter

Kevin McHale is a professional basketball player for the Boston Celtics, whose game Dylan attended after appearing on David Letterman's TV show in March 1984.

Although he plays for the big Boston side, McHale is from Hibbing, Minnesota, and, according to a friend, 'Hibbing is what Kev is all about. You can take Kevin McHale out of Hibbing but you can't take Hibbing out of Kevin McHale.'

McHale described his brief encounter with Bob Dylan (quoted in the *Minneapolis Tribune* 10 February 1985) thus:

'. . . But here's only one famous person I've met that matters. I was walking off court at Madison Square Garden and looked into the stands, and there he was. As I approached I was practically speechless, which says a lot for me. I walked up to him and said, "Dylan." And Bob Dylan smiled at me and said "Hibbing." Now that was really neat.'

1980s: Dylan and the Making of USA-for-Africa

Having been stunned by the Ethiopian situation and impressed by the efforts of Band Aid, the man for whom Bob Dylan played harmonica on his first-ever venture into a professional recording studio (June 1961) – Harry Belafonte – is determined to get something going in America too.[119] He asks manager Ken Kragen for advice, and Kragen, predictably, suggests a record.

Kragen used to manage the late Harry Chapin, himself a crusader against world hunger. Now, in addition to Belafonte, Kragen manages wealthy Lionel Richie and fabulously wealthy Kenny Rogers (and therefore has a bob or two himself). Kragen puts the idea to Rogers and Richie, and both are keen to respond. The ball is rolling. By 22 January 1985, the song that is needed has been written, but not yet polished up, by Richie and Michael Jackson, and arrangements have been made to get something down on tape.

On 22 January, then, in Kenny Rogers' Lion Share Recording Studio on Beverly Boulevard, there is a recording session to get the basic instrumental track down. They have six takes. When the backing is to producer Quincy Jones' satisfaction, Michael Jackson and Lionel Richie have to add a guide lead vocal. The idea then is to duplicate this onto fifty cassettes, to be sent out to the invited potential performers, so that they'll be familiar with the song before the upcoming main recording session.

On this guide version, the lyrics aren't finished. 'There's a chance we're taking/We're taking our own lives' is causing some worries. The second line sounds suicidal, the first self-congratulatory. Richie changes the second 'taking' to 'saving', while Jones comes up with 'There's a choice we're making'. This version of the song also has a chorus of gobbledegook: 'sha-lum, sha-lingay'. But by 1.30 a.m. this demo is wrapped up.

Two days later, the fifty cassettes are sent out to all the artists by Federal Express, which provides its delivery services free. With each cassette is a letter from Quincy Jones addressed to 'My Fellow Artists':

> The cassettes are numbered, and I can't express how important it is not to let this material out of your hands. Please do not make copies, and return this cassette by the night of the 28th. In the years to come, when your children ask, 'What did Mommy and Daddy do for the war against world famine?' you can say proudly that this was your contribution.

On 25 January there is an administrative meeting, with Kragen as concerned as Jones had been to stress the need for absolute secrecy:

> The single most damaging piece of information is where we're doing this. If that shows up anywhere we've got a chaotic situation that could totally destroy the project. The moment a Prince, a Michael Jackson, a Bob Dylan – I guarantee you! – drives up and sees a mob around that studio, he will never come in.

Secrecy is ensured, and Bob Dylan does come in. He arrives pretty early, soon after nine o'clock, on the evening of 28 January. Michael Jackson, Billy Joel and Ray Charles are there already: 'Bob Dylan slouches in, stone-faced, and sits down in the seat closest to the door.' He has just walked under Quincy Jones' sign which reads 'Please Check Your Egos At The Door'. The session is at the A & M studios, across the road from the Shrine Auditorium, where the American Music Awards ceremony is being held the same night but is due to finish at 10 p.m. Jones hopes to get things started soon after eleven.

Few seem to have noticed the irony of tables in Studio B

groaning with $15,000-worth of roast beef, tortellini, imported cheeses, fruit and delicacies: provided free by Someone's In The Kitchen Catering, but somewhat incongruous in the circumstances.

As more and more people arrive, the studio gets noisier and Dylan is not allowed to sit silent for long:

> Bruce Springsteen arrives with no entourage, no bodyguards. He simply parked his rented car across the street from the studio, breezed by security and entered the control room, where he's smothered in giggles and hugs by the Pointer Sisters. He hugs Dylan . . .

After suffering the Springsteen hug perhaps Bob finds the Diana Ross hug more comfortable. Perhaps not: 'From a dramatic dipping hug with Quincy, Diana jumps into 'Bobby' Dylan's lap for a few minutes . . .'

Some time after 11 p.m., the recording begins – choruses first, so that none of the egoless stars will walk out if they find that vocal arranger Tom Bahler hasn't given them a solo vocal line in the verses. Each performer has been allocated a particular place to stand. Each name is on a piece of silver gaffer-tape on the risers. Egoless Diana Ross has been carefully allocated a place in the middle of the front row, between Michael Jackson and Stevie Wonder.

On the other side of Michael Jackson – between him and Paul Simon – is a space marked 'Prince'. He never shows. He'd offered to play a steaming guitar part, but was asked to do the same as everybody else. ('Fuck him. What is he? A creep' – Bob Geldof.)

After several takes of the chorus, a break is announced and the company makes for the roast beef. Video screens replay the session-so-far. LaToya Jackson (one of Michael's sisters) checks her yellow head-band and make-up. Diana Ross checks everybody's make-up. Stevie Wonder remains unimpressed.

Dylan is with Paul Simon but is confronted by Billy Joel and fiancée Christie Brinkley, who looks star-struck. She begins to babble about a new scheme – Fashion For Africa: models and designers pooling their talents to relieve world hunger. Unfortunately Billy Joel is not star-stuck, and hugs Dylan.

At one in the morning, the chorus reconvenes: but there's a problem with the 'sha-lum, sha-lingay' line. Stevie Wonder has an idea. Instead of 'sha-lum, sha-lingay', why not a line in Swahili? Waylon Jennings figures that no good ole boy ever sang in Swahili and leaves the studio, never to return. Bob Geldof points out that Ethiopians don't speak Swahili (more properly, they don't speak KiSwahili). Michael Jackson votes to keep the 'sha-lum sha-lingay' line. But then he would, wouldn't he? He wrote the line in the first place.

It is tried out again, but a secret and subversive coalition is forming between Paul Simon and Al Jarreau. Cyndi Lauper wants to join in. She's not sure what a subversive coalition is but it sounds like fun – specially with Al Jarreau. The manifesto is to find something *meaningful* to sing, preferably in English. Jarreau soon produces a meaningful new line: 'One world, our world.'

Michael Jackson is stunned. He never knew that songs could be so meaningful. Nothing he ever wrote made as much sense as this new Jarreau line. But the new line's main champion becomes Cyndi Lauper, who recognizes the line's depth and message: 'That's right! Ain't what we're doing trying to unite the world?'

Stevie Wonder begins to sulk. Tina Turner says she prefers 'Sha-lum, sha-lingay' anytime. The song is eventually tried with the Jarreau line, though by this time it too has been substantially changed. Now it's 'One world, our children', which Quincy Jones thinks is the best line yet. There is no information on who came up with it. Perhaps it was Quincy. To relieve his frustration at not being allowed to sing in KiSwahili, Stevie Wonder suddenly breaks into 'The Banana Boat Song'. (This is all true.) There is later speculation that this was 'a sudden tribute to Harry Belafonte, who had first suggested this benefit recording-session'. 'The Banana Boat Song' proves much more popular than 'One world, our children' and the whole chorus defects to singing 'Day-o! Day-o!' . . . Stevie Wonder cheers up.

Meanwhile Bob Geldof 'draws a map of Africa on a piece of sheet music' to explain to Bruce Springsteen 'the logistical difficulties' of famine relief, while Willie Nelson explains to Dylan the logistical difficulties of golf:

Nelson asks Bob Dylan if he plays golf. Dylan, slightly amused, replies 'No, I've heard you had to study it.' Says Willie – who has become obsessed with the game – 'You can't think of hardly anything else.'

Huey Lewis joins in this discussion with an echoing enthusiasm. Dylan remains polite. He and Willie exchange phone-numbers and tentatively plan to meet in Hawaii during school spring break with the kids, to start working on material for a mooted joint album.

(Perhaps at this point Willie mentions that the song Bob keeps calling 'When I Think Of Her' is actually called 'Why Do I Have To Choose?' Perhaps he asks Bob why he dropped it from the '84 tour set. Perhaps he also asks why Bob accidentally took the composer-credit for 'Angel Flying Too Close To The Ground' on the B-side of the 'Union Sundown' single.)

Willie Nelson is looking cleaner and smarter than anyone has ever seen him look before. He looks ten years younger and would pass for sixty-two. Bob Dylan also looks fairly well-groomed, in a smart soft-leather black bomber jacket and a light and dark grey checked shirt which could have come from Next For Men. Photographs are taken.

Between three and four in the morning, soloists start getting organized. Stevie Wonder introduces two Ethiopian women to the performers. Things proceed slowly.

'Where's Bobby Dylan?' yells Quincy. 'Let's get Bobby in here.' It is 5.30 a.m.

Dylan is taken to Stevie Wonder for a rehearsal of his solo lines: (ahem: 'There's a choice we're making/We're saving our own lives/It's true, we'll make a better day just you and me.') Stevie wants Dylan to sound like Dylan.

Dylan is tentative. Stevie is doing a better 'Dylan' than Dylan – more whining exaggeration – and explains, 'Do it more like this.' After twenty minutes of coaching from Wonder, Dylan approaches the microphone. He barely manages a mumble. Lionel clears almost everyone out. With each successive take, Dylan gets stronger – more like himself. He asks Stevie to play the piano behind him. Quincy rushes in after the take. 'That's it. That's the statement.' Dylan, unconvinced, mutters 'That wasn't any good.' Lionel tells him: 'Trust me.' As Quincy gives him a bear hug [of course] and

213

whispers, 'It's great,' Dylan finally smiles. 'Well, if you say so.'

At exactly 5.57 a.m., Dylan's lines are played back over the monitors. Lionel Richie falls flat on his back, eyes closed, then dances awhile, waving his ladies' Reebok aerobic shoes in the air. The shoes have been manufactured in Bury, England, home of *The Telegraph*. One world.

Soon after, Al Jarreau corners Dylan by the piano. He's choked up. 'Bobby,' Jarreau says, holding back tears, 'In my own stupid way I just want to tell you I love you.' Dylan slinks away without even looking at him. Jarreau walks to the door of the studio, looks back at Dylan, cries 'My idol,' bursts into tears and leaves.

Then Bruce Springsteen finally moves forward to record his solo: 'You sounded fantastic, Dylan,' he calls to Bob as he steps to the mike. Dylan leans against the wall to watch Bruce work . . . Springsteen produces a flawless first take, and it's time to leave.

Dylan, who slunk away from Al Jarreau possibly fearing another hug, cannot evade a block tackle by linebacker Bette Midler. Midler, whose earlier attempts at seducing Dylan were reported in *The Sun* in November 1982, you'll remember (in case you don't, they were unsuccessful: 'I got close . . . a couple of first bases in the front seat of his Cadillac'), is as determined as anyone to hug Bobby. This time her determination proves irresistible: 'Bette Midler hugs Dylan, tells him, "Goodnight, dearest." '

By eight o'clock everyone is on the way home. 'We Are The World' is in the can. Some weeks later a bruised and thoroughly hugged Bob Dylan appears, improbably enough, on millions of television screens in 1985 pop music programmes all over the western world.

The Mailbox Unlocked, Part 3: Letters on Live Aid

Dear *Telegraph*...

... I was watching television early last Sunday morning when I had the surprise of my life.

Three drunks came on the stage doing some of the worst cover-versions of Dylan songs I have ever heard, and apparently trying to raise cash for the starving American farmers.

I wish that for just one time you could stand inside my shoes
You'd know what a drag it is to see you.

Glyn Worwood
Gwent,
Wales

... Bob Dylan should not have mentioned the plight of US farmers in his 'Live Aid' performance.

These farmers are not dying off in their millions with distended bellies and fly-picked flesh. They are suffering indignities and injustice at the hands of their government and the banks and corporations, making their lives hard, but not impossible, to live. Their chance of survival is pretty good.

The dying in Africa have nothing to fall back on but money raised by charities and hopelessly inadequate donations from reluctant governments. The money is still not enough to avoid many more deaths. The last thing they need is an irresponsible suggestion by someone as prestigious as Bob Dylan that some of the money be diverted from them! – an appeal to American nationalism at a time when he could have appealed to American internationalism.

I am glad Bob Dylan cares about the suffering of the farmers. But it was an abuse of the amount of work Bob Geldof, and all the others who helped, had put in, that Dylan should have mentioned this other cause. An abuse of an international audience assembled for a far more urgent cause, in aid of a far more monstrous disaster.

215

His statement showed an ignorance about the scale of the African disaster which seems representative of the state of mind of the American public in general.

I do not believe that Bob Dylan does not care about the good of the world as a whole. But I do hope he hears and thinks on these complaints.

Sunniva Darcy,
Edinburgh,
Scotland

Charity is Supposed to Cover Up a Multitude of Sins

Clive Wilshin

Bob Dylan's performance at the 'Live Aid' extravaganza before an estimated TV audience of 1½ billion people on 13 July 1985 showed the singer as unwilling to conform and as obstinately unorthodox and ungovernable as ever, at the climax of an event at which the emphasis was decidedly on conformity and unity.

With the attention of, so it seemed, the entire world focused upon the Ethiopian famine disaster, Dylan decided to remind us of an issue rather closer to the uncomfortable margin of politics that we had been trying to forget all day; it was supposed to be Africa's day, and here was 'one of America's great voices of freedom' seemingly trying to sour things at the last moment by taking the opportunity to publicize somebody else's grievances, and sounding somewhat less noble, somewhat more chauvinistic and mean-spirited, than a legend ought to.

Does his apparent suggestion that charity begins at home finally consign Dylan to the reactionary knackers-yard to which several commentators have long been trying to despatch him? Or was it a timely reminder, to his fellow-Americans especially, at the end of a day on which we felt able for once to do some *good* beyond our shores, that there were still plenty of problems we would be going home to, and nearer our own doorsteps?

This is an attempt to answer these questions, and to relate Dylan's remarks to views he has expressed both recently and throughout his career.

1 Now I'm Liberal But To A Degree . . .

Charities have never had a good press from Dylan. Mr Jones, who had no idea what was going on in the world, was happy to hand over his cheque to 'tax-deductable charity organizations', and in 'Desolation Row' the Good Samaritan is a carnival performer. In a much more recent song, 'Something's Burning Baby' (from 1985's sharply-titled album *Empire Burlesque*), Dylan refers to the pasture (of plenty?) where 'charity is supposed to cover up a multitude of sins'. This is a direct reference to the First Epistle General of Peter (IV.8), where Peter advises: 'And above all things, have fervent charity among yourselves, for charity shall cover the multitude of sins.' Dylan's change of the apostle's 'cover', meaning compensate for or redeem, to 'cover up', meaning conceal, is sardonic – and revealing, though the song was written some months before Dylan's participation in the USA-For-Africa video/single.

Dylan writes in *Tarantula*: 'Everyone knows by now that wars are caused by money and greed and charity organizations . . .' Perhaps this is, as Dylan sees it, because such organizations do not get through to the people they profess to benefit. The dirty word for Dylan here is 'organizations', which are invariably composed of faceless officials and self-congratulating liberals indulging their own consciences. As Dylan told Nat Hentoff about the people at the reception when he went to accept the Tom Paine Award from the Emergency Civil Liberties Committee:

> They were supposed to be on my side, but I didn't feel any connection with them . . . it was like they were giving money out of guilt.

In response to this discomfort, very much paralleled by his

stance at 'Live Aid', Dylan's speech at the Tom Paine Award Dinner caused uproar by expressing compassion for Lee Harvey Oswald.

Liberals have been a favourite target of Dylan's throughout his career, inspiring some of his most memorable invective. That wonderful book *Tarantula* is, among other things, a witty satire on self-styled liberals not only of the Mr Jones variety but of the hip, 'rebel' variety within Dylan's own generation too: all the people – as he put it in the celebrated 1966 *Playboy* interview – more dedicated to the hunk than to the butter, to the *cause* of 'peace and racial equality' than to peace and racial equality themselves:

> hi ya'll. not much new happening. sang at the vegetarian convention my new song against meat. everybody dug it, except for the plumbers neath the stage. this one little girl fresh out of college, and i believe president of the Don't Stomp Out the Cows division of the society – she tried to push me into one of the plumbers. starts a little fracas going. but you know me, i didn't go for that one little bit . . . i understand that they're not gonna invite me back cause they didn't like the way i came on to the master of ceremonies old lady, all in all i'm making it tho. got a new song against cigarette lighters. this matchbook company offered me free matches for life, plus my picture on all the matchbooks, but you know me, it'd take a helluva lot more than that before i'd sell out – see you around nomination time

This 'letter' is signed 'your fellow rebel, kid tiger' – a rebel of phoney integrity and with no shortage of causes.

In the songs of the mid-sixties period we also find savage attacks on people who are cut off, often socially, from the real world of pain and suffering. Miss Lonely is amused at Napoleon-in-rags, and thinks she will never have to compromise with the Mystery Tramp. When she has to stop patronizing them and 'make a deal' with them, Dylan asks her how she finds the real experience of such people as opposed to the kicks gained vicariously off their backs. Miss Lonely – with this romanticized, bogus interest in characters in whose eyes she soon finds little romanticism – points up Dylan's view of many liberals as being unable to understand those in need, because they don't need to 'make a deal' with them. As he once put it explicitly: 'People who can't conceive of how others hurt, they're trying to change the world.'

Dylan's mistrust of liberals gets expanded expression in a far more recent statement:

> It's very popular nowadays to think of yourself as a 'liberal humanist'. That's such a bullshit term. It means *less* than nothing.[120]

This hostility to the sort of liberalism Americans always equate with being 'on the left', together with his silence on topical issues at many points in his career, has led to Dylan periodically being accused of being or becoming a reactionary.

However, scrutiny of his songs and his press statements over the years shows that while he has rejected the idea that an artist must have ready-made opinions of all subjects (a nonsense the press imposes on every public figure), and has always been unwilling to play spokesperson for any orthodoxy, Dylan has been strongly consistent in his own views, giving in on the whole neither to reactionary nor radical dogma.

2 *Seems Like Every Time You Turn Around There's Another Hard-luck Story That You're Gonna Hear . . .*

In Joan Baez's 'Live Aid' appearance, she welcomed the 'children of the eighties' (as she patronizingly calls us, or some of us) to the 'Woodstock of your generation, and it's long overdue'.

Dylan, of course, decided to absent himself from Woodstock, and has recently poured scorn on that last manifestation of the love-generation's revolutionary innocence. Talking to Mick Brown in 1984 about the sixties, he regrets that by the end of the decade, the idealism of the earlier years had been 'suffocated' by mass communications:

> The TV media wasn't so big then. It's like the only thing people knew was what they knew; then suddenly people were being told what to think, how to behave. There's too much information.[121] It just got suffocated. Like Woodstock – that wasn't about anything. It was just a whole new market for tie-dyed T-shirts. It was about clothes. All those people are in computers now.

It was curious that Dylan, who spurned the chance to be part of Woodstock, was prepared to accept top billing at 'Live Aid', in the success of which mass communications, especially the TV medium he so despises as an opinion-moulder, played such a crucial part.[122] And despite his disparagement of 'liberal humanists', he was of course implicitly introduced as one himself, and as a relic from the Woodstock generation: 'one of America's great voices of freedom'. But though Dylan had agreed to be there, he clearly felt no sense of satisfaction at the prospect, and consistently-held views on his part make this understandable.

As well as the performances of the stars, 'Live Aid' also broadcast the CBS-TV news clip, introduced by David Bowie, which 'starred' the supposedly real concerns of the day. But television is an interesting medium because it allows us to 'enjoy' worldwide tragedy from the comfort of our own front rooms. The scenes on our flatter, squarer screens both demonstrate and deny our sympathy. We can see the blood of victims in technicolor and hear their screams in stereo, but we are denied the power to act or intervene. Cut off from the real situation, we tend ultimately to feel indifferent.

This is brilliantly demonstrated by Dylan in the *Desire* album's most underrated song, 'Black Diamond Bay'. After taking six verses to involve us and make us care about the curious collection of characters in the tale, and the disaster (an earthquake) that befalls them, he suddenly changes focus, switching to being someone seeing only a TV news version of the dénouement to these events, and thus dramatically pulling the carpet of involvement from under us:

> I was sitting home alone one night
> In LA watchin' old Cronkite on the
> 7 o'clock News.
> It seems there was an earthquake there
> Left nothing but a Panama hat and a
> Pair of old Greek shoes.
> Didn't seem like much was happening
> So I turned it off and
> Went to grab another beer.
> Seems like every time you turn around
> There's another hard luck

220

Story that you're gonna hear.
And there's really nothing anyone can say.
And I never did plan to go anyway
To Black Diamond Bay.

Granted, it was harrowing TV footage that alerted people in the west to the Ethiopian famine in the first place and prompted Geldof and others to action: but as everyone tacitly understood, what made it possible for a response as vast as 'Live Aid' to come from that was the very *uniqueness* of that harrowing footage *being* harrowing. The subsequent success of 'Live Aid' was that it at least persuaded people that they could do something other than simply switch off (the TV, and mentally: our mental pictures disappearing soon after our TV ones). But by then even the impact of the original footage was considered to have faded – for, as Don Watson pointed out in *NME*, the CBS-TV news pictures incorporated into 'Live Aid' itself were not allowed to speak for themselves. We were further distanced from the events by overdubbed pop music, interspersed with howls from the starving children. To quote Watson, '. . . there was something genuinely pornographic about ladling over [the pictures] the thick syrup of a pop soundtrack.'

To the American viewer idly flipping through the channels, it must have seemed like the most sensationalist pop video ever made. As the song –The Cars' 'Who's Gonna Drive You Home' – had absolutely nothing to do with the pictures, it would indeed have made a perfect video. Perhaps this indicates why Dylan has moved so hesitantly into the video age.

Dylan has said that he uses words to 'make the feelings real'. Television images satisfy the eyes' need but don't really appeal to the heart in the way that words and music can. TV images cannot bring the tragedy of human suffering back home, though 'Live Aid' was able to make, with the essential aid of television, a magnificent short-term gesture to the starving.

3   Highway 61 Revisited – We Are The World?

Dylan's remarks at 'Live Aid' should also be seen in the contexts of some of his comparatively recent remarks about what he calls 'globalism' – and of some of the songs from *Infidels*.

'Globalism' is partly an effect of the growth of mass-communications and of the media so derided in the Mick Brown interview quoted above. Dylan uses the term to include the economic colonization that is an inevitable effect of Western capitalism, and he decries the loss of cultural identity that results from the commercial exploitation of the 'One World' ideology:

> Everything is computerized now; it's all computers. I see that as the beginning of the end. You can see everything going global. There's no nationality anywhere – no 'I'm this, I'm that': we're all the same, all working for one peaceful world, blah, blah, blah.

We're all the same. 'It aint no use a-talking to me/It's just the same as talking to you.' 'You say you're better than no-one and no-one is better than you.'

Nothing to win and nothing to lose. There's no more 'I'm this, I'm that'. Expanding technology has already eroded rural folk culture in North America and the rest of the developed world. Dylan acknowledged this by picking up the electric guitar and 'going global' himself.

The title-track of *Highway 61 Revisited* takes a humorous look at this frontier erosion that has claimed America and replaced its old 'folk' communities with a new 'global' people. As Dylan explained in 1978, the Highway 61 in the song unites not just all places north to south, but past, present and future as well; there is no place or time that can preserve its own identity, that is not corrupted and commercialized by the growth of mass communications, symbolized in the song by one of those Great American Highways which stretch for vast distances through the States.

In 1984, Dylan chose to open his European concerts with a timely revival of this song. And was it not his parallel hostility to the globalizing of everywhere which caught the Dylan of *Infidels* (1983) appearing to back narrow nationalist concerns, even while raising that oppositely-focused notion that 'patriotism is the last refuge to which a scoundrel clings'?

Dylan had first linked his notion of a spiritually weakened and morally depressed America with that of the loss of her economic independence, in these notorious, xenophobic lines from 'Slow Train':

All that foreign oil
Controlling American soil
Look around you, it's just bound to make you embarrassed
Sheiks walkin' around like kings
Wearing' fancy jewels and nose-rings
Deciding America's future from Amsterdam and Paris

and there is a similar xenophobic *Zionism* firing off furiously
all through 'Neighborhood Bully'. But Dylan's argument in the
latter song is one easier for the left to sweep impatiently aside
than to answer, while the anti-Arab stance of those lines from
'Slow Train' is simply unworthy of everything the real Bob
Dylan stands for. This is not just generalization: against this
aberrant racism can be set not only Dylan's career-long fight for
racial equality in America but specific instances of this Jewish
American's effective *pro*-Arabism.

Two examples. One: in 'Got My Mind Made Up', from 1986's
Knocked Out Loaded LP, his first release since Reagan tried to
bomb Gaddhafi out of existence, Dylan doesn't hesitate to
declare his position – and with humour too – in a spirited
two-fingers to Reaganism, the like of which you'll look for in
vain in the work of America's more modishly working-class-
hero troubadours:

I'm going off to Libya
There's a guy I gotta see
He's been working there three years now
In an oil-refinery
I got my mind made up!

And listen to how purposively unAmerican (how correct) is
Dylan's pronunciation of the word 'Libya'. This carries his
recognition that American xenophobia has given the very *word*
'Libya' a power to provoke apoplexy; he knows that the way he
says it maximizes its clout of outrage. Two: Dylan's openness to
the influence of that superstar of the Middle East, Om Kalsoum
(she is Egyptian), to whom Dylan has more than once paid
tribute – and this is a real *cultural* openness not necessarily easy
for the Westerner to achieve, as you might concede if you've
heard any Om Kalsoum recordings. Perhaps this can be allowed
to balance out those other oil-slicked lines from the earlier song.

At any rate, it is to roughly the opposite theme from the one explored in 'Slow Train' that Dylan returns on the *Infidels* song 'Union Sundown'. Instead of deploring 'foreign' economic power being wielded over America, Dylan turns to an examination of America's neo-colonial power and its devastating effect on the poor everywhere.

This has been a widely-miscomprehended song. To our old-style socially aware music press (as opposed to the new-style gossip-pop press, for whom Dylan's sin is not his politics but his lack of eighties hits), Dylan doesn't do much to endear himself:

> I hear a lot of people complainin' that there is no work:
> I say 'whaddaya say that for? . . .'

This is a provocative couple of lines – but designed to provoke: to try, as Dylan has consistently done, to stop people thinking in great blocks of the ready-made and second-hand.

Yet 'Union Sundown' itself is nothing if not concrete. And Dylan actually uses terms like 'capitalism' as though they were meaningful, rather than dismissing them as stultifying labels, part of the 'surface waste' that gets deposited above the *real* issues – which were, before, always about individual spiritiuality and collective responsibility rather than political ideology. In *Street Legal*'s 'No Time To Think' (1978), for instance, 'socialism/ hypnotism' and 'patriotism/materialism' were simply part of the medley of siren voices that hindered the pilgrim with their false charms on the road to his spiritual calvary. In *Slow Train Coming*'s 'When You Gonna Wake Up?' Marx and Kissinger were tying us into knots and keeping us asleep to the real issues.

'Union Sundown', however, clearly cites capitalism as a force to be reckoned with: the lawless creed that knows no geographical or moral boundaries and applies the ruthless dictum 'It don't count 'less it sells' regardless of social cost, either in jobs at home or neo-colonialism in the Third World where a man or woman earns 'thirty cents a day'.

> What's thirty cents a day? He don't need the thirty cents a day. I mean, people have survived for six thousand years without having

to work for slave wages for a person who comes down and . . . well, actually it's just colonization.

But, see, I saw that stuff first hand, because where I come from they *really* got that deal good, with the ore.

Q: In Minnesota, on the Iron Range, where you grew up?

Yeah. *Everybody* was workin' there at one time. In fact ninety per cent of the iron for the Second World War came out of those mines, up where I'm from. And eventually they said: 'Listen, this is costing too much money to get this out. We must be able to get it someplace else.' Now the same thing is happening . . . with other products.

Dylan comes close here to putting into the mouths of the mining bosses the very words he attributed to them in his 1963 lament for the town of his birth, 'North Country Blues':

> They complain in the East they are payin' too high
> They say that your ore aint worth diggin'
> That it's much cheaper down in the South American towns
> Where the miners work almost for nothin'.

Almost for nothin'. Thirty cents a day. These two songs, though separated by more than two decades, seem companions, and show the clear consistency of a significant strand in Dylan's thinking.

But there is development too. In 'North Country Blues' the protagonist is a female working-class victim of precisely the political system denounced in 'Union Sundown' by the male middle-class observer. The heavy echo put on the vocal of 'Union Sundown' highlights the distanced, commentator's stance – giving the impression that the song might be a proclamation over the public address system at a political gathering.

Unlike the narrator of the earlier song, the narrator of 'Union Sundown' is compromised. Concerned at the greed that has corrupted his own country, he is also aware that he has benefited from its exploitation of others' labour and resources. His every material possession is evidence of his own part in America's guilt. This is a 'protest' song in which the protester's hands are dirty – perhaps the only honest protest that an American can now make.

225

Of course, having once got hold of the wrong end of 'Union Sundown's' stick as many reviewers did, one might readily misinterpret the song's chorus:

> Well, it's sundown on the Union
> That was made in the USA

(a neat pun this, for 'Made In The USA' is the only label the song's narrator cannot find on any of his goods.)

> Sure was a good idea
> Till greed got in the way.

That 'greed' is deliberately not pinned down as the province of any one faction, but it isn't intended that the main force of that 'greed' should fall on the unions, and granted that Dylan's denunciation of capitalism is the loud main theme of the song, so much misinterpretation can hardly have been anticipated.

The Union that was 'Made In The USA' is the original union of the thirteen states, which was the 'good idea' of people like Jefferson, now 'turning over in his grave'.

> Right now in the States, and most other countries, there's a big push on to make a global country – one big country – where you get all the raw materials from one place, assemble them someplace else, and sell them in another place, and the whole world is just all controlled by the same people, you know?

It's easy to see without looking too far that not much is really sacred. Even the moon is up for grabs. Soon 'even your home garden is gonna be against the law'. Jefferson's dream, the American dream, is now lurching from one absurd folly to another. Meanwhile, back on the Third World ranch, the poor must face the reality of their exploitation, for:

> A man's gotta do what he has to do
> When he's got a hungry mouth to feed.

In denouncing 'globalism', then, Dylan remains true to his folk roots, both with his detestation of the spread of mass

226

communications and the power of the media, which are such a threat to communal identity, and with his championing of the 'little people' against the big institutions and corporations which manipulate them.

4   The Whole Wide World is Watching . . .

The world produces enough food to feed every man, woman and child.[123] Enough food is available even in those countries where so many are forced to go hungry. In Mexico, where 80% of children in rural areas are undernourished, livestock consumes more grain than the entire human population – livestock then exported to the USA to be made into hamburgers. As Dylan asks in 1978's 'Señor (Tales Of Yankee Power)' – and note that key sub-title for the song: 'Señor, Señor, can you tell me where we're headin'?'

In Bangladesh, after the 1974 floods, four million tons of rice remained in storage because people could not afford to buy it. In Europe, similarly obscene stores of 'excess' foods are given the natural-sounding prettified names 'mountains' and 'lakes':

> People starving and thirsting
> Grain elevators are bursting
> You know it costs more to store the food
> Than it do to give it.
>
> ['Slow Train', 1979]

There is enough cultivatable land in Africa to feed 270% of the population. Much of it has been laid waste by soil erosion created by short-term responses to economic pressures imposed by the developed world; and much of it is used to grow cash crops for sale to the West. Truly

> Hunger pays a heavy price
> To the falling gods of speed and steel.
>
> ['Dark Eyes', 1985]

All this said, back to 'Live Aid'. Dylan's remarks followed an aptly chosen, albeit raggedly performed 'Ballad Of Hollis Brown', and were as follows:

227

Thank you. I thought that was a fitting song for this social important occasion. You know, while I'm here I hope – I'd just like to say that I hope that some of the money that's raised for the people in Africa, maybe they could take just a little bit of it – maybe *one* or *two* million maybe – and use it, say, to pay the, er, pay the mortgages on some of the farms, that the farmers owe to the banks.

If (disregarding the fact of his choosing to sing 'Ballad Of Hollis Brown' and 'When The Ship Comes In' – the latter previously unperformed since 1964 – at either end of his address) Dylan fails here to express much sympathy for the 'people in Africa', and if his remarks seem not in keeping with the event, they do serve as a reminder that poverty is not a prerogative of the Third World and that while corporate America seeks to pretend otherwise, it is responsible for squeezing people at home too. No one else at 'Live Aid' in Philadelphia got up in front of that mammoth worldwide audience, and pointed a finger straight at American banks. Dylan's remarks also show him unafraid to stay loyal, at however unpopular a moment, to the 'poor whites' whom he championed in his old 'folkie' days (often doing so in the course of attacking the exploitation of black America: reminding us then too that poor whites are also pawns in the game of the rich).

So yes, there was an inappropriateness to Dylan's remarks – but one that has been much misunderstood. And how typical of Bob Dylan it was that he should be so uncomfortable while other stars were cooing smug, glib clichés about world peace. How typical too that he should perform, in 'When The Ship Comes In' – with, as that song puts it, 'the whole wide world . . . watchin' – such a unique, visionary hymn, with its disquietingly naked joy at the coming damnation of the 'foes' who are to be defeated by the powerless ('like Goliath they'll be conquered'), and with its stress on the joy of liberation that the ship's arrival will bring to the rest of creation.

This is a long way from 'We Are The World' – as was Dylan's shaky but moving performance of 'Blowin' In The Wind', which is somehow also uniquely his song despite so many others having recorded it. Christopher Ricks has said of this seminal Dylan composition: 'It's a lonely song . . . it's about lonely political courage.' This was the quality that seems to me to have marked Bob Dylan's performance at 'Live Aid'.

Lyrics 1962–1985: A Collection Short of the Definitive

Clinton Heylin

Why now? This is an important step; one doesn't collect his life's work on a whim. There is stock-taking to such a collection. One can find the result satisfactory and complete; one can be disappointed; ... One can judge the past by it, or the future.

> Peter Knobler on *Writings and Drawings* by Bob Dylan,[124]
> *Crawdaddy*, US, September 1973

Since the release of *Infidels* one has had the sense that, not for the first time in his long career, Dylan has been entering a period of self-reappraisal.

After *New Morning* there was a three-year hiatus. In that period, though, Dylan not only chose to collect his *Writings and Drawings* but also offered a two-album career retrospection, *More Bob Dylan Greatest Hits*. At the same time the flood of bootlegs in the early seventies afforded Dylan listeners the opportunity to put together a more complete picture of his career achievement.

Since 1983 Dylan has issued only two albums of original material (and with one, *Knocked Out Loaded*, by no means all his own work). In 1984 he toured Europe presenting a set of songs which looked back to the sixties, notably to *Highway 61 Revisited*. In 1986 he used his American tour similarly. The band was in each case very much a back-to-the-starting-point outfit.

Dylan has also lately shown some enthusiasm for talking about the past – most fondly to the *News-Tribune & Herald*, Duluth, Minnesota, but most notably in the illuminating 'Westwood One' American radio interview. This was presented as 'a retrospective', as relevant as (if less accessible than) *Biograph* in the way it offered a survey of Dylan's achievement. Since that interview Dylan has presented a high profile on television – networked by ABC on '20/20' in the States – as if to remind everyone that he is still alive and creating, and there have been abundant further interviews, two being extensive: with Scott

Cohen for *Spin* magazine (December '85) and with Cameron Crowe for the *Biograph* booklet. These offer sprawling but intriguing self-assessment, self-revelation. And now we are offered (in the words of the American publishers) a 'revised edition' of *Writings and Drawings* titled *Lyrics 1962–1985*.[125]

Are the results satisfactory and complete, or is one disappointed? I think that taking the context of the book into consideration – the fact of its being only one part of a comprehensive stock-taking, but arguably the most important part of all – what *is* a great disappointment is that there is so much evidence of carelessness in the 'revision' of *Writings and Drawings* offered here.

In 1973 the editor-in-chief at Knopf said of that earlier volume: 'I know it wasn't a rushed, overnight piece of hysteria because too many books happen that way and I can recognize the signs. There was nothing sloppy or careless or rushed or hysterical about this. It seemed to me very carefully worked, and I imagine over quite a period of time.' And although that book lacked quite a few of the poems which Dylan had donated to friends' albums and to magazines in the early days of his career, there were few omissions of important song lyrics. This time, unfortunately, some of Dylan's finest lyrics from the last dozen years *have* been omitted and, unhappily, the errors in the earlier volume which ought to have been put right for this one with careful editing still remain.

Lyrics 1962–1985 offers all of *Writings and Drawings*, including the drawings, but gone are the original dedications – replaced here with a simple 'To Narette' – and the endpapers which were included only in the hardback edition of the original book. Gone too is the jotted note grumping about 'trying to please everybody'.

We do get two 'new' prose pieces: 'Off The Top Of My Head', originally printed in the Newport Folk Festival Programme of 1965, and 'Alternatives To College', which was apparently submitted to and rejected by *Esquire* in 1965. Four pages long, this latter piece is, predictably for the period, Tarantulaesque.

Some of the 'Early Songs' are made earlier, being placed in the *Bob Dylan* section rather than under *Freewheelin'*. Incongruously, the two earliest pieces, 'Song to Woody' and 'Talking New York', are given pre-1962 composition dates.

'Dusty Old Fairgrounds', an omission from *Writings and Drawings*, is happily published here. So are 'Silent Weekend', 'Apple Suckling Tree' and 'Goin' To Acapulco', but with these three all inside the *Basement Tapes* section – which most misleadingly and for no obvious reason is now placed between *New Morning* and *Pat Garrett and Billy The Kid*!

And indeed most of the reasons for disappointment in the carelessness of *Lyrics 1962–1985* do pertain to the new part of the book, the post-1971 contents. Included here are all the songs in the volume published between *Writings and Drawings* and the new book, i.e. *The Songs Of Bob Dylan From 1966 Through 1975*,[126] plus the songs on the LPs from 1978's *Street Legal* to 1985's *Empire Burlesque*.

We also get most, but not all, of the songs from this period which have been covered by other singers, and two songs which were issued only as B-sides of Bob Dylan singles. In sum: 'Seven Days', 'Sign Language', 'Coming From The Heart', 'I Must Love You Too Much', 'Walk Out In The Rain', 'If I Don't Be There By Morning', 'Trouble In Mind', 'Let's Keep It Between Us', 'Caribbean Wind' (now issued by Dylan on *Biograph*), 'The Groom's Still Waiting At The Altar' (ditto, as well as being a B-side), 'Need A Woman' and 'Aint No Man Righteous'. However, the many omissions (noted in full at the end of this review) include such powerful unreleased songs as 'Blind Willie McTell', 'Angelina', 'Aint Gonna Go To Hell For Anybody' and 'Am I Your Stepchild?'

Moreover, there are songs which *have* been released officially yet are missing here. For example, two most recently-covered songs, 'Go Away Little Boy' and 'I Don't Want To Do It'. There's no sign either of 'Champaign Illinois', 'Jet Pilot', or the two 'new' songs from the *Renaldo & Clara* soundtrack, 'Patty's Gone To Laredo' and 'What Will You Do When Jesus Comes?'

Then there are certain lyrics which have received varying degrees of official publication and which are not here collected. These are, in the main, rewritten versions of published songs – but they are major reworkings. For example, Betsy Bowden's book *Performed Literature*[127] published the lyrics to the significantly different original (New York out-take) version of 'Idiot Wind': lyrics certainly worthy of inclusion, as are the 1976 lyrics for 'Lay Lady Lay' (which were included in the Dutch lyric-sheet to the *Hard Rain* LP, on which they can be heard) and the 1984 rewrite of 'Tangled Up In Blue', performed on the *Real Live* album and included in the Japanese release's lyric-sheet.

Certainly some revised versions stand up alongside their antecedents in terms of literary merit – the 1978 'The Man In Me', perhaps, or the '76 'If You See Her, Say Hello'; and though few people might agree with him, Dylan has said of that reworked 'Tangled Up In Blue': 'It's more like it should have been . . . the imagery is better and more the way I would have liked it than on the original . . .' [*Biograph* notes] and:

> I didn't just change it cause I was singing it one night and thought, 'Oh, I'm bored with the old words.' The old ones were never quite filled in . . . so I looked at it again, and I changed it. When I sang it the next night I knew it was right. It was right enough so that I wanted to put it down and wipe the old one out.[128]

All this raises a main issue: that it is to be regretted that a section could not have been created in the book specifically for alternative versions of songs. The nature of Dylan's art clearly allows songs to be both reworked and to be constantly reinterpreted in performance – a significant aspect of the artist's writing which is simply not acknowledged in *Lyrics 1962–1985*.

On the other hand, as with *Writings and Drawings*, in the words that *are* published within *Lyrics 1962–1985* there are variations from previously published or released versions, in addition to variations in the words to songs that have not been included on the LPs. Note for instance this passage from 'Where Are You Tonight? (Journey Thru Dark Heat)':

> A full-blooded Cherokee, he predicted it to me
> The time and the place that the trouble would start

or this, from 'If You See Her, Say Hello':

> If you get close to her
> Kiss her once for me
> I always have respected her
> For bustin' out and gettin' free

These lines, though unreleased, were printed in the songbooks of the respective LPs. We may also note that 'Trouble In Mind', 'New Pony', 'Meet Me In The Morning', 'Lily Rosemary and The Jack of Hearts' and 'Never Say Goodbye' each include a verse that did not appear on the released recorded version, although again these lyrics were given in the songbooks of the time. In each case we get the extra verse included in *Lyrics 1962–1985*.

However, other opportunities to include missing verses have not been taken. 'She's Your Lover Now', which has always lacked its final verse in print, continues to do so, despite the emergence of a complete take, now in circulation among collectors. Both 'Ballad Of Hollis Brown', and 'Aint Gonna Grieve' had extra verses (never seen since) in their original forms published in small magazines,[129] while the complete 'Watered-Down Love' also warrants inclusion, rather than the version which is shorter by virtue of the recording having been edited down for the LP. And the original copyrighted version of 'Union Sundown' had two extra verses, including a marvellous final one castigating 'The man in a mask in the White House'.

Why complete verses have not been used is unaccountable, and goes against a practice adopted in the original *Writings and Drawings* of combining lyrics from two different takes – witness, for example, 'Babe I'm In The Mood For You' which incorporates sections from both the Witmark Demo and the take finally released on *Biograph*.

There's also something odd, and a little disturbing in what it augurs, about what has happened to 'Caribbean Wind' as it appears in *Lyrics 1962–1985*. It looks as if the lyrics have been transcribed from the recording published on *Biograph* (the song has been recopyrighted 1985) – but they seem to have been misheard in several places. 'Were we sniper bait' has become, in *Lyrics*, 'Did we snap at the bait'; 'Redeemed men who have escaped from the noose' have turned into 'Arabian men'; and Dylan's lovely phrase 'chrome brown eyes' seems to have been misheard as 'lone brown eyes'. If these were indeed mistranscriptions then a major disservice has been done to an important song.

In other songs where changes have occurred in one or two lines, one can presume that this indicates Dylan's own initiative, or dissatisfaction with the original or previous version.

233

Watching this process at work is really fascinating. In the cases of 'When You Gonna Wake Up?' and 'Sweetheart Like You', for example, we find evidence that Dylan has always been dissatisfied with the LP versions. In 'When You Gonna Wake Up?' the released version has:

> There's a Man up on a cross
> And He's been crucified for you
> Believe in His power
> That's about all you got to do

In concert that verse became:

> There's a Man on the cross
> And He been crucified
> You know who He is
> And you know why He died

In *Lyrics* we get a further change, to:

> There's a Man up on a cross
> And He's been crucified
> Do you have any idea why
> Or for who He died?

The opening lines of 'Sweetheart Like You' seem to have been equally unsatisfactory. In the original unreleased studio take we are told that the boss has 'gone to that lighthouse beyond the bend'. In the released version it's the vaguer 'He gone north for a while', and *Lyrics* has:

> He gone North, he ain't around
> They say that vanity got the best of him
> But he sure left here after sundown.

There's another change later in this same song, making for a *slightly* less chauvinistically brazen verse than before:

> A woman like you should be at home
> That's where you belong
> Watching out for someone who loves you true
> Who would never do you wrong.

234

Some of the other changes offered in *Lyrics* are interesting too. The opening section of 'The Groom's Still Waiting At The Altar' has changed – in this case because it does incorporate two versions (1980 live and 1981 studio), producing the tremendous

> Prayed in the ghetto with my face in the cement
> Heard the last moan of a boxer, seen the massacre of the innocent
> Felt around for the light switch, became nauseated
> She was walking down the hallway while the walls deteriorated.

Perhaps the most intriguing version of a song in *Lyrics 1962–1985* is that of 'Need A Woman'. Although the version cleared by Dylan's office for publication in *The Telegraph* (issue 19, 1985) and the lyrics printed to accompany Ry Cooder's recording of this song (on his LP *The Slide Area*) are identical, Cooder has claimed that for his version he changed some of Dylan's lyrics. Now of the other two known versions of 'Need A Woman' (i.e. Dylan's 1981 demo-tape recording, and the printed lyric sheet which was sent out to accompany that demo and yet had very different words) *neither* corresponds at all closely to Cooder's, which suggests either a major rewrite or that Cooder's source was different. Although the *Lyrics* rendering is close to Cooder's, it is far from identical. The entire last verse as on his recording is omitted (and appears in neither other version), suggesting that it was this which was Cooder's contribution. There are a few more minor changes too: we have wet trenches instead of wet mouths, for example, and we are given this attractive variation: 'Seen you turn the corner, seen your boot-heels spark'.

'Coming From The Heart' (co-written with Helena Springs) gets a couple of 'new' verses and perhaps these additions explain the re-copyrighting of the song in 1979, six months after its composition. Minor changes are to be found in the foreshortened 'Watered-Down Love' and in 'Legionnaire's Disease' (perhaps not so minor in this case, with maidens turning into old maids and the loss of the priceless simile 'Whatever it was, it hit him like a tree'); and there's an awful rewrite at the end of 'Isis': 'She said "You gonna stay?", I said "Yeah, I jes might." '[130]

235

Curiously too, 'I Must Love You Too Much' as published in *Lyrics* would seem to be predominantly Greg Lake's work rather than Dylan's: it corresponds neither with the version Dylan performed in concert nor with the version published in *The Telegraph* issue 17. This would seem to expose sloppiness indeed.

The song that it is most surprising to see changes in at all (suggesting that Dylan himself is far from careless in these matters) is surely 'Silent Weekend'. This song, as far as I'm aware, has never been released by anyone, yet it is included in both *The Songs Of Bob Dylan From 1966 Through 1975* and here in *Lyrics 1962–1985*, even though the four other songs copyrighted at the same time have all been omitted. As obscure a song as this is, it has had the last three lines of its second and third verses changed (though in my opinion these alterations add nothing to the song).

And what interesting changes 'Goin' To Acapulco' has been through, since its publication in *The Songs Of* – with neither printed version bearing much resemblance to the song as it appears on *The Basement Tapes*. That LP release has as the last four lines of the first verse:

> It's a wicked life but what the hell
> Everybody's got to eat
> And I'm just the same as anyone else
> When it comes to scratching for my meat

In *The Songs Of* this has become:

> It's a wicked life but what the hell
> Everybody's got to keep it neat
> And I'm just the same as the Taj Mahal
> When it comes to standing on my meat

while for *Lyrics* the force of that Taj Mahal has been retained yet shifted – made less incongruous, more physically present – as Dylan moves the song away from that patent Basement Tape milieu, giving instead:

It's a wicked life but what the hell
The stars ain't falling down
I'm standing outside the Taj Mahal
I don't see no-one around

The changes we're taken through in the second verse are as substantial. On the LP version we hear:

I just make it down to Rose Marie's
And get something quick to eat
It's not a bad way to make a living
And I ain't complainin' none
For I can [go] my plum and drink my rum
And then go on home and have my fun.

In *The Songs Of* (in this case removing it already from its Basement world) we read:

I just make it down to Rose Marie's
On my faithful white steed
It's not a bad way to get there
And I aint complainin' none
If the wheel don't drop and the train don't stop
I'm bound to meet the sun

while in *Lyrics 1962–1985* this is further amended, the second of these lines becoming ' 'Bout a quarter to three' and the fifth 'If the clouds don't drop and the train don't stop'.

As if mystery was meant to be an integral element in *Lyrics*, two albums-worth of songs are arranged in a very unusual order. *Infidels* has 'License To Kill' coming after 'Jokerman' and 'Man of Peace' moved to seventh place, after 'I And I'.

The running-order of the *Blood On The Tracks* material is even stranger: 'You're Gonna Make Me Lonesome When You Go', 'You're A Big Girl Now', 'Tangled Up In Blue', 'Simple Twist Of Fate', 'Shelter From The Storm', 'Meet Me In The Morning', 'Lily Rosemary And The Jack Of Hearts', 'Idiot Wind', 'If You See Her, Say Hello' and 'Buckets Of Rain'. (Except that 'Idiot Wind' and 'If You See Her, Say Hello' would need swapping round, this running-order is actually reversed alphabetical order: but why?)

Finally, when we come to the poems and prose pieces, there are similar unaccountable inconsistencies. The sleeve-notes for *Desire* have rightly been included but the more extensive writing Dylan published on the original album sleeve of *Planet Waves* has not – a bad oversight indeed. And, as mentioned earlier, there are many poems and prose pieces from the early years missing here, and it is likely that these omissions simply show up poor research.

Bob Dylan is a major literary artist. Whatever other claims may be made for him he is a great user of words. A volume which offers those words to posterity ought to have been more carefully edited than *Lyrics 1962–1985* has been.

The editor of the next revision might note the following appendix of omissions and consider the appropriateness or otherwise of claims for their inclusion.

Meanwhile, and until it becomes possible to publish the unabridged annotated Bob Dylan, *Lyrics 1962–1985* will have to do.

Appendix: Omissions From Lyrics 1962–1985

Here are:

1   Songs that have had official record release (not always by Dylan himself) and yet are excluded.

2   Songs that have had some form of official publication elsewhere.

3   Songs where there are earlier alternate versions, and where these variations are substantial enough to warrant inclusion. (In the case, say, of 'Caribbean Wind', the 1980 version is effectively a wholly different song.)

4   Songs where there are later alternate versions – i.e. those songs which Dylan has changed substantially in concert performance. (Most songs in this section have been tampered with more than once.)

5   Those songs which have been included yet changed significantly for publication in *Lyrics* (so that there are omissions of known passages from previous versions).

6   Those songs which have been included but for which there are known extra verses *not* included in the book.

7 Songs which I believe have been copyrighted but which have still been excluded from *Lyrics*. (There are a number of Dylan-Springs songs amongst these, plus many leftovers from what were at time of the book's publication the two most recent studio albums *Infidels* and *Empire Burlesque*. No extra (i.e. unreleased) tracks have been listed for either record. In the case of *Infidels* this seems an especially poor time to break with the established practice of including extra tracks from LP sessions, since Dylan kept back significant amounts of what many people feel is more major and important work than much of the contemporaneous material chosen for release on the album.

8 All excluded poem and prose pieces, including several written interview-features which seem to me valid as prose pieces written by Dylan.

9 Arrangements or versions of 'public domain' songs where Dylan has claimed copyright and/or published them as being his own arrangements in past songbooks but which have nevertheless been excluded from the book. Certainly 'Rocks and Gravel' and 'Gospel Plow' are – or are not! – as much Dylan songs as are 'Corrina Corrina' and 'All Over You'. (I do not list cases where the arrangement is essentially of music rather than words.)

10 Excluded songs known to be by Dylan though apparently not copyrighted.

11 Those songs (and a poem) which may well be by Dylan, but for which there is no definite evidence of his authorship.

NB. Some items will therefore get more than one listing: e.g. the omitted version of 'Idiot Wind' is an Earlier Alternate Version, and is also a Song Published Officially Elsewhere; the 1984 'Masters Of War' is a Later Alternate Version and also (on *Real Live*) a Song Officially Released.

1 Songs Officially Released

All I Really Want To Do [1978], All The Tired Horses, Champaign Illinois, Go Away Little Boy, Going Going Gone [1978], I Don't Want To Do It, Jet Pilot, Masters Of War [1984], Patty's Gone To Laredo, Talkin' Devil, What Will You Do When Jesus Comes?, You Ain't Goin`Nowhere [1971].

2 Songs Officially Published Elsewhere

Idiot Wind [earlier version], I Must Love You Too Much, Lay Lady Lay [1976], Let's Keep It Between Us, Need A Woman, Talkin' Hava Naghila Blues, Tangled Up In Blue [1984].

3 Alternate Versions – Earlier

Abandoned Love, Caribbean Wind, Clean Cut Kid, Corrina Corrina, Do Right To Me Baby, Dreadful Day, Driftin' Too Far From Shore, From A Buick 6, The Groom's Still Waiting At The Altar, Hurricane, Idiot Wind, If You See Her Say Hello, Jokerman, Need A Woman, Paths of Victory, Phantom Engineer, Slow Train, Something's Burning Baby, Sweetheart Like You, Tangled Up In Blue.

4 Alternate Versions – Later

All I Really Want To Do [1978], Billy 4, Buckets of Rain, Going Going Gone [1976], Hero Blues [1974], If You See Her Say Hello [1976, 1978], Knockin' On Heaven's Door [1975, 1981], The Man In Me [1978], Masters Of War [1984], Simple Twist Of Fate [1975, 1978, 1980, 1981, 1984], Tangled Up In Blue [1978, 1984], Tonight I'll Be Staying Here With You [1975], When You Gonna Wake Up [1984].

5 Published in Lyrics But With Very Different Words

Apple Suckling Tree, Coming From The Heart, Goin' To Acapulco, I Must Love You Too Much, I Shall Be Free, Killing Me Alive, Minstrel Boy, Need A Woman [× 2, as it were], Sign On The Cross, Silent Weekend, Sweetheart Like You, When I Paint My Masterpiece, You Angel You.

6 Songs with Known Extra Verses

Ain't Gonna Grieve, Ain't No Man Righteous, Ballad Of Hollis Brown, Billy 7, Heart Of Mine, Knockin' On Heaven's Door, Love Is Just A Four Letter Word, Need A Woman [though this verse is probably not Dylan's but Ry Cooder's], Pressing On, Sara, She's Your Lover Now, Union Sundown, Watered Down Love, Ye Playboys and Playgirls.

7 Other Copyrighted Songs

Ain't Gonna Go To Hell For Anybody, All American Boy, Angelina, Baby Give It Up, Blind Willie McTell, Bourbon Street, Brown Skin Girl, Call Letter Blues, City Of Gold, Coverdown Breakthrough, Death Is Not The End, Don't Ever Take Yourself Away, Driftin' Too Far From Shore, Enough Is Enough, Foot Of Pride, Fur Slippers, Goodbye Holly, Her Memory, I Can't Leave You Behind, I'm Not There (1956), Jesus Is The One, Julius and Ethel, Lord Protect My Child, More Than Flesh and Blood, New Danville Girl, On A Rainy Afternoon, Responsibility, Santa Fe, Someone's Gotta Hold Of My Heart, Someone Else's Arms, Stand By Faith, Stop Now, You Treat Me Like A Stephchild, Tell Me, Tell Me The Truth One Time, There's A Thief On The Cross, The Wandering Kind, What's The Matter, Who Loves You More, Wild Wolf, Without You, Ye Shall Be Changed, Yonder Comes Sin, You Changed My Life.

8 Poems and Prose Pieces

Blowin' In The Wind [*Hootenanny*, March 1964], The Bomb Song, For Dave Glover, Endpapers and prologue in *Writings and Drawings*, In The Wind [*Hootenanny*, December 1963], In The Wind [Peter, Paul & Mary LP cover], *LA Free Press* spoof interview [April 1965], A Letter to *Broadside*, Letter to Ralph J. Gleason, Letters to Tami Dean, Lifeline [*NME*, May 1965], A Message to the ECLC, Pageant [March 1965], Sleeve notes for The New World Singers, Sleeve notes to *Planet Waves*, Sleeve notes for Ric von Schmidt, Talkin' Folklore Center, Ten Things I Like [*Rolling Stone*, July 1969], Walk Down Crooked Highway.

9 Arrangements Copyrighted and/or Published in Songbooks

Baby Let Me Follow You Down [1966], Blessed Is The Name Of The Lord Forever, Gospel Plow, Man Of Constant Sorrow, Pretty Peggy-O, Rocks and Gravel, That's Alright Mama [1964], What Kind of Friend Is This?

10 Uncopyrighted Songs

All You Have To Do Is Dream*, Baby Won't You Be My Baby*, Ballad Of Easy Rider, [not, in this case, an uncopyrighted song per se, but a song where one verse, the first, was actually written by Dylan but on which he waived his copyright and by-line], Ballad Of The Gliding Swan [aka Swan On the River], Blackjack Blues, Bound To Win, Cuban Blockade, Gates of Hate, I Was Young When I Left Home, Kingsport Town, Medicine Sunday, One-Eyed Jacks [aka Queen Of His Diamonds], Ramblin' Down Thru The World, Troubled And I Don't Know Why. [*At the time of writing [December 1986] these are newly-emerged Basement Tape songs of unstated authorship but almost certainly Dylan's.]

11 *Compositions Which May Be By Dylan but Which Cannot Be Verified As Such*

All You Have To Do Is Dream, Baby Ain't That Fine*, Don't You Try Me Now*, Down On Me*, Gonna Get You Now*, I Can't Make It Alone*, I Love You Darling, I'm Alright*, Lock Your Door*, A Night Without Sleep*, An Observation Revisited (poem), One For The Road, One Man's Loss*, One More Night, Talking Hugh Brown, Take It Or Leave It, They Talk About Me, This Way That Way, Try Me Little Girl*, You'd Love Me To Go, Your Rocking Chair. (* At time of writing these are newly-emerged Basement Tape songs of unknown authorship.)

The Mailbox Unlocked, Part 4

Dear *Telegraph* . . .

. . . My dear friends: my homeland is Hungary. I speak another language but my thoughts are very similar to yours. Bob Dylan is one of my models. I love his songs. I have many records from Dylan and I like to listen to him many times. I feel his music and try to understand what he says in essence. So I like when there are matching songbooks in the record jackets because it's a big assistance to understand the message of his songs. I learn and read English a lot but I don't speak and write well and I don't understand the modern living language and the slang. I used to translate Dylan's poems with dictionaries if I have texts. I used to make translations of poems because you cannot read Dylan's lyrics in Hungarian. You know that many people would like to read Bob Dylan in Hungary but unfortunately there isn't a book.

I am very fond of poetry. I read all kinds of poems. And Bob Dylan's poetry is the greatest to me in our days, which tells me about the world and people and his feelings. He warns me about the false, worthless and stupid things, but he shows me the right, precious and true things too. And his music transmits all that to me, through the frontiers and régimes, quicker than anything else.

Bokor Laszlo
Veszprem
Hungary

. . . I like Bob Dylan's music because it enlightens my soul. I regard him as one of the greatest songwriters in the world. One of his best contributions to music is on the album *Slow Train Coming*.

Though we are far away across the seas, Bob Dylan's music is *Desire*d in Zimbabwe. Yours in music power,

Lovejoy Gavaza
Bulawayo
Zimbabwe

. . . Every now and then something happens which puts the whole business into perspective. When I played the Keith Green album, with Dylan's brief harmonica solo on one track, to a fellow collector we laughed ourselves silly. Ten dollars for a few seconds' worth of harp playing! We realized we must both be mad. Then he sent away for it too.

Christer Svensson
Molkom
Sweden

Fans, Collectors and *Biograph*

Roy Kelly

The title *Biograph* does suggest the summary of a life through a careful selection of songs and/or performances. The inclusion of many items previously known only to tape collectors of bootleg material further suggests an, as it were, autobiograph – with Bob Dylan himself involved in the material's selection.

Yet Dylan wasn't at all concerned in *Biograph*'s genesis. The people to thank are Bruce Dickinson of Columbia Records and Jeff Rosen, a Dylan office lawyer, whose idea it was. In *USA Today* he said that the selection was made to 'illustrate every facet of Dylan's talents.' Meanwhile Bob was saying: 'I didn't pick the material, I didn't put it together and I haven't been very excited about it.' (Geminis blow hot and cold: I don't know if you've heard that . . .)

So what is it? Well, it's an imposing semiotic object, designed to convey cultural messages. Here, it says, is no fly-by-night Bobby-come-lately on the Adult Oriented Rock scene; here is no lightweight pop flimsy. Here is an artist of weight, density and history. Here is a man who can fill a box with albums, like Wagner or Mozart or any of those old Europeans. Here is a man who can be written up in Necessary Enclosed Booklets. A man of hidden depths, replete with unearthed aural treasures. (And, at its moment of release at the end of 1985, here is the object of a marketing exercise with Christmas in its sights.)

All of this is true. And to be beamed out to a general public. It was not a tease for collectors: not the record company saying, 'Look what we have in store that we could turn loose if we wanted to.'

American reviews suggested that Columbia was trying to bridge a generation gap: that with Bob's high visibility on the 1985 scene ('USA-For-Africa', 'Live Aid' and 'Farm Aid'!) he might once again be perceived as an artist of social awareness, of 'relevance'. Older fans were imagined as wanting to renew worn out copies of songs, and younger buyers as suddenly realizing what a warehouse of goodies awaited them.

It's true that any artist desiring longevity has to keep attracting new fans, but it seemed to me that a non-Dylan fan would be unlikely to spend the money it takes to own *Biograph* on impulse; that people wanting to renew a worn-out *Blonde On Blonde* or *Desire* would do just that; and that most Dylan collectors would find the contents of *Biograph* inadequate for one reason or another. But did this cloudiness of purpose mar the collection?

In the accompanying booklet Dylan is scornful of bootleggers and tape-collectors, deploring the way they invade his privacy in order to produce sub-standard music sold at inflated prices. He compares the process to the drug trade, so strongly does he feel. In concurrent interviews to publicize release he wonders who will buy the set because those 'in the know' will already have the material. . .

(Of course in the end *Biograph* was so long in the making that even if no one had any of the rarer songs previously, almost the whole of *Biograph* itself was circulated on tape well in advance of official release! In any case surely Bob (and Jeff Rosen) must be aware that unofficial tapes and official releases are bought by the same people. Who else would bother with the *Real Live* album?)

Arguments are inevitable as to what should have been put in or left out. My own objections happen to be that more should have been included from unreleased studio material from *Shot Of Love* onwards, once it was clear to the compilers that their original target date had been missed. Celebrating twenty years' association between an artist and a record company (the initial impetus to the project) is OK when that's the relevant time-span, but once it goes by there's no reason not to update. And like most people I feel that the 1966 live acoustic and electric songs could have been increased to a whole disc's worth, although I understand the disinclination to emphasize material two decades old as if it were the only high point of a career. I regret that more *Street Legal* songs weren't included, because I've always felt that the work on that LP indicated the most fruitful direction Dylan's work could have taken had not evangelical Christianity come stepping in. And it's a shame there are no details of recording bands. And so on.

It's inevitable, yet also sterile, to whinge about what's missing. Better to note the striking way that with what's *there*, even familiar songs – I'm talking about the ones that have bred contempt – are made new. Everything having been re-mastered digitally, the sound quality is for the first time Dartington clear. Some songs are so changed by this that one wants to elevate them from minor to major. Almost everything sounds better. Some sound *different* because of the clarity. The anthem 'Like A Rolling Stone' is changed by making the acoustic guitar, organ and piano so sharp that the tempo of the piece seems to have slowed. (The drums, unfortunately, still have the dissolved quality of the stereo album mix rather than a hardness I remember from the original single – but memory may not be serving me well here.)

The immediate result, when the set came out, was the enormous pleasure of playing all of the sides through, one after the other, granted the time (and understanding companions): because no song is exactly as it was. Even something previously judged inconsequential, like 'If Not For You', can seem transformed with newly revealed felicities of voice and instruments.

What *this* suggests is that a better (or subsequent) way of marketing Bob Dylan and his record company's twenty-plus years together would be to do what Capitol have done with Frank Sinatra: digitally remaster the entire back-catalogue. That way old fans are more certain to replace their scuffed, worn-out copies, and the all-important new blood might better be drawn to the tracks too. It's not an idea that can wait until Bob hits seventy.

Meanwhile, along with the records, the two booklets which are part of the *Biograph* package are a vital part of *its* idea. They do offer fresh (in both senses) information:[131] indeed a treasure-trove. Hands up those who knew before that Johnny Ray was an idol of the young Bob Zimmerman, or that a Brecht poem provided the stanzaic model for 'The Lonesome Death Of Hattie Carroll', or that Dylan auditioned some of *New Morning*'s songs for an Archibald MacLeish play? Well I didn't.

Despite his reservations, Dylan clearly gave willingly of his time and of his memory, and, wholly against his stance of two decades, of his family photo-album, to make the booklets worthwhile. Indeed without the booklets perhaps *Biograph* would be meaningless. If we're looking at the recent past and sampling some of Dylan's social and musical history, we need the testimony only he can give.

It's interesting that in a year when Bob was very public – playing for charitable enterprises, going to Russia, coming to London, and releasing a new studio album – the only widespread good reviews he got at all in 1985 were for *Biograph*. Even Richard Williams in *The Times*, notable in recent years for his apostate posture, and viciously dismissive of *Empire Burlesque*, smiled upon this enterprise.

Empire Burlesque did not mean much to anyone outside a small circle of friends. Nearly all the reviews were short and disagreeable. (Even *The Telegraph*'s Mailbox carried a brief, comprehensive rubbishing.) Yet that album marked a real change in Bob's approach to recording. For the first time he used current technology to supplement instruments and to shape songs: and it was clear from this as much as from recent interviews and the *Biograph* texts that his comparative lack of sales success – not only alongside Bruce Springsteen but alongside someone as evanescent as Cyndi Lauper – does bother Dylan.

More than this, it seems to affect what he thinks he can put out. A couple of times he alludes to the difficulty of placing album tracks, or having singles released which he wouldn't choose. He mentions wanting a children's album, or one of instrumentals. What are we to make of this? If he has such reduced artistic control, who holds the rest of it? And how much more material is hidden away, and what will it take to release it properly? Ah, but that way Dakota paranoia lies. We have to allow Dylan, the artist, the chief prerogative of artists – selection (and so does the record company, of course). An album doesn't exist until the songs are selected, and it seems there are always more than enough songs.

What Dylan is trying to create when the contents of an album are decided, whether in unconvinced consultation with industry jobbers or not, is always a mystery. It is a mystery we are supposed to allow to work within us. What else is art for? If Dylan can't be judged fairly on his official albums, why does he deserve the attention devoted to him by collectors of the unofficial?

(In this context – indeed in any – I find startling John

247

Hinchey's notion that Dylan deliberately left good work off *Shot Of Love*, the better to present his burnt-out case and evoke his spiritual dilemma.[132] Yet this offers a novel instance of what may be relevant in reflecting on what official releases mean – and what relationship they may have to an undertaking like *Biograph*.)

Dylan can't, wouldn't want to, release everything he's ever recorded, and there is a variety of commercial and artistic forces at work on creating an album. In retrospect, some of these contexts change, the compunctions of the moment drop away. Those albums judged as failures in the past are always likely to get some degree of favourable later reassessment.

Biograph itself can help in this process. I play the sparkling remastered 'Time Passes Slowly' from the supposedly mediocre *New Morning* LP, and think how marvellous it sounds. *Saved* was quickly consigned to the cut-price bins, but here 'Solid Rock' comes out sizzling: a joyful, powerful vindication of the band-and-chorus interplay Dylan was seeking. All of Dylan's albums are afloat on critical judgements, and there everything passes, everything changes.

Dylan emphasizes this in the unusually high number of interviews given to send *Biograph* out into the world – more than at any time since *Renaldo & Clara*:

'I'll know a hundred years from now,' he says when asked about the value of the songs.

The continuum and the flow are intrinsic aspects of Dylan's creative imagination, hence the way the songs mix persons and tenses to produce not a linear chronology but an artistic no-time where anything can happen, or might already have happened. 'When did Abraham break his father's idols,' Bob asks in the song notes: 'I think it was last Tuesday.'

What *Biograph* does is recreate in its rag-bag of contents, its hotch-potch attempts at thematic tracking, the random nature of memory. Major nuzzles against minor, screaming electric against wistful folk. What makes this piquant is that it replicates the resources that the collector has to call on. Everything is right next to everything else, in the same dimension: just as in Collectors' Cornerland little 1961 Canadian clubs are neighbours of 1986 stadiums.

The conjunction is paradoxical, given the contrast between

248

the attitudes of mind evinced by Dylan and by the (or by at least one sort of) archetypal collector. In the *Time* interview Bob says: 'I feel like it's all right in front,' and what he seems to mean is the purpose of life. But he could equally mean the future, always looking to what is ahead and leaving the dead behind. Of a released record he says: 'I listen to it once or twice before it's out, and then once it's out I don't really listen to it anymore.' He leaves the records to their own devices because he has to make the songs new anyway every night of a tour. He says he can't name his first five albums. Compare this with the stance of one kind of collector, where so much energy, time, frustration, and, I don't doubt, love, is devoted to a hoarding of trainspotter fact. Worse: not simply fact but newsprint fact. Art becomes a paperchase, a paperchain. What shirt was he wearing on this gig? Was he present at that nightclub in 1975? Can anyone out there help, has anyone out there got it in yellowing black and white? As if fugitive clippings, misinformation and misinter- pretation are art and life. All Dylan items are accorded the same regard, and so all become trivial.

Biograph is both a monument to, and a mockery of, information-amassing. This neat box-set of records shows us that life is a mess of mistakes and more. More of what? More of more. Its greatest gift is that it shows you what it's like not to be a collector. (Dylan says those in the know won't want it because they have it already. Put it the other way around: why should collectors moan about what is or isn't included when they have everything anyway – and in first-generation copies if they're obsessive enough?)

Biograph tells you that a collector is never going to be satisfied. It also tells you that Dylan has done more than enough to satisfy anyone. All caveats noted, the *Biograph* package is impressive evidence of a prodigal largesse of talents in one individual.

The collection's second gift is to demonstrate the range and quality of singing Dylan is capable of – a useful reminder when not only can everyone in the world parody him but all too often he seems happy to do it himself. Here we can check the variety of accomplishment, from the rueful magnanimity of 'You're A Big Girl Now' to the exquisitely camouflaged, mellifluous vituperation of 'Positively 4th Street', a song perfect in the way

249

that everything works. The state of his voice is crucial to Bob Dylan's art, quite as much as his writing. I wish some of the care devoted to the 1984 re-writing of 'Tangled Up In Blue' – inferior though I still find it to the original – had been brought to its performance on *Real Live*: so pinched, mean and throwaway does it sound there. 'My little voice,' he says in the *Time* interview, and elsewhere speaks of his sense of greater achievement singing harmony – something likely to bring a wry smile to anyone knowing his duets with Joan Baez (none of which are included here).

So what *Biograph* certainly raises, in a myriad of niggles, doubts, misgivings, asides, enthusiasms and – let us say it clear – gratitude, is the issue of what it *means* to be an admirer, a fan, a critic, a collector. It invites us to reassess what response is appropriate to Bob Dylan's work.

He knows that, of course, as he knows most things surrounding him. In the song booklet he becomes most animated when railing against interpreters: 'Stupid misleading jerks sometimes these interpreters are . . . Fools, they limit you to their unimaginative mentality. They never stop to think that somebody has been exposed to experiences that they haven't been . . . contrary to what some so-called experts believe, I don't constantly "re-invent" myself – I was there from the beginning.'

A slap in the face, this, for the Chameleon Poet school of shape-changing. (Fools, jerks, interpreters? Are you talking to me? Well, I don't see anyone else around. I suspect that Bob has been reading back numbers of *The Telegraph*, and not liking much that he finds there. Could it be that these fools and jerks are also the bloodhounds of London, sniffing out his life along with his songs – London here emblematic of England, home of us interpreters by self-appointment? We get a name-check in the *Biograph* booklet, where we are referred to as 'pouring over lists': like cream perhaps or on troubled waters?)

Bob Dylan's reaction to foolish interpretation, as he sees it, is symptomatic of the peculiar, private, public, obsessive relationship performers have with audiences. Performers know more than their audiences. In 1966 Dylan was booed though he knew the music was strong and true. In 1974 the crowds were ecstatic, but it was too late: 'When we needed the acceptance it wasn't there'.

So he says, 'Don't forget John Lennon was murdered by a so-called fan – I know it gives them all a bad name but so what?' and he dislikes the mindlessness of some reaction to his work. And yet he continues to make records, to go out on tours to countries where his language is foreign, and hence his power is reduced, to present his work to a largely indifferent world.

Presumably because that's what he has to do. But if he doesn't like the stupid jerk interpreters and if fans are potential assassins, of the spirit at least, if not of the flesh, then who does he sing to? Who does he think he sings to? Who are the people who go to Dylan concerts? Fans of his? Concertgoers? Tourists?

Like all poems and songs, his are presented to whoever cares to be interested. If Dylan wanted, he could sing to friends and lovers and family alone. He doesn't choose to. Something in him needs to perform, as it needed to when he was a teenager in Hibbing. 'You got to be strong and stay connected to what started it all, the inspiration behind the inspiration, to who you were when people didn't mind stepping on you . . . easy to say, but the air gets thin at the top, you get light-headed.'

Here he sounds the note that reverberates throughout *Biograph* and the interviews done to publicize it (an effort which showed that whatever his non-involvement in its genesis, he was concerned about the project's success). What people think he is, the myth people have, the false glamour attached to the sixties: all this seems to mean little to him. The long perspective is his forté. The man whose favourite time to have lived, he says, would have been that of the biblical King David, can look back with detachment on what happened to him over two fast decades. And how fast were those first four years. Difficult not to believe in chameleons looking at the mutations from Chaplinesque cherub to Medusa The Acid Queen.

Now he looks at the current music scene with sour, cutting insight, mistrustful of the interplay between music, advertising and video, wary of synthesizer hi-tech. But he is warm and affectionate about all of the musicians who inspired him, seeing music as a chain of inspiration.

Alongside this musical common sense persona, there is also the Bob Dylan capable of saying '. . . the dead have eyes and even the unborn can see and I don't care who knows it': a little something to bear in mind when he talks about having had experiences we may not have shared, and when he complains about fans laying their own little worlds on him.

So we fans and collectors should seize upon *Biograph* as an opportunity not to be proprietorial, not to think because we may know every interviewed word he's said over the last twenty-plus years (how dreadful if someone confronted you with the same documentation) that Bob Dylan should be somehow under our control. All we should do, all we can do, is try to listen with an intelligent heart to what is produced, and to know what may make it good or bad.

Somewhere in this 'biograph' Dylan is described as the kind of man he always was: someone with a guitar and a point of view. He's also a mystery and a funny wonder, and there's no-one else like him. Bruce Springsteen is sociological and writes about what it's like to be American, coming to terms with age and flawed heroes. Bob Dylan is a mystic and writes about what it's like to he human, seeking God and coming to terms with flawed human love.

'I is another,' said that other old European, Rimbaud, and Dylan agrees with that. *Biograph* blends this view with the Americana of Whitman. So I contradict myself, he agrees in passing – I am large, I contain multitudes.

The multitudes he contains, amongst others, are us; because he has lived something that we only glimpse: an American myth and a universal one, like a fairytale of the gods. Nice Jewish storekeeper's kid is stolen by music as a child, dreams that he is Bob Dylan and sets off in a snowstorm to create the dream in the magic city, New York. New York – fabulous as Samarkand. A year or so later he has written (adapted/remembered/stolen) the folk anthem of the age – destined, paradoxically, to become part of the repertoire of every supper-club chanteuse and nylon-headed crooner in the world for a while.

And Bob Dylan, the dream come true, has been in exile ever since, travelling in the parallel world of music: professional music, that is. Recent photographs show him losing his grip on anorexic charm, looking like a bleary gypsy vampire, face baggy with booze and camera-boredom. How many shows, how many parties is it? After a while everything blurs. Especially the past.

Biograph and the interviews are attempts to retrieve that past.

Various photographs in the booklet help show it to us – some well-known, some newly donated by Bob Dylan. Two of these are particularly striking. One shows Robert Zimmerman's parents before he was born, clothed in the fashions and the black and white light of 1939. They look proud and hopeful and (naturally) quite unaware that their union will have so much meaning for so many other unborn people. Then there is one of four photographs showing Bob and Suze Rotolo. The presence of the four in the booklet hints at the strength of feeling he has for those times and that girl: someone who has never traded on her unique association with him.[133] In three of the pictures Bob affects cool, hip, try-on poses with a cigarette; but the fourth time around he is wrinkling into a Punchinello smile, looking very unhip – the kid who dreamed Hibbing dreams.

These photographs show the respect Bob Dylan is paying the past, and the people who live there. And whatever its faults, *Biograph* is paying respect to his own extraordinary achievements too. Play these records and they send you back to the previous albums; but also, after all these years, make you look forward to his next.

Into the Future, Knocked Out and Loaded

Nigel Hinton

Joseph Conrad, to whom Dylan tips his hat on the cover of *Desire*, talks about the aim of art in his preface to *The Nigger Of The Narcissus*. He says that the task of the artist is to attain a 'clearness of sincerity'. 'If I succeed,' he adds, 'you shall find there, according to your deserts: encouragement, consolation, fear, charm – all you demand – and, perhaps, also that glimpse of truth for which you have forgotten to ask.'

For me Bob Dylan is someone who has sometimes attained a 'clearness of sincerity' that has given me glimpses of something extraordinary. Such moments come rarely for me. They have come from a few – a very few – passages in books. They have come from conversations with some people. They have come from Bob Dylan: and from no one else in music. Which is why I value him so highly.

What are they, these moments? As far as I can tell they are not moments of heightened emotional intensity, though there are similarities. Dylan is certainly capable of arousing intense emotions in me – he does it frequently: a thrill can charge through me at the way he phrases a line; or the way in which he hits an unexpected note; sunlight can seem to come shafting down through the notes of his harmonica. At such times my heart swells and lifts. But I'm not talking of such moments. They are thrilling and very pleasant and I'm grateful for them but they are merely sensuous and I'm aware that intense emotion can be stirred by many things.

No, the moments I am talking about are not emotional. Nor are they, strictly speaking, intellectual, though they seem to be received by my mind rather than by my senses. They are moments when all Dylan's talents – as a singer, writer and musician – combine to produce something other than what is there, something which is invisible and unknown. For example, he can write a line which has one clear and obvious meaning but which, often as a result of the way he sings it, suddenly reveals another meaning. In the tension between the two meanings there is, unstated, something more. He can sing a tune, or play it on the harmonica, then play or sing a variation on it that is like the mirror image of the original. Not only are there then two versions of the melody but between the two, suggested but unheard, is a third – perhaps a fourth; perhaps, it leaps in on me, a multitude. At such moments there is an undeniable emotional charge, but there is something else: something that is not there in an ordinary sense. These sudden switches of perception seem to scramble my brain out of its pedantic rut and activate it to sense that I might be able to see what I normally don't see. It's evident that any attempt to express this in words is going to fall a long way short of what it's like, but it's as if the effect of Dylan's words and music on my emotions and my intellect somehow breaks down a barrier and momentarily gives me a glimpse of something that is not music, words, emotion or intellect. I don't know what it is, but I do know that it is not like anything else.

I'm not claiming that Dylan gives me any 'answer' in these moments where his art heightens my perceptions. At one time I looked for, and thought I was finding, answers, but now I realize that what he manages to do is inspire me to keep working. He knows that he has no answers and has frequently gone on record (in both senses) as saying so, but he has said, 'The highest purpose of art is to inspire. What else can you do? What else can you do for anyone but inspire them?' (*Rolling Stone*, 1978).

Strangely, not long after he made that statement, he found what he thought was the answer and began to present it as such to his audience: it was Jesus Christ.

> Believe in His power
> That's about all you've got to do.

Coincidentally to his finding belief in Christ's power, I found that Dylan's power to inspire me began to diminish. He could raise my emotional temperature but, except in concerts when he reinterpreted some of his old songs, he no longer gave me moments of insight. He seemed more concerned with making statements. The lyrics and the overall tone with which he delivered his message were quite specific and simple and did not have room for multiplicity of meaning.

'You're gonna have to serve somebody' is unequivocal. 'Nobody feels any pain', on the other hand, is not. As 'Just Like A Woman' progresses we learn that there is 'pain in here', so that that opening line doesn't mean what it appears to mean: it doesn't mean 'nobody at all', it means 'nobody except the singer'. From there, and in the context of the song in which its multiple meanings indicate that the singer feels that he is trapped inside a human personality – 'Ain't it clear/That I just don't fit' – it becomes apparent that the line means 'no *body* feels any pain', but that perhaps the spirit or soul does.

So, since 1979, I have found Dylan's work to be largely lacking in that quality that put him in another class from everyone else. Even when his songs in this period had been clever (and many of them have been clever `and` beautiful) they have always been explicit. The meaning is all there on the surface and there has not been that elusive, ambiguous quality with which he used to

255

manage to invest even simple words so that they would suddenly open up to a new meaning. Even rich and complex songs such as 'Jokerman' are rich and complex only on the surface – they do not have resonances that suddenly bloom to reveal something previously unthought of by the listener. There has been no mystery in his art and, simultaneously, he has been less musically and vocally inventive.

As far as I'm concerned, this process reached a low-point on *Empire Burlesque*, which I find cold and artificial. Images such as 'Madame Butterfly, she lulls me to sleep' are mere words – nothing about the picture is really *known*. The same sense of words arbitrarily brought together is found throughout the 'love' songs:

> I'll remember you
> When I've forgotten the rest
> You to me were true
> You to me were the best.

There's nothing living in such lines; they don't ring with truth. Truth about how things are was what always distinguished Dylan's lyrics no matter how perilously close he stepped to cliché:

> I don't need to be no doctor, babe,
> To see that you're madly in love.

'Madly in love' is a cliché, but the mention of 'doctor' frees it from cliché: this girl is so emotionally entangled that her mental balance is disturbed. That's what gives the power to his plea, 'Baby, please stop crying'.

There's nothing like even this kind of subtlety and truth to be found in the 'love' lyrics on *Empire Burlesque*. Instead, there is a feeling of formula about the writing. A girl is a 'living dream' and the songs are full of vague statements, some of which seem to be there merely to fit the rhyme:

> I could be unravelling
> Wherever I'm travelling

Just as there is a lack of lived-in, experienced truth about the emotions in the 'love' songs, so there is a lack of compassion in the 'political/religious' songs. This unfortunate tendency to crow about the fate of infidels has been present in Dylan's work since 1979, when he stood back from his 'so-called friends' and threatened that a time would come:

> When men will beg God to kill them
> And they won't be able to die.

I find the same tone in *Empire Burlesque*. The night is going to come falling from the sky and Dylan seems to relish the prospect: 'It'll fit you like a glove'. It's the same bitterness that ran through 'Positively 4th Street' but on a global, apocalyptic scale. And, crucially, there's none of the compassion that mitigated the sneering in that much earlier song:

> No I do not feel that good
> When I see the heartbreaks you embrace . . .

In 'Something's Burning, Baby' he may say that he's waiting for baby to ring down, but at the heart of this excellent yet unpleasant song is the sense of being addressed by a doom-laden, holier-than-thou preacher: 'I know what you need but it aint what you deserve'. I'm suspicious of such preaching, just as I'm slightly suspicious of people who declare that they '. . . Live in another world/Where life and death are memorized.'

All that said, I can come to what is, at the time of writing, the *new* album. I like *Knocked Out Loaded* very much indeed. It has given me more sheer pleasure than any other Dylan album for years. After the cool *Infidels* and the positively frosty *Empire Burlesque*, what struck me on first hearing *Knocked Out Loaded* was the relaxed warmth of the sound and the returned richness of Dylan's voice. Then, on repeated listenings, I heard, almost with disbelief, the wit and affection and liveliness, not only in the lyrics but in the singing and the music. I found that a Dylan album was making me happy, making me smile – something that hadn't happened in a long, long time. And then as I got to know the album better I realized that those very qualities which I have tried to describe above were back in his writing and in his performance – the compassion, the truth, and the mystery.

I must stress that I like the *whole* album, including the two songs which other people, I know, find hard to swallow: 'They Killed Him' and 'Precious Memories'. Indeed 'Precious Memories', arguably a rather soppy song, seems to me to sum up much of what I like about the album. I like the kind of company Dylan is on *Knocked Out Loaded*. I like his mood. He's not alienating me by hectoring or threatening and I'm prepared to listen to whatever he has to say. Over long years he has used his art to speak so frankly and directly that his work has become for me like letters from a friend. As with other friends, I'll listen to whatever he wants to talk about – love, religion, hopes, fears, memories – as long as there is a sense that the friend is alongside, talking to me, not lecturing me from some aloof position.

After a number of years in which his principal tone has been of judging from a remote and superior platform, he seems to have remembered his own injunction:

> If ye cannot bring good news
> Then don't bring any.

On *Knocked Out Loaded* Dylan is back on the earth with me, 'caught between heaven and hell'. He no longer assumes a superior position. He, too, is 'in a bit of a jam'. He, too is in a world where 'the desert is hot, the mountain is cursed' and he needs my prayers, just as I need his, to avoid dying 'of thirst/Two feet from the well'. We may both be 'in some kind of a test' and we may both be failing to 'do what we do best' but it is *both of us*.

Just as 'Down Along The Cove' and 'I'll Be Your Baby Tonight' come as a welcome relief from the severity of the rest of *John Wesley Harding*, so this album comes as an antidote to Dylan's more recent work. There's hope and encouragement in abundance. There are no threats of a vindictive God who will ignore men's pitiful plea to kill them; instead:

> You will be alright girl
> Someone's watching over you

258

and the corollary bite of the two lines that follow:

> He won't do nothing to you
> Baby that I wouldn't do

is shared, humorous bite.

This more human, more humane Dylan seems to have re-opened his eyes to what it's really like to be down here on the planet scrabbling around trying, and failing, to live right and make sense of it all. A note of genuine surprise appears time and again in 'Brownsville Girl':

> I can't believe we've lived so long
> And are still so far apart.

> Strange how people who've suffered together have
> Stronger connections than people who are most content.

> You know it's funny how things never turn out
> The way you had 'em planned.

On recent albums I've felt talked at; on this one I feel I'm being talked to. Like a friend. I will listen to a friend when he talks to me, even about subjects on which we don't see eye to eye. (I'll listen to a friend who thinks highly of Mahatma Gandhi even though I've always been puzzled by how a man who set such store by non-violence always acted in a way that stirred up such violence around him.) I'll certainly listen when he does this talking in such beguiling style: singing and playing with freshness and drive and commitment. And I'll listen when he is prepared to risk sounding simple-minded and banal by talking about memories and fathers and mothers.

In 'Precious Memories' Dylan dares to do what he's done before – particularly in *Nashville Skyline*: say simple things that can easily be mocked as mawkish. But I'm not inclined to mock, any more than I would with a friend who was feeling sentimental about 'precious father, loving mother' and 'home scenes of my childhood'. High Art it is not, but I'm not always after High Art. Sometimes sentimentality has its place, especially when expressed with such 'clearness of sincerity' and in such warm, nostalgic music. In 'Precious Memories', as throughout this album, the music is vibrant. After the dead, mechanical

259

production on *Empire Burlesque*, *Knocked Out Loaded* is filled with lovely sound. It is living music, played joyously by people who are in the mood to be inventive and who seem to savour the chance to try out so many styles and moods.

The music on this album reminds me of the innocence of fifties rock 'n' roll, and there even seem to be passing homages to that period – the Duane Eddy guitar on 'Got My Mind Made Up', the Buddy Hollyish 'Maybe Someday', and the Chuck Berry relish with which Dylan attacks such tempting place-names as 'Libya', 'San Antone' and 'Tallahassee'.

And there's another thing: he's found his sense of humour again – the witty fade as 'she' drifts away at the end of 'Driftin' Too Far From Shore' when he has declared 'I can finish this alone, honey'; the laughing way he rhymes 'completeness' and 'sweetness'; the light, glancing put-down of his girl's flight to San Francisco ('I always liked San Francisco/I was there for a party once'); and the delightful mocking of the stupidity of roles and of the games people play:

> I don't like playing cat and mouse.
> No gentleman likes making love to his servant
> Specially when he's in his father's house.

Put a capital letter on 'Father', of course, and there are all kinds of other resonances there. For, above all on this album, Dylan has miraculously rediscovered the ability to make points with discretion and subtlety. He makes his lines ring with mysterious possibilities: where one level works perfectly but where, if you care to switch contexts, the whole thing works on another level too. Thus 'Maybe Someday' is a warning farewell to a girl but it is so artfully written that it needs only a slight sideways step to see that each line carries a moral/spiritual implication. No sledgehammers, no breaking down no bedroom doors, and no moralizing contempt needed here: 'The love that I had for you was never my own.'

When Dylan is working at this level of creativity – a level that sets him head and shoulders above everyone else – there's a magic evocativeness about everything he writes that gives the words enormous possibilities. In one of the numerous examples to be found in the marvellous 'Brownsville Girl' he sings

'We got him cornered in the churchyard!' I heard somebody shout.
Well, you saw my picture in the *Corpus Christi Tribune*;
Underneath it it said 'A man with no alibi'. . . .

Now this sequence fits perfectly into the wonderful narrative of
the song as one of the chance encounters that the narrator has
on his wide-space, time-shifting voyage across the land – but the
language is so precise and evocative that it opens up other levels
of meaning. The shots that have just rung out remind us of the
shooting in the back of the gunfighter from that film which
haunts the narrator and which threads through the song as a
kind of reference point to which we can relate all the actions of
the characters. The choice of 'churchyard' and 'Corpus Christi'
(Body of Christ) are no accident – he could have sung 'junkyard'
and 'Fort Lauderdale' – and they imbue that remembered
fragment of film, and therefore, the whole song, with added
significance. At the same time the lines are so packed with
possibilities that, if one chooses, they can be heard as an
evocation of Dylan's recent religious position: he's got no alibi –
he's been cornered in a churchyard with the body of Christ.

I'm not saying it does mean this – I'm using it to show how
Dylan's language is once again charged with imaginative potential. Certainly for me the religious possibilities in those lines are
an underlining of the themes that run throughout the song (and
the album as a whole). Prompted by the never-to-be-forgotten
image of the dying gunfighter, the narrator looks compas-
sionately at the fate of friends, lovers and himself as they go
through their lives. Dylan, as he made clear to that *Time*
journalist so many years ago, has always been concerned with
how one lives in the face of the knowledge that one will die.
That's why the dying gunfighter's last gasped words made such
an impression on him: 'I want him to feel what it's like to every
moment face his death.'

How one lives. Bob Dylan has always been singing about
that. In the last few years, he has tended to berate and cajole.
I've listened, but found the tone off-putting and lacking in an
essential ingredient: love. On *Knocked Out Loaded* love is
omnipresent: for mother, father, childhood scenes, Gandhi,
Martin Luther King, Christ, Ruby, and 'You'.

> You'll never get rid of me
> As long as you're alive.

It's not an uncritical love. The album is filled with the awful things people do. They beat kids to a bloody pulp; they desert you and go off to San Francisco, or run out on you way down in Mexico; they might blow your head off; they take all your money and then drift off too far from the shore; they lie so well that they can even act real tears; they all plan to get something for nothing; they break every vow; they lead secret and shady lives and then have to invent false names, names like Henry Porter; they try to *win* names for themselves by shooting people in the back; they even assassinate great leaders. ('My God, they killed him!')

It would be tempting to abandon such people to their fate – to 'let the dead bury the dead' because, no doubt about it, this is 'the land of the living dead'. But, crucially, behind their apparent indifference to this fact, Dylan recognizes that people are really 'so brokenhearted'. Anyway, he has no choice. It may be almost more than he can take but 'There's somethin' about you that I can't shake'. He's under no illusions. The stars have been 'torn down'. The heroes are gone, the dreams are finished, we're under a starless sky in the 'naked night'. And 'You', he knows all about 'You':

> Everywhere you go, it's enough to break hearts
> Someone always gets hurt, a fire always starts.

He knows, however, that you can get your mind made up not to trespass but that 'sometimes you just find yourself over the line'. And besides, he has 'noticed your light'. He stares at your picture and hears your words. He wants to do something. 'I'd like to help you'; and he pleads 'Turn back, baby'. You know where he's staying: that same old Heartbreak Hotel. And he's promised to 'call you tomorrow if there's phones where I am'. And all this because 'There was no greater love than what I had for you'.

Dylan's moral concerns are as serious as ever. His analysis of the situation is still as urgent. How to live? He's not turned his back on that search and he still believes there 'must be some

262

way out of here'. This time, however, his view has had a shot of love. This time he is on a whole other level with this listener. We're side by side, joker and thief together, and *Knocked Out Loaded* fills me with pleasure, hope and inspiration.

Some Bob Dylan Lists

A   Nineteen Great *Bob Dylan Songs He's* Never *Done In Concert:*

Dear Bob, please consider the pleasures of the fresh . . .

Black Crow Blues
Black Diamond Bay
Blind Willie McTell
Buckets of Rain
Dirge
Dear Landlord
Drifter's Escape
Farewell Angelina
I'll Keep It With Mine
Never Say Goodbye
No Time To Think
Odds and Ends
Sad-Eyed Lady of the Lowlands
She's Your Lover Now
Sign on the Window
Tears of Rage
Tell Me That It Isn't True
Went to See the Gypsy
Wigwam

B I'm Seeing Your Picture, I'm Hearing Your Words:

All those works of art, in order of appearance, in Dylan's 'Jokerman' video.

Self Portrait as the Redeemer, Dürer (1500)
Sumerian idol (2700 BC)
The Slave Ship, Turner (1840)
Minoan snake goddess (1500 BC)
Bob Dylan poster, Glaser (1966)
Moses, Michelangelo indeed (1514)
Man In Bondage, from *The Book Of Urizen*, Blake (1795)
Dead Christ, Mantegna (1490)
The Delphi Charioteer (Greece, fifth century BC)
Weeping Woman, Picasso (1937)
Woman And Man, Lindner (1971)
The Musicans' Hell, Bosch (1510)
Jewish illuminated manuscript (Germany, 1300)
Island Man of New Guinea, Kirk (1970)
The Battle Of San Romano, Uccello (1435–50)
David, Michelangelo again (1504)
Cow's Skull – Red White And Blue, O'Keefe (1931)
Chief Joseph of the Nez Perce, Curtis (1903)
The Third Of May 1808, Goya (1814)
The armour of Henry VIII (1520)
Muhammed Ali as St Sebastian, Lois (1969)
Colossal Head (from the Palazzo Orsini, Bomarzo, Italy)
Slain Heroes At Arlington, Lois (1969)
The Joker (DC Comics)
The Scream, (Münch (1893)
Goddess of Earth and Procreation (Aztec, 1400)

C It Used To Go Like That And Now It Goes Like This
Early titles that became something else . . .

Freeze Out (Visions Of Johanna)
Just A Little Glass Of Water (She's Your Lover Now)
New Danville Girl (Brownsville Girl)
The Old Man (Man On The Street)

Over The Cliff (Sitting On A Barbed Wire Fence)
Phantom Engineer (It Takes A Lot To Laugh, It Takes A Train To
  Cry)
Reminiscence Blues (Ballad For A Friend)
Someone's Got A Hold Of My Heart (Tight Connection To My
  Heart)

D   *Things You Didn't Necessarily Expect to Know About Bob Dylan's LP Sleeves*

1   The photograph on *Bob Dylan* is printed the wrong way
    round.

2   The cuff-links he wears on *Bringing It All Back Home* were
    the ones Joan Baez gave him, mentioned years later in her
    song about him, 'Diamonds And Rust'.

3   The legs and striped T-shirt with the camera behind Dylan
    on the back of *Highway 61 Revisited* is Bobby Neuwirth.
    (The photo was taken on the steps of the The Breakers, a
    mansion in Newport, Rhode Island.)

4   Two of the women inside the original issue of *Blonde On
    Blonde* are Claudia Cardinale and Edie Sedgwick.

5   As well as tiny pictures of The Beatles and of Dylan
    himself, the *John Wesley Harding* photo has a 'hand of God'
    hidden in the tree bark.

6   The people standing with Dylan in that picture are mostly
    the Bauls of Bengal.

7   The guitar held by Dylan on the sleeve of *Nashville Skyline*
    belongs to George Harrison.

8   That sleeve photographically echoes *The Folk-Blues of Eric
    Von Schmidt*, which actually appears on Dylan's *Bringing It
    All Back Home* cover.

9   The photograph for *The Basement Tapes* was taken in the
    boiler-room of the YMCA in Los Angeles. (The models
    include David Blue, Neil Young and Ringo Starr.)

10   The sleeve photograph of *Desire* is a photographic echo of
     John Phillips' LP *Wolfking of LA*.

11   On the back of that sleeve in the top right hand corner, the
     man with the moustache is producer Don DeVito speaking
     to his brother Richard DeVito, who was head of the street
     crime unit of the New York City Police.

E   *World's Worst Cover-Versions Of Bob Dylan Songs*
Listed in alphabetical order by song-title.

1   Anything by the Four Seasons or The Hollies
2   'Blowin' In The Wind' by Trini Lopez
3   'I Shall Be Released' by Telly Savalas
4   'Lay Lady Lay' by Melanie
5   'Like A Rolling Stone' by Dino Desi and Billy
6   'Like A Rolling Stone' by Lanne and The Leekings
7   'Maggie's Farm' by Solomon Burke
8   'The Mighty Quinn' by Lulu
9   'Mr Tambourine Man' by The Tweets
10 'Mr Tambourine Man' by William (Captain Kirk) Shatner

F   *Eight Lines Stolen From Humphrey Bogart Movies*
And All Used On *Empire Burlesque* . . .

1   'I don't mind a reasonable amount of trouble' *The Maltese
    Falcon*

2   'Don't look for me, I'll see you.' *The Maltese Falcon*

3   'Think this rain would cool things off, but it don't.' *Key
    Largo*

4   'There's some people that you don't forget even if you've
    only seen them once.' *The Big Sleep*

5   'I don't care who loves who . . . maybe you love me and
    maybe I love you.' *The Maltese Falcon*

6   'Didn't I take chances?' *Key Largo*

7   ' "We wanna talk to you, Spade." "Well, go ahead and talk".' *The Maltese Falcon*

8   'I'll have some rotten nights after I've sent you over, but that'll pass.' *The Maltese Falcon*

G   Well, Well, Well . . .

This information emerged from Presley-fanatic sources. Here is the songlist from the Presley-Dylan session of May 1971 in Nashville! Elvis was booked in to do Christmas songs; for atmosphere's sake, they had santas and angels, Christmas trees and holly and – not duetting on all titles, we believe (no tape has yet surfaced) – they sang:

All I Really Want To Do	My Garden Of Prayer
Blowin' In The Wind	The Ghetto
Carolyne	One Too Many Mornings
House Of The Rising Sun	She Belongs To Me
It Aint Me Babe	Say You Love Me One More Time
Jodie And The Kid	Silent Night
Like A Rolling Stone	Subterranean Homesick Blues
Me And Bobbie McGee	Walking Down The Line
Mr Tambourine Man	Satisfied

Reportedly they got together again, some time in 1972, at which session they managed only 'If Not For You'.

H   Allen Ginsberg Poems About Bob Dylan

'Postcard To D––––' [1972]
'Blue Gossip' [1972]
'On Reading Dylan's Writings' [1973]
'Bob Dylan (1941 –)' [1986]

Then there's

Gates of Eden welcomed in in   Who Be Kind To   1965
   same year September
      surprise documentation of hearing

on car radio near Oregon
　　mistake release of Please Crawl Out Your Window
plus misquote Positively 4th Street　both inside Beginning Of
　　A Poem To These States.
citation Hiway Poesy: L.A.–Albuquerque–Texas–Wichita
　　　& verse of Wichita Vortex Sutra
　could-be allusion-wish　Iron Horse　1966 all three
mention too in 68 in course of Crossing Nation　and
　　small part
　　　　end of decade
　　　　　　　Ecologue.

Finally, if Ginsberg's inside-sleeve-notes for *Desire* (1975) aren't
poetry, very little is.[134]

I　Pardon, Monsieur, Am I Hearing You Right?
Selected reported mishearings from the lyrics:

1　You're the queen of my flesh girl
　And you torture the night
　[Precious Angel]

2　She's delicate and seems like veneer
　[Visions of Johanna]

3　Do you need me half as bad as you say
　Or are you just feeling ill?
　[Is Your Love In Vain?]

4　Their religion of the lilting women
　[Can You Please Crawl Out Your Window?]

5　And the one-eyed undertaker
　He blows a feudal horn
　[Shelter From the Storm]

6　My Iranian Beethoven once unwrapped a bedroll
　[Tombstone Blues]

7　The lava flowed down from about a mile above
　[Black Diamond Bay]

8　Half asleep 'neath the stars
　With a small dark look on your face
　[Jokerman]

9 Down in South Asia
  Packaging of the soul
  [Trouble]

10 Rosemary combed her hair
   And took a cabbage into town
   [Lily, Rosemary and the Jack of Hearts]

11 You're the other half of what I am
   You're the mess 'n' peas
   [Wedding Song]

J Dogs Bob Dylan Seems To Have Abandoned

1 Hamlet: the pedigree shepherd-dog that turned out not to be; acquired by Dylan (a sibling went to Albert Grossman) in the Woodstock era. Dogs were a fashion then – see also items 2 and 3 on this list. Hamlet was given away to Band member Rick Danko when the unfortunate animal's pretensions to good breeding were exposed as phoney.

2 The Collie that Dylan owned, again in Woodstock, in 1968. It is pictured in the middle of the 1986 Australian Tour Programme.

3 The St Bernard ditto; pictured in *The Telegraph* (issue 15).

4 Sasha: the dog A.J. Weberman found evidence of in Dylan's garbage on MacDougal Street, Greenwich Village, in 1970. A.J.'s unique research established that the Dylans gave this wretched creature Gainsburgers and Ken-L Ration (she was well fed . . .), and that they had to call a vet in to treat her for an upset stomach.

5 Rover: the dog that was part of the family in 1972, and which was taken across the borderline down to Durango, Mexico, and installed as part of the Dylan entourage in his trailer on the set of *Pat Garrett and Billy The Kid*.

6 Peggy: the Beagle puppy mentioned in the *Rolling Thunder Logbook* by Sam Shepard as being less than fully housetrained, and which can be seen in *Renaldo & Clara* trying to insinuate herself between Shepard and Sara Dylan on the sofa in *that* trailer. Or caravan, as we say in Britain.

7   The black Labrador which Dylan had with him in his
     station-wagon (or estate-car, as we . . .) when he revisited
     his childhood home in Hibbing, Minnesota in April 1984.

     NB. Dylan's current dogs are two Great Danes called
     Brutus and Baby. How much longer?

K   *Four And Twenty Windows And A Woman's Face In Every
One*
Significant women in Bob Dylan's life and art:

Ra Aranga
A Maori Princess: Bob chatted her up when they met while
jogging on a New Zealand beach, 1978; then, delaying the
scheduled start of recording *Street Legal*, he flew back to her
after his Sydney shows and stayed a couple of days.

Mary Alice Artes
A Religious Influence: a black actress, first mentioned on *Street
Legal* LP cover (billed tellingly as 'Queen Bee'), who helped
bring Bob to Christianity, after calling a halt to living with him
after her own conversion; subject of 'Precious Angel' and a
focus in 'Slow Train'. Dylan reportedly bought her an engage-
ment ring in early 1980; later that year he wrote relevant
versions of 'Groom Still Waiting At The Altar' and 'Caribbean
Wind'.

Avril the Dancer
New York girlfriend: a dancer and actress who saw Dylan
perform at a Gerde's Folk City Monday night Hootenanny,
perhaps as early as mid-February 1961. Dylan lived with Avril
on East 4th Street for the last weeks of his first stay in New York
City, March-April of that year.

Joan Baez
Folk-music lover.

Carole Bayer-Sager
Song co-writer ('Under Your Spell', *Knocked Out Loaded*, 1986;
own success in 1977 with co-penned hit 'You're Moving Out
Today', also a US hit for the incorrigible Bette Midler).

Bonnie-Jean Beecher
Minneapolis girlfriend.

Carole Childs
Girlfriend; around Dylan back in 1974 and still there in Australia in 1986; had worked for Columbia; now working for David Geffen, whose Asylum label Dylan used briefly in 1974.

Emily Dickinson
A favourite poet: never published till after her death; in retrospect a major American nineteenth century voice; lived 1830–1886.

Anna Dylan
Daughter.

Maria Dylan
Step-daughter.

Sara Dylan
Wife.

Gypsy Fire
Sexsational gossipmonger (no smoke without Gypsy? See 'My Sexy Nights As A Slave To Bob Dylan',*The People*, UK, 27 July 1986).

Echo Helstrom
Hibbing girlfriend: subject of 'Girl Of The North Country' and maybe of 'Hazel'.

Om Kalsoum
A favourite singer: a powerhouse-voiced 20th-Century-spanning Egyptian superstar and, as Bob put it affectionately, a 'fat old lady that smoked a lot of hash'; gave an annual concert in Paris; did last show aged eighty-two and died at eighty-three.

Clydie King
Back-up companion as, from February 1980.

Malka
The Last Straw Other Woman: who, according to Sara, was sat calmly with Bob at breakfast one morning right there in the marital Malibu home when Mrs D came downstairs.

Bette Midler
A Persistent Failure As Seductress: see 'Bob Dylan and The Making Of USA-For-Africa'.

Carla Rotolo
The 'Ballad In Plain D' 'parasite sister'. She was, despite it all, a Dylan enthusiast (unlike her mother, who called him 'Twerp').

Suze Rotolo
New York girlfriend: first saw Dylan perform on Wednesday 5 April 1961, at the Loeb Student Center on Washington Square, Greenwich Village. Dylan was nineteen, she was seventeen. Later put proudly on the cover of *Freewheelin'* and the subject of 'Boots Of Spanish Leather' and more.

Edie Sedgwick
Brief companion, 1965–6: see 'In The Factory'.

Helena Springs
Song co-writer (of several songs, including 'Coming From The Heart', which Bob sang live in '78) and the only back-up singer to work the whole 1978 tour, from Japan and Australia–New Zealand in February–March, thru Europe June–July, to Florida in December, *and* still be there for the 1979 religious concerts.

Elizabeth Taylor
Dream-girl (1964) to dinner-date (1986).

Beatty Zimmerman
Mother

Queen Esther Marrow
Crazy name, crazy gal!

Back In New York City, Summer of '86

Backstage at Madison Square Garden, summer 1986, Bob Dylan is being interviewed by a British music journalist. Part way through, the journalist gets called away to take a phone call.

At this point a friend of Dylan's asks him: 'How's the interview going, Bob?'

'Not so good.'

'Oh. Why's that then, Bob?'

'He keeps asking me *questions* . . .'

Notes

NB. Each note is by the author of the relevant section of the book, except where otherwise initialled.

1   Two Jim Marshall photographs document Dylan at this workshop; they appear on p.51 of *The Art Of Bob Dylan*, Michael Gray, Hamlyn, UK, 1981/St Martins Press, US, 1982; and on the Contents Page of *Bob Dylan – The Illustrated Record*, Alan Rinzler, Harmony, USA, 1978. They catch Dylan doing both songs: only the second photo shows a capo on his guitar.

2   Silber's article was reprinted in *Bob Dylan – A Retrospective*, Craig MacGregor, Morrow, US, 1972, but omitted from the UK edition; Picador, 1975. MacGregor fails to mention that in a 1968 issue of US left-wing weekly *The Guardian*, Silber published a full and gracious retraction (MG).

3   The obscuring of Newport 1964 by events the following year was understandable *then*; subsequent neglect is less so. There are few retrospective accounts at all; those that there are (aside from that in Robert Shelton's *No Direction Home*, Beech Tree/Morrow, US, and NEL, UK, 1986) draw on Scaduto's, itself essentially reprocessed from one 1966 Ralph Gleason piece ('Children's Crusade', *Ramparts*; reprinted US by MacGregor, as 2.)

4   Interview with Cameron Crowe, *Biograph* booklet, 1985.

5   Steven Goldberg, 'Bob Dylan & The Poetry of Salvation', in *Bob Dylan – A Retrospective*, MacGregor, as 2.

6   *Popism*, Andy Warhol, Harcourt Brace Jovanovich, US, 1980.

7   *Uptight: The Velvet Underground Story*, Victor Bockris and Gerard Malanga, Omnibus Press, UK, 1983.

8   *Rolling Stone*, 26 January 1978.

9   *MacLeans*, Canada, 29 March 1978.

10   *Los Angeles Times*, 22 January 1978.

11   As 7.

12   As 7.

13   *Edie; The Life and Times of Andy Warhol's Superstar*, Jean Stein, Knopf, US; Cape, UK, 1982.

14 As 7.

15 As 13.

16 *The Philosophy of Andy Warhol*, Warhol, Harcourt Brace Jovano-vich, US, 1975.

17 As 6.

18 As 6.

19 As 7.

20 As 6.

21 As 13.

22 As 16.

23 The tune of 'Living The Blues' is, however, the same as that of 'I'm Feeling Sorry', recorded in the late fifties by Jerry Lee Lewis and composed by Claud DeMetrius, writer also of the classic 'Mean Woman Blues' (MG).

24 *Writings and Drawings by Bob Dylan*, Dylan, Knopf, US, 1972; Cape, UK, 1973.

25 *The Poetry Of Rock*, David Pichaske, Ellis Press, US, 1981.

26 *Rolling Stone* No.134, 10 May 1973.

27 *Rolling Stone* No.116, 17 August 1972.

28 *Rolling Stone* No.121, 9 November 1972.

29 'The Man Called Alias', Michael Watts, *Melody Maker*, 3 February 1973.

30 Dylan must have filed it fast too, because it was officially copyrighted 18 December 1972.

31 *Rolling Stone* No.130, 15 March 1973.

32 As 29.

33 As 29.

34 *Crucified Heroes: The Films of Sam Peckinpah*, Terence Butler, Fraser Publishing (further details unknown).

35 *Rolling Stone* No.138, 5 July 1973 and as 31.

36 As 29.

37 As 31.

38   As 34.

39   As 31.

40   As 29.

41   As 29.

42   *Bob Dylan: An Illustrated History*, Michael Gross, Elm Tree Books, UK, 1978.

43   As 29.

44   *Rolling Stone* No.135, 24 May 1973.

45   *Rolling Stone* 23 February 1973.

46   As 31.

47   As 29.

48   As 31.

49   Dylan had been playing 'Will The Circle Be Unbroken?' since he was a very young man, and would soon re-introduce it: as a duet with Neil Young at the SNACK Benefit, San Francisco, 23 March 1975 and again as an encore at a San Antonio concert with Willie Nelson, 11 May 1976.

50   All as 31.

51   *Rolling Stone* No.140, 2 August 1973.

52   *Rolling Stone* No.142, 30 August 1973.

53   *On The Road With Bob Dylan*, Larry Sloman, Bantam Books, US, 1978.

54   *Bob Dylan*, Miles, Big O, UK, 1978.

55   As 29.

56   As 29.

57   *Pat Garrett and Billy The Kid*, Rudy Wurlitzer, NAL, US, 1973.

58   As 29.

59   As 31.

60   As 24.

61   Rinzler; as 1.

62   As 51.

63   As 35.

64   Gordon Gow, *Films and Filming*, August 1973.

65   Gray; as 1.

66   Yes: a commentator with an eye on both Billy's romantic old West and Garrett's pragmatic new one (Peckinpah's theme). Landau misses the point: Alias is not offered as heroic cowboy, with Dylan not noble or tough enough. Alias is observer of the imperatives of the moment: his heart rides out with Billy but his realism accepts the ascendancy of the Garrett/Chisum era. Because this character, this Greek Chorus functionary, is played by Dylan a special emphasis is given to those key lines of film dialogue which come straight out of two crucial songs from Dylan's own history. They occur in the mouths of the film's two main characters even before the opening credits roll:
   Billy: How does it feel?
   Garrett: It feels like times have changed.   (MG)

67   As 34.

68   As 34.

69   *Rolling Stone* No.131, 29 March 1973.

70   Stanton, Luke in *Pat Garrett*, reappeared in *Renaldo & Clara*. He subsequently appeared in *Repo Man*, on the soundtrack of which were The Plugz, some of whose members had backed Dylan on his unannounced David Letterman TV Show performance, New York, March 1984. (MG)

71   As 44.

72   As 31.

73   Republished, with introduction by Frederick Christian, Sphere Books, UK, 1973.

74   Source: an unidentified newspaper cutting, US, no date.

75   So did Johnny Ace, who wrote 'Never Let Me Go', sung by Dylan and Baez in *Renaldo & Clara* and issued as a track on a for-DJs-only 12" EP.

76   NB. Edie Sedgwick was dead long before the making of *Renaldo & Clara* (see 'In The Factory: Dylan and Warhol's World' in this volume). But cf. remarks by that earlier Dylan film-maker, D.A. Pennebaker: 'All the right people to see it [some mid-sixties footage] are dead. Like Edie. I shot a lot of film with Edie, did you know that? She was around

my studio a lot. She was so smart and so stupid about her life. I told her if she wanted to be a rocket she couldn't be anything else. She knew that, but she was completely devoted to acting her life out.' (*Heavy Metal*, late 1983).

77 As 55.

78 *Bob Dylan: An Intimate Biography*, Anthony Scaduto, Grosset and Dunlap, US; W. H. Allen, UK, 1972.

79 Interview with Howard Alk, *Take One* magazine, March 1978.

80 *Fourth Time Around* fanzine No.1.

81 'Don't Look Back Revisited', *High Times* magazine, December 1983.

82 *The Telegraph*, issue 16, 1984, and/or the present volume, p.71.

83 *Sing Out!* magazine, October/November 1968. ('The Eye' was Dylan's nickname for Pennebaker.)

84 As 29.

85 Sloman; as 53.

86 As 83.

87 As 53.

88 *Festival*, the film.

89 *Eat The Document*, the film. (See *Endless Road* fanzine, No.5)

90 'Putting *Janis* Together: The Inside Story', *Take One*.

91 *American Revolution II* in *Take One*.

92 'The Murder of Fred Hampton': interview with Alk in *Take One*.

93 Ibid.

94 Ibid.

95 Ibid.

96 As 79. But this is misleading. The Dylan who stays quiet about his reluctant meeting with the Panthers stays so about many things, mistrusts organizations and orthodoxy ('. . . There is only up wing and down wing,') and will have understood his own inevitable irrelevance to the Panther programme. And just as the *power* of Alk's politics derives not from dogma but from his affection for, and trust in, those 'who have been stepped on and victimised', so there is nothing apolitical in Dylan's consistent and similar solidarity with the pawns

black and white dispossessed is an honourably clear strand through his work, from Greenwood Mississippi and the Washington Civil Rights March of 1963 to the Martin Luther King Birthday Commemoration of 1985. While Alk made *The Murder of Fred Hampton*, Dylan had made 'The Lonesome Death Of Hattie Carroll'. The unsatisfactory Panthers meeting didn't put Dylan off visiting Hurricane Carter in jail five years later; and in the same era in which Alk made his Panthers movies, Dylan came out with 'George Jackson'. So the notion that Alk inserted politics into *Renaldo* despite Dylan is absurd. The 'Hurricane' sequence is clearly a co-production. Whatever the film achieves or doesn't, it offers a survey of North America: and while TV reportage deliberately keeps non-WASP America invisible, the special strength of *Renaldo*'s survey is the high visibility it insists on giving to this other America. Two things about this insistence are clear: it makes for a politically radical act, and it reflects Bob Dylan's vision as much as Howard Alk's. (MG)

97 'Won't You Listen To The Lambs, Bob Dylan?', Scaduto, *New York Times*, 28 November 1971.

98 *Toronto Sun*, 29 March 1978.

99 As 83.

100 As 53.

101 As 98.

102 As 79.

103 *Fourth Time Around* No.2.

104 As 79.

105 As 98.

106 For a substantial interview with Dylan on his writing (conducted March 1985), see the relevant section of *Written In My Soul*, Bill Flangan, Contemporary Books, US, 1986; including Dylan on Jacques Levy, plus a paragraph on 'Brownsville Girl' being in part a response to Lou Reed's 'Doin' The Things That We Want To', which incorporates a reference to Shepard's play *Fool For Love*. (MG)

107 For a fuller account of the planning and failure of *Gene Tryp* see *Timeless Flight: The Definitive Biography of The Byrds*, John Rogan, Scorpion/Dark Star, UK, 1981.

108 The main sources of this piece are: Larry Sloman, as 53; 'Oh! Jacques Levy! Dylan's Co-writer!', Steve Weitzman, *Rolling Stone*, 7

April 1977; 'Dylan's Write-Hand Man', Chris Charlesworth, *Melody Maker*, 24 January 1976 and 'Jacques Levy's Psychology of Songwriting', Jim Bohen, *The Aquarian*, 21 February 1979. (Songs written by Bob Dylan and Jacques Levy are published in *The Songs of Bob Dylan 1966–1975* and *Lyrics 1962–1985*: for publishing details see notes 126 and 125 respectively.)

109 The quote is from 'Enter the Tambourine Man', Pete Oppel, *Dallas Morning News*, 22 November 1978; for a round-up on the impact of 'Norman' on Dylan, see 'Dylan's Mysterious Man Called Norman', Bert Cartwright, *The Telegraph* issue 23, 1986.

110 The TV session, *Freetime*, aired mid-November 1971, PBS-TV, New York, comprised: 'Nurse's Song'; 'A Dream'; 'Mantra'; plus 'September On Jessore Road'. The studio session, late November 1971, at the Record Plant, New York, comprised: 'September On Jessore Road' plus 'Jimmy Berman'; 'Vomit Express'; 'Going To San Diego'; 'Many Loves'; 'Om My Soul Shalom'; 'Nurse's Song'; 'Prajnaparamitra Sutra (Rashupate Rayham)'; 'The Tyger'; plus (rumouredly) 'Sacred Cow' and perhaps a second 'Jessore'. Dylan variously played guitar, organ and piano. Only the first two listed studio tracks have been issued: 'September On Jessore Road' as a *Sing Out!* flexidisc, 1972, and 'Jimmy Berman' on the LP *Disconnected*, issued by Giorno Poetry Systems, 1974. (JB)

111 This session consisted of two takes of 'Do The Meditation' and one of 'Airplane Blues'; none of these have been released. Dylan played bass. (JB)

112 'Meat universe' is Allen Ginsberg's term for what we ordinarily call 'the material world'. He had used it at his poetry reading the previous night, to describe the thorny rose in William Blake's 'My Pretty Rose Tree', contrasting it with the visionary/mental rose 'that May never bore'. The term has a very lively comic flavour to it, unlike the moral solemnity of 'the material world'.

113 There was a 1974 reissue: *Allen Ginsberg*, MGM Archetypes (M3F–4951), US.

114 Peter Orlovsky, Beat Poet and long-term lover of Ginsberg's, still tours with him (and doing so in Scandinavia, winter 1984–5, wore shorts and no shoes throughout). He can be seen early on in John Lennon's 'Give Peace A Chance' video: the camera moves in on Lennon over Orlovsky's left shoulder. (JB)

115 Tell all the truth but tell it slant/Success in circuit lies
Too bright for our infirm delight/The truths's superb surprise

As lightning to the children eased/With explanation kind
The truth must dazzle gradually/Or every man be blind.
(Emily Dickinson: see also 'Some Bob Dylan Lists', p.263.)

116 'Ginsberg is both tragic and dynamic, a lyrical genius, con man extraordinaire, and probably the greatest single influence on the American poetical voice since Whitman' – Bob Dylan. Used as an ad for *Allen Ginsberg Collected Poems 1947–1980*, Harper & Row, US; Viking Press, UK, 1985. (MG)

117 Since this writing, Dylan has released one such track: 'Dark Eyes', concluding the otherwise very unacoustic *Empire Burlesque*, 1985. In concert, on the first tour since 1984 (the 1986 Far East and American tour) only one attempt at 'Dark Eyes' alleviated what turned out to be more of this same predictability. Other virtual one-offs were limited to the *earlier* than usual acoustic song 'Song To Woody' and a band-version 'House Of The Rising Sun'. And though 'Maggie's Farm' and the all-time most-performed song, 'Just Like A Woman', were dropped at long last (and then only for the tour's last leg), 'Ballad Of A Thin Man' and 'It Aint Me Babe' again ground on throughout, while 'Blowin' In The Wind' and 'Knockin' On Heaven's Door' stayed put as formulaic encores. The process continued of ignoring seventies material almost entirely, as did neglecting new material. Before the American leg began, Dylan finished work on a new album, *Knocked Out Loaded*, which was rush-released – yet he featured only one song from it on the tour. On the other hand he did give some prominence both to nearly-new material and to songs he hasn't recorded at all. (MG)

118 In contrast, see the Levon Helm interview elsewhere in this book for a whole-hearted expression of the enjoyment an alert and responsive musician can derive from working with Dylan's on-stage unpredictability. Or see *The Last Waltz*, where Helm's love of riding that moment shows through strongly: indeed respectful relish of this special quality of Dylan's is all over The Band's faces. Or, a more recent example, see footage of 'Farm Aid' (1985), where the Heartbreakers' drummer and guitarist also rise to the occasion, beaming. (MG)

119 This article has been almost entirely winkled out of a thorough account of the relevant events by freelance writer David Breskin in *Life* in April 1985, plus a tiny bit from the *We Are The World* book, Perigree Books, USA, 1985.

120 Kurt Loder interview, *Rolling Stone*, 21 June 1984 (and quoted from several times hereafter); the interview took place that March, in a Greek café on 3rd Avenue, New York City.

121   And note these lines from the *Infidels* out-take song 'Someone's Got A Hold Of My Heart': 'Getting harder and harder to recognize the traps/Too much information 'bout nothin', too much educated rap'.

122   Echoing (unknowingly) the presenter of the Russian 'Live Aid' contribution, British Prime Minister Margaret Thatcher praised the use of new technology to restate the ideal of the 'brotherhood of man'.(!)

123   The statistics used in this section are taken from *Cultivating Hunger*, an Oxfam publication. They give emphasis to the picture of the world sketched by Dylan in 'Union Sundown' – a world in which 500 million people are starving or malnourished, while the developed world careers out of control. 'They call this religion capitalism . . .', as the alternative take of the song has it.

124   As 24.

125   *Lyrics 1962–1985*, Knopf, US, 1986; Cape, UK, 1987.

126   *The Songs Of Bob Dylan From 1966 Through 1975*, Knopf, US, 1976.

127   *Performed Literature*, Betsy Bowden, Indiana University Press, US, 1982.

128   As 106.

129   See 'Bob Dylan's Publications in *Broadside* Magazine', David Pichaske, *The Telegraph* issue 20, 1985.

130   This jes might be a *joke*. (MG)

131   Two points. First: in the US package there is *one* booklet: the material that in Europe makes up the second booklet, i.e. the track-by-track comments on the songs, is in the US printed on the inner sleeves of the five records. Second: as many people have noted, you get more records and better notes for less money with *The Complete Buddy Holly*, a far more scrupulous boxed-set from MCA: but that was put together (a) not by record company officials and the like but by expert fans and (b) not till twenty-five years after Holly's death. (MG)

132   *The Telegraph* issue 22, 1985.

133   Suze Rotolo finally talked in 1986, being an interviewee in the imprecisely-titled *Rock Wives*, Victoria Balfour, Beech Tree, US; Virgin, UK, 1986.

134   For 'Blue Gossip' (reprinted in this volume), 'On Reading Dylan's Writings' (badly reprinted in *The Telegraph* issue 20) and 'Postcard To D————' see *First Blues: Rags, Ballads and Harmonium Songs*

1971–74, Allen Ginsberg, Full Court Press, NY, 1975. For 'Bob Dylan (1941–)' see a 1986 *Esquire*, (badly reprinted in True Confessions Tour Programme, East West Touring, US, 1986). For the rest (with apologies to AG), see 116.

The Contributors

Bill Allison lives in Lancaster and teaches English in a secondary school. A longer version of his 'Bob Dylan's Neglected Newport Year: 1964' was published in a different format in *The Telegraph* issue 9.

Derek Bailey and David Hammond are independent film makers from Belfast, Northern Ireland. Bailey's latest work is a film of Harrison Birthwhistle's opera *Yan Tan Tethera*, shown on Channel 4 at Easter '87; work by Hammond (also a distinguished folk song collector), includes the prizewinning film *Steelchest, Nail in the Boot* and the *Barking Dog*. Their interview with Dylan has been condensed from the one conducted for their 1984 documentary on The Clancy Brothers & Tommy Makem and published in *The Telegraph* issue 18.

John Bauldie's work appeared as follows: earlier versions of the Information material appeared in *The Telegraph* issues 1–8, except 'Bob Dylan's Favourite Electric Guitars' (issue 15) and 'Dylan and the Making of USA-For-Africa' (issue 20). 'Dirge' and 'Jacques Levy and the *Desire* Collaboration' were in issue 11. Longer versions of 'A Meeting With A.J. Weberman, Summer of '82', 'The Oppression of Knowledge: No One Can Sing The Blues Like Blind Willie McTell' and 'The Motorcycle Crash' appeared in issues 8, 18 and 20 respectively; some 'Bob Dylan Lists' and other small items were written specially for this book (some jointly with Michael Gray).

Aidan Day teaches English Literature at Edinburgh University. His 'Reels Of Rhyme: Mr Tambourine Man' first appeared in *The Telegraph* issue 24.

Michael Gray's interview with Ronnie Hawkins was published in *The Telegraph* issue 22, and 'Deaths Around Bob Dylan's Life' in *The Telegraph* issue 24; some 'Bob Dylan Lists' and other small items were written specially for this book (some jointly with John Bauldie).

Clinton Heylin is the author of the *Rain Unravelled Tales* series of collated Bob Dylan rumours. His 'Profile Of Howard Alk' (with research assistance by George Webber) first appeared in *The Telegraph* issue 18 and '*Lyrics 1962–1985*: A Collection Short Of The Definitive' in *The Telegraph* issue 23.

John Hinchey is a former professor of American Literature at Swarthmore College, Pennsylvania, and writes for the *Ann Arbor Observer* in Michigan, US. His Allen Ginsberg transcript was first published in *The Telegraph* issue 12, as was his single-song study 'Slow Train'.

Nigel Hinton is a novelist (*Heart Of The Valley*, Constable, UK, Harper & Row, USA, 1986) and children's author, and has adapted his book *Buddy* for the TV series of the same name, starring Roger Daltrey. His 'Into The Future, Knocked Out And Loaded' appeared in *The Telegraph* issue 25.

Patrick Humphries is a freelance journalist and the author of books on Simon & Garfunkel, Bruce Springsteen and Alfred Hitchcock. His Liam Clancy feature was part of a longer interview published in *The Telegraph* issue 18.

Roy Kelly writes poems, short stories and radio plays. *Drugstore Fiction*, a book of poems, is due from Harry Chambers/Peterloo Poets, UK, in 1987. He has been a regular correspondent of *The Telegraph* since its inception. A longer version of 'Fans, Collectors and *Biograph*' was published in *The Telegraph* issue 23.

Michael Krogsgaard is author of the authoritative *Twenty Years Of Recording: The Bob Dylan Reference Book*, Scandinavian Institute for Rock Research, Denmark, 1981. His interview with Allen Ginsberg first appeared in *The Telegraph* issue 11.

John Lindley is a poet and a sales rep for an industrial thread company. 'Highway 84 Revisited' is a revised and updated version of the essay that first appeared in *The Telegraph* issue 18.

Shelly Livson is a financial controller in local government and lives in White Plains, New York State. An even longer version of his interview with D.A. Pennebaker was published in *The Telegraph* issue 16.

David Pichaske is Chairman of the English Department at Southwest State University, in Bob Dylan's home state of Minnesota. He is the author of several books, including *A Generation In Motion* and *Beowulf To Beatles*. His essay 'Bob Dylan and the Search For the Past' was published in *The Telegraph* issue 14.

Christopher Ricks teaches at Boston University. While a revised version of the material in his 'Clichés That Come to Pass' was later incorporated into his book *The Force Of Poetry*, first publication was in *The Telegraph* issue 15. 'What He Can Do For You' was written for *The Telegraph* issue 22.

284

Wes Stace is an undergraduate at Jesus College, Cambridge, and a musician in the group The Accelerators. His Allen Ginsberg interview appeared in *The Telegraph* issue 20.

Patrick J. Webster is a violin-maker and guitar-maker and lives in Yorkshire. 'In The Factory: Dylan and Warhol's World' is a revised version of a piece first published in *The Telegraph* issue 17.

Chris Whithouse lives in London and has a daughter called Corrina. An earlier version of his 'Alias, Pat Garrett and Billy The Kid' originally appeared in *The Telegraph* issue 19.

Bob Willis is a former England Cricket Captain and fast bowler, and has recently been a British and Australian TV cricket commentator. While he has written a number of books about cricket, his Introduction to the present volume marks his writing début on the subject of the other great influence on his life.

Clive Wilshin is an undergraduate studying Russian and French at Manchester University. An earlier version of his 'Charity Is Supposed to Cover Up a Multitude of Sins' appeared in *The. Telegraph* issue 22.

NB. Subscriptions to The Telegraph *magazine can be taken out by writing to* Wanted Man/The Bob Dylan Information Office, PO Box 22, Romford, Essex RM1 2RF, England. *Write to this address with SAE/International Reply Coupon for current subscription rates in the UK, Eire, Europe and outside Europe.*

Index

For practical reasons which will be apparent from the relevant passages, the contents of the following three items have not been indexed: The Appendix to 'Lyrics 1962–1985: A Collection Short of the Definitive', p.238–42; List B in 'Some Bob Dylan Lists', p.264; and 'The Contributors', p.283–5.

286

Rock on with Futura . . .

JOHN LENNON
Ray Coleman

The first detailed and definitive biography of the man whose
genius revolutionized rock music. Written with the co-operation
of Lennon's friends and family, including Cynthia Lennon and
Yoko Ono, Ray Coleman's book is a revealing and highly readable
portrait of one of the twentieth century's most enduring cultural
heroes — and a moving tribute to a man whose music and
complex personality won him the love of millions.

Futura Publications
Non-Fiction/Biography
ISBN 0 7088 2740 3

THE BEATLES LYRICS
'There's a lot of random in our songs . . . writing, thinking, letting others think of bits — then bang, you have the jigsaw puzzle'

THE BEATLES: heroes and superstars of our time, whose meteoric rise to fame in the sixties made them a legend overnight. From their dazzlingly versatile music to the eccentricities of their private lives, the Beatles have mirrored the changing trends of the century as no other group before or since.

Now almost 200 of their lyrics have been collected to form one volume of poetry. From the ambiguity of 'Lucy in the Sky with Diamonds' to the surrealism of 'Eleanor Rigby', from the style songs of John Lennon to the psychedelic brainstormers of Paul McCartney, poetry with astonishing breadth of vision and depth of meaning.

Futura Publications
Poetry
ISBN 0 8600 7478 1

McCARTNEY: THE BIOGRAPHY
Chris Salewicz

Here, at last, is the complete biography of the most successful
composer and recording artist of all time: Paul McCartney —
Liverpool lad, Beatles superstar, solo artist, husband and father.
Chris Salewicz takes us from Paul's early days of struggle through
a long career which has in turn been enormously successful
and deeply acrimonious. McCartney is revealed as the driving
force within the Beatles, yet his contribution has often been
misunderstood and undervalued, particularly in the light of his
sometimes stormy relationship with John Lennon.

Meticulously researched and with 16 pages of photographs, this
rich and revealing biography redresses the balance and leaves
no stone unturned in its portrayal of the real Paul McCartney.

'Without losing his balance, Salewicz pulls Paul out from under
John's shadow'
Dave Marsh, author of *Springsteen: Born to Run* and *Glory Days*.

Futura Publications
Non-Fiction/Biography
ISBN 0 7088 3374 8

SURVIVOR: THE AUTHORIZED BIOGRAPHY OF ERIC CLAPTON
Ray Coleman

In the sixties the legend ran: Clapton is God. Guitarman in such seminal British groups as John Mayall's Bluesbreakers and Cream, catalyst in that decade's rock revolution, Clapton was always more than just another pop hero. A musician of exceptional talent, ability and passion, Clapton is arguably the greatest guitarist of his generation.

But the price of success is often high — and for Clapton it almost proved too high. Ray Coleman's authorized biography examines the career and the private life that was shielded from prying eyes for so long, the pressures that culminated in heroin addiction, the seven years lost to alcoholic torpor. Slowly and painfully Clapton kicked drugs and drink and reclaimed his career and his life. This is his story. The story of an incomparable guitarman. The story of a survivor.

'Fascinating . . . A story of resilience' *Daily Telegraph*

'Sensational' *Mirror*

'The perfect present for that Clapton fan' *Melody Maker*

Futura Publications
Non-Fiction/Biography
ISBN 0 7088 3080 3

Fiction with a difference from Futura

DAYS BETWEEN STATIONS
Steve Erickson

He woke nine years later remembering nothing. Not his name,
nor what he was doing in that room, nor whatever it was that
had blotted out his identity. For it wasn't so much that he couldn't
remember, but rather as though it was gone, his life before that
morning, disappeared. And to get it back he would have to
journey through not just space but time itself. To get it back he
would have to find *her*.

'Sometime in the not too distant future, the planet Earth is going
rapidly to the dogs, Los Angeles is swept by sandstorms . . . a
pall of smoke hangs over Paris . . . The canals of Venice have
inexplicably dried up . . . The landscape is fabulous, bleak; the
lovers who travel through it are just the opposite — romantically
alienated and drunk on their own eroticism . . . Richly convoluted'
— *The New York Times Book Review*

'Steve Erickson has that rare and luminous gift for reporting
back from the nocturnal side of reality . . . an engagingly romantic
attitude and the fierce imaginative energy of a born storyteller.
It is good news when any of these qualities appear in a writer
— to find them all together . . . is reason to break out the
champagne' — *Thomas Pynchon*

'Fascinating' — *The Philadelphia Inquirer*

'There isn't a risk that Steve Erickson hasn't taken in this novel
. . . interesting . . . ambitious . . . lovely and peculiar' — *Los
Angeles Times*

'Erickson is brilliant. Period' — *The Los Angeles Weekly*

Futura Publications
Fiction
ISBN 0 7088 3758 1

In some ways Shark Trager was more than a Hollywood legend.
In some ways Shark Trager was Hollywood itself . . .

BOY WONDER
A novel by James Robert Baker
Author of FUEL-INJECTED DREAMS

Shark Trager wanted everything Hollywood had to offer — the
fame, the fortune, the thrills, even the perfect California blonde.
And one way or another he got — and lost — it all . . .

Born in the back of a Chrysler at the Flying Wing Drive-In during
a showing of the B-movie film noir *Gun Crazy*, Shark Trager
was arguably *the* quintessential Hollywood wunderkind producer
of the last quarter of the twentieth century. Which means that
he was probably the definitive narcissistic genius-as-monster of
the entire movie industry, if not of the entire civilization, as well.
Trager's controversial career (*Sex Kill á Go Go*, *Mondo Jet Set*,
etc.), his obsessive love for heiress Kathy Petro, his outrageous
(some might even say despicable) behaviour in both his public
and private life, his immense popularity and equally immense
vilification, his sudden filmably spectacular death, all epitomized
the culture he did so much to enrich. Here is a man who accepted
James Dean into his soul as a Christian must accept Jesus into
his heart. Here is a man unscrupulous in his pursuit of Art;
unprincipled in his pursuit of Love; untempered in his pursuit
of Life. Here is Shark Trager as he is remembered by those who
loved and loathed him most.

BOY WONDER
James Robert Baker's blackly hilarious satire of the movie
business — a masterpiece of invention, wit and style.

Futura Publications
Fiction
ISBN 0 7088 4191 0

All Futura Books are available at your bookshop or
newsagent, or can be ordered from the following address:
Futura Books, Cash Sales Department,
P.O. Box 11, Falmouth, Cornwall, TR10 9EN.

Please send cheque or postal order (no currency), and
allow 60p for postage and packing for the first book plus
25p for the second book and 15p for each additional book
ordered up to a maximum charge of £1.90 in U.K.

B.F.P.O. customers please allow 60p for the first book,
25p for the second book plus 15p per copy for the next
7 books, thereafter 9p per book.

Overseas customers, including Eire, please allow £1.25
for postage and packing for the first book, 75p for the second
book and 28p for each subsequent title ordered.